Edited

The Teaching of Classics

p. 60   dealing c̄ weaknesses and
strengths (q. OCIA)

pp. 121-22   the very nature of the
sources teaches us to
peer c̄ great suspicion
at them...

p. 123   truth, like time, is
irredeemable

CAMBRIDGE
UNIVERSITY PRESS

PUBLISHED BY THE PRESS SYNDICATE OF THE UNIVERSITY OF CAMBRIDGE
The Pitt Building, Trumpington Street, Cambridge, United Kingdom

CAMBRIDGE UNIVERSITY PRESS
The Edinburgh Building, Cambridge CB2 2RU, UK
40 West 20th Street, New York, NY 10011-4211, USA
477 Williamstown Road, Port Melbourne, VIC 3207, Australia
Ruiz de Alarcón 13, 28014 Madrid, Spain
Dock House, The Waterfront, Cape Town 8001, South Africa

http://www.cambridge.org

First published 2003

Printed in the United Kingdom at the University Press, Cambridge

Typeface Palatino, *System* QuarkXPress®

A catalogue record for this book is available from the British Library

ISBN 0 521 52763 5 paperback

ACKNOWLEDGEMENTS

Thanks are due to the following for permission to reproduce photographs:
p. 129, Vatican Museums and Galleries, Vatican City, Italy/Bridgeman Art
Library; p. 130, Ancient Art and Architecture Collection; p. 132, Museo
Archeologico Nazionale, Naples; p. 134, Verlag Ernst Wasmuth.

The publisher has used its best endeavours to ensure that the URLs for external
websites referred to in this book are correct and active at the time of going to press.
However, the publisher has no responsibility for the websites and can make no
guarantee that a site will remain live or that the content will remain appropriate.

Contents

Notes on contributors

Judith Affleck is Head of Classics at Harrow School, where she has been since 1996. Before that she taught at Eton College from 1987. She has been involved in summer school teaching at the JACT Greek summer school since 1988. She is co-editor of the Cambridge Translations from Greek Drama and has contributed two volumes to the series as author (*Philoctetes*) and co-author (*Oedipus Tyrannus*).

Maurice Balme was Head of Classics at Harrow School and is now retired. He has written several books on the classics, including the Oxford Latin Course (with James Morwood), *Athenaze* (with Gilbert Lawall) and, most recently, *The Plays and Fragments of Menander* (Oxford World's Classics).

Robert Bass is Head of Classics and Director of Studies at Orwell Park, a preparatory school near Ipswich. He is the classics subject co-ordinator for IAPS (Incorporated Association of Preparatory Schools). He is chairman of the Latin Common Entrance and Common Academic Scholarship examination setting panel of ISEB (Independent Schools Examinations Board) and is currently engaged in producing support materials for those teaching Latin in prep schools.

Barbara Bell is the Head of Classics at Clifton High School in Bristol. She is the author of *Minimus – Starting Out in Latin* and the Director of the Primary Latin Project. She has taught classics for nearly thirty years, mostly in the Bristol area. From 1994 to 1998 she was the executive secretary of the Joint Association of Classical Teachers. In 1980 she established the JACT Latin summer school and she regularly teaches Greek at the JACT summer school in Durham.

John Claughton has been Headmaster of Solihull School since 2001. For the seventeen years before that he was a teacher of Greek, Latin and ancient history at Eton College. During that time he was master in charge of cricket for eleven years, and a housemaster for four. He has produced no published work, although he has written cricket and rugby reports for the *Independent on Sunday* (and has a Herodotus text for schools, if he could only find a publisher!).

Brenda Gay is PGCE Course Director and Lecturer in Classics Education at the Department of Education and Professional Studies, King's College London, which she joined in 1996. She has taught in both the independent and maintained sectors, was headmistress of a girls' independent school and has worked in teacher education and educational research. She has published in a wide range of areas, including religion in the independent school, the global dimension of teaching and learning in classics, accountability and the management of conflict in the classroom. Her current research interests are focused on teacher induction, classics teaching and learning as part of global communication, and the religious dimension of independent schools.

Marion Gibbs is Headmistress of James Allen's Girls' School, London. She is the author of *Greek Tragedy: An Introduction* (under the name Baldock) and numerous articles on classics, inspection and education. She taught and examined classics in schools and at the Open University for many years before becoming an HM Inspector of Schools, a post she left for headship in 1994. She has been actively involved in many classical organisations since the late 1970s, including being joint secretary of the Classical Association and chairman of the council of JACT.

David Goodhew is the Head of Classics at Bristol Grammar School; previously he taught at Bancroft's school, and then at Eton College. At Eton he initiated the Greek Software Project and established the department's intranet site, in addition to overseeing the introduction of laptops and data projectors into classroom teaching. He has been book reviews editor for JACT, and is currently the secretary of BACT (Bristol Association of Classical Teachers).

Lorna Hardwick teaches in the Department of Classical Studies at the Open University where she is Professor of Classical Studies and Director of the research project on the Reception of Classical Texts in Modern Drama and Poetry. One of her first teaching appointments was as a part-time tutor on the very first Open University classical studies course. She subsequently joined the permanent staff and has served as head of the Department of Classical Studies and on many course teams in classical and inter-disciplinary studies. From 2000 to 2003 she was also the subject director for classics and ancient history in the learning and teaching support network. Her publications include *Translating Words, Translating Cultures* and *New Surveys in the Classics: Reception Studies*.

David Hargreaves has been Chief Inspector of the Inner London Education Authority, Chief Executive of the Qualifications and Curriculum Authority and Professor of Education in the University of Cambridge. Currently he is Chairman of the British Educational Communications and Technology Agency (BECTA), a senior associate of the think-tank Demos, and visiting professor of medical education research at the University of Keele.

Catherine Hobey graduated in Greek and Latin from Bryn Mawr College, USA and in classics from Cambridge University. She earned her PhD in Greek art at the University of London. She taught classical subjects for the Open University and Greek and Roman art at the University of London. She teaches Latin and Greek at the London Oratory School. She has published articles on Greek painters and sculptors for the Macmillan Encyclopedia of the History of Art.

Tony Hubbard is Director of the Independent Schools Inspectorate. He is co-author of *Plato's Protagoras: A Socratic Commentary*. After ten years as Head of Classics at Downside School in Somerset, he spent seventeen years as an HM Inspector of Schools in England. During that time he had responsibility for the monitoring of classics in the South West and in the Metropolitan area and contributed to a range of HMI publications on the provision and teaching of classics. He was a regional and then national point of responsibility for provision for gifted and talented pupils.

Peter Jones, co-founder of Friends of Classics, was a school teacher and university lecturer before taking early retirement to concentrate on writing and broadcasting. He wrote *Learn Latin* and *Learn Ancient Greek* (originally published in *The Daily Telegraph*), *An Intelligent Person's Guide to Classics* and co-authored the *Reading Greek* and *Reading Latin* series. He recently revised E.V. Rieu's *Iliad* for Penguin, and wrote a commentary on it. He writes a weekly *Ancient and Modern* column in *The Spectator*.

James Morwood (editor) was the Grocyn Lecturer in the classics faculty at Oxford, in charge of language teaching. He is co-author of the Oxford Latin Course and co-compiler of the *Pocket Oxford Dictionary of Classical Greek*. Among his many other publications are Greek and Latin grammars for the Oxford University Press. He spent thirty years teaching in secondary education (at Harrow School), seventeen of them as Head of Classics, and has been associated with the JACT Greek summer school since 1970. He is the Dean of Wadham College, Oxford.

Robin Osborne is President of the Hellenic Society, Professor of Ancient History in the University of Cambridge and Fellow of King's College. He has published extensively in the fields of Greek history, Greek archaeology and the history of Greek art, including *Greece in the Making 1200–479 BC* and *Archaic and Classical Greek Art*. He was chairman of the JACT ancient history committee during the revision of the specifications for the new AS and A level, and is one of the editors of *Omnibus*.

Richard Shannon is an Additional Inspector for the Office of Standards in Education (OFSTED) and a Reporting Inspector for the Independent Schools Inspectorate. He served as an HM Inspector of Schools (HMI) from 1988 to 2001. He has been a Moderator and Chief Examiner and was a Head of Classics for eighteen years.

Pat Story has been a member of the Cambridge School Classics Project team since 1967. She was its Director for nine years and most recently has been Revision Editor of the fourth edition of the Cambridge Latin Course. She taught in both independent and state schools and for twenty-four years trained classics graduates at the Oxford and Cambridge Departments of Education. She is a Life Fellow of Hughes Hall, Cambridge.

Christopher Stray is Honorary Research Fellow in the Department of Classics and Ancient History at University of Wales, Swansea. He has published on the history of classical education and scholarship, on the history and sociology of textbooks and on private and family languages. His *Classics Transformed: Schools, Universities, and Society in England 1830–1960* was published in 1998. He is editing a centenary history of the Classical Association, to be published in 2003.

John Taylor is Head of Classics at Tonbridge School. He is secretary of the JACT Greek committee, Director of Studies for the JACT Greek summer school at Bryanston (where he has taught annually since 1986), and a regular tutor on Greek courses at Madingley Hall, Cambridge University's Institute of Continuing Education. He is editor of *New Testament Greek: A Reader* and co-editor of *A Greek Anthology* (both forming part of the JACT Greek Course); co-compiler of the *Pocket Oxford Dictionary of Classical Greek*; and author of *Greek to GCSE*.

David Tristram is head teacher at the Kingswood School in Corby, a comprehensive school. He has taught classics in the maintained sector throughout his career of over twenty-five years and was Advisory Teacher for Classics in Northamptonshire during the late

1980s. He was Chief Examiner for GCSE Latin for ten years and also taught for many years at the JACT Latin summer school. He continues to teach Latin at his school, and at Madingley Hall, Cambridge University's Institute of Continuing Education.

Henry Wickham (assistant editor) is Head of Classics at King's College Junior School, Wimbledon. Before taking up his current post he spent several years as an opera singer, and can thus testify to the advantages of a classical education in picking up modern foreign languages quickly! In 1999 he turned to teaching and was appointed Head of Classics at Chinthurst School, Surrey, where he gained an in-service PGCE from the University of Surrey, Roehampton, through the Council for British Teachers (CfBT).

Julie Wilkinson is Head of Classics and Year Coordinator at Nower Hill High School, a mixed comprehensive that happens also to be a Beacon school and has Arts College status in the London borough of Harrow. There she established the current classics department. She has been INSET coordinator for JACT and a member of the Roman Society Schools Committee. She is currently on the Latin committee and a member of JACT council. She has been involved in the revision of book one of the Cambridge Latin Course and the piloting of the 'Result' digital materials that will accompany it. She is a classics mentor on the Cambridge PGCE course and a member of the Cambridge Schools Classics Project committee.

Richard Woff is Deputy Head of Education at The British Museum, where he has responsibility for provision for schools, teachers and children. Before joining The British Museum, he spent sixteen years as a lecturer in classics education, first at the University of London Institute of Education and then at King's College London. He frequently gives talks to school students on Greek art and is author of several books for young readers on aspects of the classical world.

Foreword

Peter Jones

The classical community has made mistakes in the past forty years, but there are no fashionably tearful, lip-trembling apologies in this unsentimental, straight-talking collection of essays. No surprise: two thousand years ago, Cicero observed that 'nothing dries more quickly than a tear'. This book squarely addresses the record, considers where we are now, and speculates about where we could go from here.

Classicists in schools have, in fact, played with considerable skill the increasingly thin hands that have been dealt them over the years by myopic governments and educators. The teaching of the core subjects – the Latin and Greek languages – has been entirely re-thought to meet new constraints: in particular, new timetables. The non-linguistic subjects – ancient history and classical civilisation – have been developed to dramatic effect. Classicists in universities too, institutions not usually renowned for their advanced educational thinking and themselves under increasing pressure, have not only constantly reconstructed their own courses in response to school developments but have also worked tirelessly alongside teachers in the subject's evolution, to the very great benefit of both.

All this raises an important question. As we begin to think about where we are now and where we go from here, how are those outside the school loop – parents, educators, opinion-formers – to get to know of the changes that have taken place, and the value and pleasure of what we now have to offer? Many will be quite unaware of the radical reforms of the past twenty or thirty years.

One thing is certain. If we do not blow our own *tubas* (acc. pl.), no one else will. Let me therefore add another straw to the classicists' back, and urge the teachers among you to grasp the chance of trumpeting abroad what you are doing, 'abroad' being in this case the UK. The classical cause can never get enough publicity, and the most authoritative source for this is you.

It is always a good idea to go, rather like Pompey, straight to the top. The education correspondents of our national papers are (in my experience) a friendly and honest lot. They live off stories about education, and if stories do not come to them, they have to find them. Being only human, they much prefer stories to come to them.

Their only need is that the story is newsworthy in itself. The key test is that the journalist will say to him/herself 'Now that really is different', 'This is incredible!', or 'Are you crazy?' (Teaching Latin in primary schools or over the internet passes all these tests brilliantly.) It can also help to inject a story with 'human interest'; that means articulate students, preferably quite young, or, if older, good-looking and appallingly dressed (by my old git's standards) who will support your angle on the topic. If you have such a story, get (i) the school's agreement, (ii) all the details, names and phone numbers, and (iii) on the phone. Ask for the education correspondent. Be incisive and to the point. They are busy people.

Mutate the *mutanda*, and the same applies to letters. If you see an issue with a classical point to be made, educational or historical, write about it to the organ concerned. The more letters of this sort they receive, the more they will be aware of public interest; papers thrive on keeping their fingers on the pulse and responding to it. Not merely is a journalist's reputation enhanced by a big mailbag; it makes him/her feel more inclined to write about the subject again.

Here are the addresses, general phone numbers and letters fax/e-mail addresses for the most likely national newspapers. They require daytime contact number and address:

The Daily/Sunday Telegraph 1 Canada Square, London E14 5DT. Tel. 020 7538 5000; *DT* fax 020 7538 6455; dtletters@telegraph.co.uk; *ST* fax 020 7538 7872; stletters@telegraph.co.uk

The (Sunday) Times 1 Pennington Street, London E98 1TA (*Sunday* E98 1ST). Tel. 020 7782 5000; *Times* fax 020 7782 5046; letters@thetimes.co.uk; *Sunday* fax 020 7782 5454; letters@sunday-times.co.uk

The Independent (on Sunday) 191 Marsh Wall, London E14 9RS. Tel. 020 7005 2000; *Daily* fax 020 7005 2056; letters@independent.co.uk; *Sunday* fax 020 7005 2628; sundayletters@independent.co.uk

The Guardian/Observer 119 Farringdon Road, London EC1R 3ER. Tel. 020 7278 2332; *Guardian* fax 020 7837 4530; letters@guardian.co.uk; *Observer* fax 020 7713 4250/4286; letters@observer.co.uk

The Daily Mail 2 Derry Street, London W8 5TT. Tel. 020 7938 6000; fax 020 7937 7493; letters@dailymail.co.uk

The Daily Mirror 1 Canada Square, London E14 5AP. Tel. 020 7510 3000; fax 020 7293 3975; mailbox@mirror.co.uk

The Daily Express 245 Blackfriars Road, London SE1 9UX. Tel. 020 7928 8000; fax 020 7620 1643; expressletters@express.co.uk

The Times Educational Supplement Admiral House, 66–68 East Smithfield, London E1W 1BX. Tel. 020 7782 3000; fax 020 7782 3200; letters@tes.co.uk

Do not be disappointed if you do not score. All national papers have three or four times the number of stories they actually use; journalists commanding their own pages can fill them many times over; letters could fill the whole paper. Inevitably, what may strike you as a great story may not look like one to a journalist. It is a hit and miss business, mostly miss. But papers take *weight* of correspondence on any topic very seriously.

Regional papers, however, are under less pressure. Check, in particular, if your local paper has an education correspondent; if it has, invite them to see what you are doing. Journalists are (it is, I know, hard to credit) humans. The personal contact can make all the difference. Further, a good story in a regional may well make it into a national a day later (the Laura Spence story first broke in the Newcastle *Journal*); and *vice versa*.

Again, a story which catches the imagination can spread across the media for as much as a week or so, not just in the papers but into radio and TV as well (local or national). *Minimus* is a good example.

It goes without saying that your first responsibility is to your schools. But to be where you are now, you must have developed some pretty silky arts of persuasion. My point is that it is well worth trying them on a wider public which is still unaware of the riches we have to offer.

To end with, a chestnut which, lacking the practical touch, rather contradicts the spirit of the above (therefore making this whole Foreword excitingly 'post-modern'). It also proposes a false antithesis, but never mind. As an expression of one sort of sentiment about our subject, it gives me at any rate intense pleasure:

Evelyn Waugh's *Scott-King's Modern Europe* (1947) introduces a disillusioned Mr Chips figure in the person of the eponymous hero, who teaches classics at Grantchester. An expert on the (invented) seventeenth-century Latinist Bellorius, Scott-King is invited in the summer holidays to give a paper on him at a conference in Neutralia. It all goes horribly wrong, and Scott-King only just gets away. The book ends – sorry, negotiates closure – at the start of the new term, when the head master summons Scott-King for a chat. The head, 'an old Greats man myself', points out that the number of classical specialists has dropped and goes on:

'Parents are not interested in producing "the complete man" any more. They want to qualify their boys for jobs in the modern world. You can hardly blame them, can you?'

'Oh, yes,' said Scott-King. 'I can and do.'

'I always say you are a much more important man here than I am. One couldn't conceive of Grantchester without Scott-King. But has it ever occurred to you that a time may come when there will be no more classical boys at all?'

'Oh, yes. Often.'

'What I was going to suggest was – I wonder if you will consider taking some other subject as well as classics? History, for example, preferably economic history?'

'No, head master.'

'But, you know, there may be something of a crisis ahead.'

'Yes, head master.'

'Then what do you intend to do?'

'If you approve, head master, I will stay as I am here as long as any boy wants to read the classics. I think it would be very wicked indeed to do anything to fit a boy for the modern world.'

'It's a short-sighted view, Scott-King.'

'There, head master, with all respect, I differ from you profoundly. I think it is the most long-sighted view it is possible to take.'

Introduction

James Morwood

When I started teaching classics in 1966, it never occurred to me that the subject would still have a significant position in UK schools at the start of the new millennium. How wrong I was! Our profession's inventiveness and adaptability in the face of constantly shifting circumstances have combined with a sense of realism and a dogged determination to ensure that we have both a present and a future, however fraught with danger they may be.

This collection of essays, written a quarter of a century after the last book of its kind, John Sharwood Smith's *On Teaching Classics* (Routledge and Kegan Paul, 1977) is in part a celebration of that remarkable achievement. It should also serve as some kind of summation of where the teaching of classics stands as we enter the 2000s. It covers the whole educational spectrum: *From 'Minimus' to Madingley*, the latter referring to Cambridge University's Institute of Continuing Education, was an early working title. And while the book grapples with the adventure of our past, it also suggests some strategies for the future. Much of it – and not only the chapter on ICT – will date fast. Many admirable initiatives find no mention in these pages. (I shall come back to this.) But I hope that at the very least they give an impression of the commitment and resilience that have taken us so far and will certainly take us further.

The book is aimed most specifically at practising and aspiring teachers of classics. Some of it could usefully find its way into the hands not only of head teachers and governors of schools but of parents too. In its focus on classics, it is inevitably parochial, but some parts of it may be of interest to a wider educational world. The enthusiasm for the project shown by Professor David Hargreaves, currently chairman of the British Educational Communications and Technology Agency, who has written so heartening an epilogue, gives some grounds for such optimism. Whatever the book's weaknesses, it gives a voice to a significant number of people, the vast majority of them practising teachers of classics, who care deeply about their subject. Their passion and dedication, a mirror of those qualities which pervade our profession, will, we hope, not only shed light but reflect it too.

Peter Jones, that unflagging proponent of our cause, has already trumpeted his call to arms in a noble foreword. The first two chapters that follow my introduction tell the story of the development of classics from the nineteenth century to the 1990s. Christopher Stray deals with the changing face of the subject up to the 1960s, to *Aestimanda* and the Cambridge Schools Classics Project, while David Tristram takes us on to the eve of the new millennium with a lively account of those roller-coaster years which saw the introduction of the National Curriculum and much else too. To put the matter simplistically, Stray's is an account of initiatives, some of them – such as W.H.D. Rouse's propagation of the direct method – genuinely exciting, Tristram's a tale of strategies for survival.

In her chapter 'Classics teaching and the National Curriculum', Brenda Gay covers some of the same ground as Tristram but surveys it from a very different angle. She argues impressively that classics is fully entitled to a place in the revised National Curriculum of 2000 both within its programmes of study for core and foundation subjects and as a means of promoting pupils' spiritual, moral, social and cultural development. This chapter could profitably be drawn to the attention of head teachers, whether well disposed or hostile to our subject. Marion Gibbs, a head teacher herself, discusses the place of classics in the curriculum of the future, keeping her feet on the ground – there is some splendidly trenchant writing here – but nonetheless finding reason for optimism. Next Richard Shannon, who as an HMI must have sat in on more classics lessons in the UK than anyone else, gives examples of good teaching practice in the various areas of our subject. He has clearly witnessed much excellent classics teaching and his chapter is indeed a heartening one. Finally in this opening section of pieces on classics in the curriculum comes Tony Hubbard's chapter on provision for special needs in classics. Insisting that classical subjects must be made available not only to the most able but also to those traditionally viewed – too easily, as he properly emphasises – as the least gifted, he gives a clear picture of how classics can prove rewarding across the whole intellectual spectrum.

We now move on to a survey of the teaching of classics from the primary to the tertiary level. This section begins and ends with the two great success stories of recent years. First, in a chapter of infectious enthusiasm, Barbara Bell gives us a lively account of the triumphant adventure that is *Minimus*. This course is serving a far wider market than primary schools, but it is for that age group that it was designed and here it is centred. At the time of writing, it has found its way into 5 per cent of the country's primary schools. Lorna Hardwick has an equally inspiring story to tell of the growth of classics in the Open University. Here, astonishingly, over 4,000 students a year are now studying classical subjects.

The chapters that come between are less buoyantly optimistic. Nevertheless, they too make it clear that the show is still very decidedly on the road. Writing of the situation of classics in prep schools, Bob Bass deals frankly with the problems that confront teachers there; it is plain, however, that they are showing determination and adaptability amid unnervingly fluid circumstances.

We now move on to the secondary sector. Brenda Gay discusses the theoretical underpinning of the main Latin courses used today, and is followed by Pat Story who gives an account of the responsive and innovative development of the Cambridge Latin Course, whose central importance to the survival of Latin comes over very clearly in this book. In her footsteps there tread Maurice Balme and James Morwood on the Oxford Latin Course. (*Ecce Romani* is discussed on pages 79–82.) And next John Taylor conducts a magisterial and kaleidoscopic appraisal of the situation regarding Greek courses and related published material.

The title of Julie Wilkinson's chapter, 'Working at the chalk face', is not intended to imply that the other practising teachers who have written in this volume are in any way remote from reality. Certainly, however, there is an impressive grittiness about her reintroduction of Latin in a north London comprehensive school twelve years ago and the success she has made of this. Like other contributors, she rightly insists on the fundamental importance of good teaching but argues that this by itself is not enough.

We now move on to ancient history. Here two writers discuss the JACT A level syllabus, with Robin Osborne describing how it came into being and John Claughton discussing what it means for the teacher, with a lively appreciation of the problems. Some may feel that their concentration on the JACT syllabus is unreasonably limiting. The fact remains that in 1968 there were eight A level syllabuses on offer in England and Wales. By the mid-1990s this total had sunk to three. Now only the JACT one survives. That is because it was only the JACT ancient history committee – the two key figures being its supremely resilient chairman Robin Osborne and the doggedly resolute John Murrell – that had the adaptability and persistence to respond to the constant shifts of government policy and work with what was then the Oxford and Cambridge Board to produce an appropriate syllabus. As I write, even that is under threat, but I am confident that this doughty committee will take on all comers.

In the chapter that follows, Catherine Hobey celebrates classical civilisation, our subject's great growth area in secondary schools, and suggests strategies for teaching the challenging topics in a stimulating manner while at the same time steering clear of superficiality. She also writes interestingly of the possibility of participation in the International Baccalaureate. Then David Goodhew rounds off the chapters on secondary education with a piece entitled 'Using ICT in classics'. He leaves us in no doubt of the vast and exhilarating range of opportunities offered to classics teachers by this medium, while at the same time alerting us to some of the dangers. James Morwood then writes of the great variety of classics courses now available at our universities but wonders whether this *embarras de richesse* brings problems in its wake. His tempering of optimism with realism is characteristic of the volume as a whole.

We now move outside the curriculum. Judith Affleck gives eloquent expression to a view that I imagine all of us share – that every student should have the opportunity to study classics at secondary level. Indeed, hers is one of the book's two most explicit statements of the reasons for studying classics, and readers who wish to make use of this are referred to pages 162–3. (The other is Julie Wilkinson's on pages 109–10.) She then goes on to discuss various ways in which the opportunity is in fact being offered to those who do not get the chance to study the subject at school. The dedication of teachers motivates the twilight teaching which offers ever-increasing access to our subject. For Affleck, the twilight can at times seem perilously close to a Götterdämmerung. However – or perhaps therefore – hers is basically an inspiring story.

The question remains of how a potential student who has never heard of classics – and there are substantial areas of the UK where this is only too likely to be the case – can be fired with the enthusiasm to track down such opportunities. For such classically disenfranchised students – my expression for where they dwell is 'beyond-JACT', and JACT is of course ever eager to find ways of reaching them – a museum could provide the necessary inspiration. And it is in a museum that our journey ends. Richard Woff, Deputy Head of Education at The British Museum and formerly lecturer in classics education at King's College, London, is ideally placed to tell us how teachers can make the best use of such a wonderful resource. Indeed, his eminently user-friendly chapter provides a splendidly affirmative conclusion to a series of essays which aim to tackle serious problems with a hard-nosed realism while at the same time insisting that there are solutions to most of them.

Near the start of this Introduction, I made the point that many admirable initiatives remain unacknowledged in these pages. This is no doubt inevitable – quite simply there is too much happening – but it is all the more regrettable in that I firmly believe that the accumulation of all those individual and collective initiatives is what has kept us going thus far and will continue to do so. We are getting along pretty well under the benevolent and far from *dirigiste* leadership of JACT with its council and subject committees, some of which are extraordinarily effective, of the Association for Latin Teaching with its annual refresher day and summer school for teachers, of the Classical Association with its splendid commitment to young scholars, and HM Inspectorate with its continuing support and monitoring of the teaching of the subject.

Not all of the classical initiatives have proved successful, of course. Many of them have fizzled out. A number of them promised much but delivered less. Language awareness should no doubt be numbered among the latter. Many will remember that in 1985 David Corson produced a book (*The Lexical Bar* (Pergamon Press)) which argued that there is 'a lexical bar in the English lexicon which hinders the members of some social groups from lexical access to knowledge categories of the school curriculum in their oral and written language and perhaps in their thinking as well' (p. 28). Since much of the vocabulary used in these knowledge categories derives from Latin and Greek, exposure to classical languages would take children from every social background across the bar and give them access to the 'semantically precise and educationally appropriate lexes of the knowledge categories of the secondary school curriculum' (p. 117). An experiment conducted in elementary schools in the USA (in Indianapolis) in 1973 had shown that some basic knowledge of Latin could very significantly advance children's ability to learn, not only in language skills but also in mathematics, science and social science (*American Education*, June 1978). Adrian Spooner published an article on the subject in the *JACT Review* (Spring 1986, pp. 16–19) and in 1987 JACT and the Centre for Educational Studies held a day's conference on it in London, at which both Corson and Spooner spoke.

Two school textbooks communicating awareness of the Latin and Greek languages subsequently appeared, Spooner's *Lingo* (Bristol Classical Press, 1988) and James Morwood and Mark Warman's *Our Greek and Latin Roots* (Cambridge University Press, 1990). However, language awareness failed to secure a significant foothold in the school curriculum. Even so, both books are still in print and *Lingo* has sold between 10,000 and 11,000 copies, *Our Greek and Latin Roots* almost 18,000; indeed the latter is the only survivor of the Awareness of Language series for which it was written. The project in fact proved a modest success and was surely well worth embarking on. Now some ten years later Barbara Bell has found a triumphantly successful format to communicate language awareness in *Minimus*, her book for primary schools. Sales for this now total over 42,000 and it is being used in Kent as a means of delivering the National Literacy Strategy (see p. 65).

One current initiative promises particularly well. In the National Curriculum for English, Key Stage 1 has story-telling as a component and this continues in KS2, which should include 'texts drawn from a variety of cultures and traditions and myths, legends and traditional stories'. A project run by the Cambridge Schools Classics Project and coordinated by Grant Page and Bob Lister is developing stories from the *Iliad* to provide material for these Key Stages. This important work has got off to a highly successful start. It is yet another exciting development in the story of determination, inventiveness and renewal which is told in the pages that follow.

And fortune seems to favour the brave. For the first time, a government has directed serious money towards classics for schoolchildren. It has given more than £1.5 million towards the Cambridge Online Latin Project. In addition it has granted JACT funds to develop a website and to produce a Good Practice guide in ICT for teachers of classics.

Furthermore, the government's wish to see state and independent schools in partnership rather than rivalry is a decided boost for a subject such as ours in which so high a proportion of the teaching is in the latter. The worrying teacher-training situation in classics (see pp. 167–8) has significantly improved with the development of in-service training. Teachers already in post can gain a PGCE through the course developed by the Council for British Teachers (CfBT).[1] Candidates can train anywhere in the country, not just in areas accessible to tutors at the excellent Departments of Education at Cambridge, King's College London, and Strathclyde. They are overseen by an external tutor and by a mentor at their own school. Moreover, as classics is deemed a shortage subject, the government pays the course fee. Usually candidates are awarded the PGCE after a year of study, and after another year they can achieve Qualified Teacher Status (QTS), armed with which they may teach at maintained or independent schools alike. The breaking down of the barriers between the two sectors is not the least indication of hope for the future.

---

[1] See Henry Wickham in *JACT Review* (Spring 2003). Contact: www.cfbt.com. The Ofsted inspection – and endorsement – of the course is at http://www.ofsted.gov.uk/reports/ittreports/705.htm

Acknowledgements

In 1998 R.A. LaFleur published a collection of essays entitled *Latin for the 21st Century* (Scott Foresman–Addison Wesley). From a UK point of view, the only problem with this admirable book was that it is about Latin in the USA! When I first saw it at the American Classical League's Institute in San Francisco in that year, I found myself regretting that we had not produced such a volume on our side of the Atlantic. Then, when I was President of JACT in the millennium year, my regret hardened to a determination to do something about it. I am most grateful to Fiona Kelly of Cambridge University Press for taking on this project and giving it her consistent support.

My two qualifications for editing such a volume are perhaps worryingly negative. One of them is that plainly nobody else was going to do so. The other is that I take no doctrinaire position on any aspect of the teaching of classics. I simply believe that teachers should follow the methods that best suit their circumstances and themselves. I hope that some readers may feel that that negative is up to a point a plus!

A number of people apart from the contributors have given me invaluable help, above all Pat Easterling, John Murrell, Clare Roberts, Charlotte Roueché, David Taylor and Linda Woodward. I express my warmest thanks to them. My most profound debt is to Henry Wickham, who has proved the most conscientious and efficient assistant editor in the final stages of the enterprise.

Three editorial matters need to be mentioned. One of them concerns the plethora of acronyms. I considered devoting a page to the clarification of these, but then felt that this would appear somewhat comic; the Department of Education alone, for example, has had four titles in recent years, DES, DfE, DfEE and now DfES. I very much hope that all such abbreviations are clarified in the text. Secondly, three of the chapters, John Taylor's and both of Brenda Gay's, have full bibliographies at the end. It seemed sensible to keep these intact as they provide useful reference points. Thirdly, I am conscious that some information is given two or even three times over. The justification for this is that, where the repeated material occurs, it is a key part of the writer's argument and thus cross-referencing would damage and obscure the flow of thought. Cross-referencing has in fact been kept to a minimum since it could easily have proliferated to an unhelpful degree.

I give my thanks to the Oxford classics faculty for granting me a sabbatical term to work on this book. Part 1 of Richard Shannon's article incorporates the classics section in 'Good teaching, effective department', OFSTED 2002 (reference no.: HMI 337). Crown copyright material is reproduced with the permission of the Controller of HMSO and the Queen's Printer for Scotland. Julie Wilkinson quotes with permission from the Qualifications and Curriculum Authority booklet *Classics in the Curriculum* (1997).

James Morwood

Classics Faculty   Wadham College
Oxford   Oxford

1 | Classics in the curriculum up to the 1960s

Christopher Stray

At the beginning of the nineteenth century, classics was firmly embedded in the schools and universities of England, Wales, Scotland and Ireland (which had just joined the Union). It is worth emphasising just how it was embedded. First of all, this was no system of education like those of France or Germany, where centralised control had produced state-run systems of schooling. In England, this did not appear until 1870 for elementary schools, and 1902 for secondary schools. Secondly, knowledge of Latin, and even more of Greek, was an important marker of social status. From the middle of the eighteenth century, a wave of protest against the domination of secondary schooling by classics had led to the foundation or revival of schools teaching English, accountancy, surveying and other practical subjects. But the expansion of middle-class numbers and power after the industrial revolution gave a boost to the declining rural grammar schools which became what we know as the Victorian public schools, led by the Rugby of Thomas James (1778–94) and the Shrewsbury of Samuel Butler (1798–1836).

Through the nineteenth century, as successive waves of newly aspirant groups struggled to assert their social status and distinguish themselves from their inferiors, further groups of schools were founded – many as proprietary schools, whose owners held shares and secured preferential entry for their sons. All this activity went unexamined by the state until the Royal Commissions of the 1860s, beginning with the Clarendon Commission of 1861. Having investigated the nine leading schools, the Commission reaffirmed the central role of classics in the education of English gentlemen, but suggested that its share of the curriculum might be reduced to about three-fifths. A later Commission on endowed schools (Taunton, 1864) looked at the 800 or so grammar schools and found that while some local parents wanted a more practical curriculum, many of them were keen to retain classics, which was seen as a sign of social status. The Commission recommended three grades of schools marked by differences in leaving age and the amount of classics taught.

Meanwhile the classical curricula of the two ancient universities had developed in different ways from their Renaissance origins. Oxford was dominated by classics, which was tested in a university examination founded in 1800 and whose climax after 1850 was the course in Literae Humaniores (Greats). This was a broadly conceived course which included ancient history and ancient (and modern) philosophy, but marginalised literature.[1] Cambridge, which had since the Newtonian days of the eighteenth century been dominated by mathematics, set up the Classical Tripos in 1822. This examination was only available to honours men in maths, and such restrictions were not completely removed until the 1850s. The reforms of the 1870s, which introduced specialised courses in a new Part II of the Tripos, went with an intellectual style of solid but circumscribed effort. The Oxonian ethos, in contrast, was one of effortless superiority and high-flown thinking – a style which matched its continuing involvement with national politics and the empire, a field where Cambridge had a much lower profile.

By 1900 new universities had been founded, in London, Durham and the industrial midlands and north. All taught classics (or rather 'Greek and Latin'), but some concentrated on science and technology and also offered English and modern languages. The map of knowledge was changing. The less complacent supporters of classics recognised that their subject now had to be fought for, and the battle was opened with the passage of the 1902 Education Act setting up municipal secondary schools. As John Postgate of Cambridge warned in November 1902, 'It is clear that classics will not be allowed to retain the lion's share which has been theirs in the past, and the question is, how much we must struggle to retain.'[2] The standard public school curriculum was based on large quantities of grammar learning and repetition, followed by constant practice in Latin and Greek composition, in prose and verse. The work was largely linguistic, with very little discussion of literary value. How was this to be cut down while remaining effective? And effective for what?

Those who advocated reform rather than retrenchment were divided. The moderates urged a reduction in the amount of composition – what was needed was to read the ancient authors, not to imitate them. A few radicals offered to reinvent the classical curriculum. Notable among them was W.H.D. Rouse, who became headmaster of a declining grammar school in Cambridge, the Perse School, in 1902. Inspired by reforms in modern language teaching, he

---

[1] Philosophy moved out of the Faculty of Literae Humaniores in 2001.
[2] J.P. Postgate, 'Are the classics to go?', *Fortnightly Review* 72 ns (1902), 866–80.

determined to teach Latin and Greek by speaking them. This was, he claimed, not only a desirable return to the Renaissance world when Latin was a medium of communication, but also an efficient way of learning – it would bring proficiency more quickly, so leaving time for other subjects. Rouse and his pupils, and the Association for the Reform of Latin Teaching (ARLT) he founded in 1913, made a considerable impact on the Board of Education and on teaching manuals. Many teachers who tried to use the direct method, however, found that it demanded more knowledge of the languages than they possessed.[3] A broader-based defensive body, the Classical Association (CA) of England and Wales, was founded in 1903, a year after its Scottish counterpart. It built bridges with politicians and attempted to link school and university classicists, though in time the latter came to dominate its activities.[4]

The hard thinking occasioned by the First World War generated fierce debate. Scientists argued that better provision for science education rather than classics would have helped to win the war; humanists replied that the war was fought for moral ends, and that these were the province of the humanities, and classical civilisation their great exemplar. The four committees on Science and Modern Languages (both 1916) and on English and Classics (both 1919) all made demands for their own subject areas; the Board of Education responded in the 1920s by withdrawing from full curricular prescription and leaving supply and demand to solve the problem. The specialised curriculum characteristic of twentieth-century British schools and so unlike others was firmly launched.

Within this curriculum, the fates of Latin and Greek were very different. The Classics Committee, which reported in 1921, had found that while Latin was taught to nearly 45 per cent of pupils, the comparable figure for Greek was less than 5 per cent.[5] Latin, which had always had a broader social base than Greek, became the acceptable face of classics, the symbolic exemplar of the academic world of the grammar school. In an inter-war world of competing extremisms, totalitarian and fascist, it represented the right thinking of the orderly, self-controlled citizen. Greek was more ethereal, more exciting, more dangerous. It was taught largely in the public schools, which clung to 'full classics' – Latin, Greek, ancient history – rather than a single specialism. (It was notable, however, that a few girls'

---

[3] For Rouse and his campaigns, see C.A. Stray, *The Living Word: W.H.D. Rouse and the Crisis of Classics in Edwardian England* (Bristol Classical Press / Duckworth, 1992).
[4] A centenary history of the Classical Association, including an account of that of its elder Scottish sister, is provided by C.A. Stray (ed.), *The Classical Association: the First Century 1903–2003* (Oxford University Press, 2003).
[5] *The Classics in Education* (HMSO, 1921), 43–6.

schools took the bold step of starting Greek before Latin.) By the 1950s, the classical course inherited from the nineteenth century and gradually attenuated rather than reformed was becoming fossilised. New courses based on intelligent reading rather than the rote learning of grammar had appeared, the best known being *Latin for Today*, a course developed in the USA in the 1920s and adapted for English schools in 1933. But they had a limited impact on the large numbers of pupils who struggled through compulsory Latin courses, leaving them as soon as they could. The situation was made worse by the fact that the platoons of teachers employed included many whose knowledge and qualifications were very limited. In the 1950s, Her Majesty's Inspectors of Classics agonised in private over the irreconcilable tension between the twin aims they ascribed to Latin teaching: the humanistic (what were the Romans like? what was their literature about?) and the disciplinary (grammar as an unrivalled means to mental training, a training which could be transferred to other subjects).

The wartime debates over reform in the organisation and curricula of schools ended in a veiled reassertion of hierarchy in both areas. The grammar schools were protected by selective entry and by the residual definition of secondary modern and technical schools. The new GCE examination (1951) took specialisation to new heights. Recruitment to Latin rose in absolute (though not relative) terms, on the back of a general expansion of secondary schooling. The demand for 'compulsory Greek' from Oxford and Cambridge had been abandoned after the First World War, to be replaced by compulsory Latin. Now the tide began to turn, as the Cold War fuelled demands for science education, and at the end of the 1950s, the ancient universities ceased to demand Latin from all students.

The impact of these decisions emerged clearly in the next few years. The numbers of entrants for O level Latin and Greek dropped immediately, to be followed by A level numbers. Many teachers held to their belief in the immortality of a subject which transcended time and place, but were persuaded to debate options other than a last-ditch reassertion of tradition. The Classical Association's booklet *Re-appraisal* (1962) reflects, largely in ways which now seem complacent, some of the contemporary discussion. Behind the scenes, reformers were trying to find a way to break through complacency to new modes of organisation and of teaching. The Joint Association of Classical Teachers (1962), largely engineered by John Sharwood Smith, brought together the CA, the ARLT and the smaller Orbilian Society in a slightly uneasy but increasingly firm alliance. JACT promoted discussion of problems and solutions, and encouraged debate through its journal *Didaskalos* (1963–77), which Sharwood Smith edited.[6]

The 1960s also witnessed a direct attack on a central cause of continuing hostility to classics: the O level Latin course. Initial moves to produce a new course were led by Charles Brink, Professor of Latin at Cambridge. A German Jew, Brink had been trained in the austere continental tradition and had taught at schools and universities in Oxford, Liverpool and Cambridge. Though personally devoted to the higher reaches of linguistic scholarship, he could see that radical change was necessary if the universities were to continue to receive a supply of competent students. His campaign led to the support of his university and of the Nuffield Foundation, and in the later 1960s to the production of linguistic and non-linguistic courses by the Cambridge School Classics Project.

The crisis of the 1960s belonged to a wider climate of change which included student revolts and educational reform, abroad as well as in Britain. Rethinking was the order of the day, and Latin discipline and the courses claiming to produce it were easily, and commonly, seen as the lingering symbols of an old order on its last legs. For teachers brought up to believe that life was essentially stable, and that classics embodied eternal symbols of stable value, the collapse of compulsory Latin and the declining recruitment which followed it were existential shocks difficult to comprehend. But for those who did not retreat into the mechanical reassertion of traditional slogans, the decade offered a chance to rethink and to explore not only new ways of teaching, but their own subject. A text could now be read not just as a corpus of linguistic phenomena, but as the artful construction of human beings with literary and cultural ends, created in social and historical contexts. Such approaches, developed by scholars like John Sullivan and Kenneth Quinn, reached schools though Maurice Balme and Mark Warman's *Aestimanda* (Oxford University Press, 1965). On a different front, a transformation of ancient history and classical civilisation courses was attempted under the leadership of Moses Finley. This American Jewish economic historian had, like Charles Brink, a width of experience which enabled him to see the English situation in perspective. The JACT ancient history A level course he masterminded threw a great stress on the use of evidence, though this radical thrust was weakened by the reluctance of examiners to penalise good traditional answers. Overall, then, the 1960s were for classicists a time of shock and dismay, yet also of opportunity and radical reform in their subject.

---

[6] The final volume (1977) was edited by Robin Barrow.

2 | Classics in the curriculum from the 1960s to the 1990s

David Tristram

This chapter looks at the position of classics – and particularly Latin – in the curriculum of this country's secondary schools throughout the period from the 1960s to the 1990s and the factors which have affected its survival. The emphasis is on classics in the maintained sector, since its position in independent schools remained relatively secure during that period – despite being subject to some of the pressures mentioned here.

In the maintained sector, the 1960s were a time for reassessment of many facets of the educational process and classics came under scrutiny from many quarters – not least from within the ranks of its own practitioners.

> All subject specialists are faced from time to time with the necessity to reassess and modify their teaching methods so as to make them more efficient and to bring them into line with advances in knowledge and with the changing patterns of curricula and examinations.

So began Sidney Morris – Lecturer in Education at the University of Birmingham – in *Viae Novae: New Techniques in Latin Teaching* in 1966.[1] Morris was calling for a reappraisal of traditional teaching methods and citing as his prime reason for doing so the number of school pupils who began studying Latin at age 11, yet did not continue beyond their first two years of compulsory study. There were other reasons for his call: the O level syllabus had been criticised by teachers for some time as being unsuitable, containing as it did a mixture of sterile grammar questions, English to Latin translation, and Latin to English translation devoid of context. Understanding and interpretation of literature – taken for granted now – played little part in the examination and thus in the teaching of Latin. Morris' plea for some form of reappraisal of Latin teaching in schools came amidst a welter of educational changes in the 1960s – a time of revolution and social change. However, the declining number of pupils taking O level Latin was but one of the major challenges facing the teaching

---

[1] Sidney Morris, *Viae Novae: New Techniques in Latin Teaching* (Hulton, 1966).

of classics in this decade. In the 1960s, classics was under threat from external factors which might prove to have a more lasting effect than the decline in interest from its own 'customers'.

Martin Forrest in *Modernising the Classics*[2] identifies at least two further major factors – which he refers to as Crisis One and Crisis Two – as being the fundamental reasons for the nature of classics teaching in schools to undergo necessary and rapid change. The first of these 'crises' was the decision by the universities of Oxford and Cambridge to abolish Latin (or Greek) as a requirement for entry to their respective universities. Their decisions were different: the University of Oxford had decreed that Latin (or Greek) would no longer be a compulsory entry requirement for those wishing to study the sciences; in Cambridge the decision was that Latin was no longer to be a specific requirement for admission to the university. These decisions contributed strongly to a movement for a re-examination of the purpose and nature of the teaching of classics – and of Latin in particular – which was to have major consequences in terms of the place of these subjects in the secondary school curriculum and in terms of the teaching materials available to classroom practitioners.

The second major crisis – according to Forrest – was of a more political nature: the accelerating move towards comprehensive education. Throughout the 1960s, many Local Education Authorities (LEAs) had begun to reorganise their education systems along comprehensive lines. The abolition of the majority of grammar schools and the introduction of a non-selective system would inevitably have a detrimental effect on classics, for so long viewed as an essentially linguistic discipline and hence as the sole domain of the 'more able' in the education system – and even of the 'more able' within the grammar schools themselves where many schools maintained a 'Classical Sixth'.

In the event, the introduction of comprehensive schooling was not a nationwide phenomenon: even after some forty years of 'comprehensive education' there are still numerous counties and LEAs with grammar and secondary modern schools, or with hybrid systems. However, the possibility that it might be so did prompt a minor revolution in Latin teaching methods and materials, which was eventually to give rise to the Cambridge Latin Course, and the Scottish Classics Group's *Ecce Romani*. It also spawned other new courses such as J.A. Harrison's *Latin Reading Course*, as well as revised versions of old favourites such as Paterson and Macnaughton's *The Approach to Latin*.

---

[2] Martin Forrest, *Modernising the Classics: A Study in Curriculum Development* (University of Exeter, 1996).

What was happening in schools at this time? The change in curricular structures was relatively slow. Head teachers wishing to implement changes in their schools were often constrained by the existing staffing structures and so had to wait until the opportunity arose to do so. Sometimes, the nature of the change depended on the inclination of the head teacher: had the head come from a grammar school system? If so, he or she might have wanted to maintain a curricular structure that mirrored the grammar school – and thus retain the 'traditional' subjects. Others might have grown up with the comprehensive ideal and wished to introduce a more revolutionary approach more quickly. LEAs too played a more critical role in the curricular structure of schools and had much greater influence on *what* was taught in schools than perhaps they had during the 1970s and 1980s. Those LEAs actively promoting a comprehensive system also promoted a curricular structure offering equality of opportunity which did not always include a place for classics. So it was that areas such as Leicestershire – with its pioneering 'Leicestershire Plan' for school and curricular reorganisation conceived in the 1950s – were at the forefront of educational change, whereas the pace of change in some other LEAs was less hurried.

In an article entitled 'Classics in the UK' in the 1985 issue of *Latin Teaching*,[3] Peter Jones made the following observations about 'comprehensivisation' and its results:

> under the old pre-60s system, classics had a pretty good deal. Virtually all Grammar, Direct Grant and Independent schools would have had Latin, some even Latin and Greek. But comprehensive schools did away with all that. The process of social and intellectual equalisation had no room for these ancient subjects. Of Classics teachers who had been 'comprehensivised', some panicked early and retired. . . Others, thank heavens, were given furiously to think about the place of Classics within the new comprehensive system. They were the fighters, bless them, and this is where the quiet revolution in Classics in England has taken place.

Jones cited some chilling statistics in the article: in 1968, he recalled, some 46,000 students had sat O level Latin and 6,500 had sat A level. By 1979 the number sitting O level had slipped to 33,000 and A level to a mere 3,000. A glance at the statistics towards the end of this chapter will show just how much the picture has changed since 1979. It was certainly the acceleration of the introduction of large-scale 'comprehensivisation' that contributed in large measure to that

---

3 Peter Jones, 'Classics in the UK', *Latin Teaching* XXXVI, No. 5 (ARLT, 1986), 35–44.

decline in numbers. The Wilson governments of the early and mid-1970s – through Reg Prentice, as Secretary of State for Education – gave notice to LEAs that they should set in motion plans for wholesale change to a comprehensive system. Though many of the direct grant schools chose to become independent and thus were able to maintain their classics departments, there were many schools where the change meant the end for classics. Jones was most certainly correct in his observation that those classics teachers who remained in the maintained sector had a fight on their hands. However, they had allies. The seventies saw a lifeline for classics teachers in the maintained sector with the rapid development of the Cambridge Latin Course.

The trials and tribulations that the project went through in its gestation are charted fully in Forrest's *Modernising the Classics*.[4] However, the real story is perhaps to be found in what was actually going on in the new comprehensive schools. Where a classics department – or in many cases, Latin as part of a languages department – could continue to exist, most teachers chose to move over to CLC, if they had not already done so. It offered a fresh dimension to teachers: a course which contained a substantial background element, which was more accessible to classes of mixed ability, and which concentrated on reading skills from Latin to English – without the necessity for English to Latin translation. CLC was not without its critics, of course. As Reader pointed out in his article in *Hesperiam* 1,[5] the course was popular with students, though not always with teachers:

> Criticism of CLC from pupils is comparatively rare: with few exceptions their interest is aroused and their attention is held by the material in the course; in that respect CLC is successful. Criticism comes rather from teachers and examiners, and I think not only from those who would fall most readily into the category of 'narrow-minded linguists'.

Whatever the criticisms might have been, it was seen as the only option for those teachers who were now teaching a wider ability range for the first time. However, although there were a few schools brave enough to introduce Latin *ex nihilo*, it was usually an option only where Latin had already existed. Jones made that point clearly in the article already quoted[6] – a transcript of an address given to the Classical Language Teachers' Association of New South Wales:

---

[4] Forrest, *Modernising the Classics*, ch. 9.
[5] T.R.A. Reader, 'The Cambridge Latin Course: linguistic principles and course design', *Hesperiam* 1 (1978), 56–73.
[6] Jones, 'Classics in the UK', 35–44.

But that is the golden picture. Here's the catch. The scenario I have just sketched applies, I guess, to about 20% of comprehensive schools, largely those which were once grammar schools, had a good classical tradition and whose staff were able to adjust to the new demands.

The scenario – the golden picture – Jones spoke of was not, in fact, the teaching of Latin, but of non-linguistic classical civilisation. He was here making a plea that, if classics were to survive beyond the 1970s and 1980s, it would need to be in the form of classics in translation. One of his arguments was that those thought unlikely to benefit from studying Latin or Greek would be gripped by a study of Greek and Roman civilisation and might later take up the opportunity of learning the languages when they went on to university to pursue their interest in the ancient world.

Classics did survive in some maintained schools. To take one LEA as an example – Northamptonshire – during the 1980s some form of classics was taught in only a handful of secondary schools – five out of a possible forty-three. It only survived where the head teacher was in sympathy with classics and where there were teachers who could continue the teaching. One by one those schools have discontinued the teaching of classics – as a result of either a change in head teacher or the departure of the teacher responsible for it. In one of Northamptonshire's comprehensive schools – where the school's head teacher had come through grammar school and was himself an Oxford classicist – the classics department consisted of three teachers; *all* pupils followed a mythology-based language awareness course in Year 7, half of Year 8 started Latin and continued to study it into Year 9; and Latin and classical civilisation were popular options at GCSE and A level. This department withered and died away to nothing in the space of five years on the retirement of the head teacher and the departure of the specialist teachers. That fate was surely shared by other such departments up and down the country.

The Department for Education and Science (DES) Circular 6/81 published in October 1981 required all LEAs to review their policies for the school curriculum and their arrangements for making their policies known. Each LEA was given two years in which to do so and, as promised, DES Circular 8/83, published in December 1983, required the LEAs to report on their progress towards this, together with a description of the consultative procedures followed, and an outline of the practical implications for schools. Most LEAs had set up working parties to determine the nature of the curriculum and the approach that would be used in defining the LEA's curriculum policy. Likewise, most had held consultations with teachers of all age groups of children, governors, parents, older students, employers' representatives and other interested parties. The results of these deliberations and consultations were curriculum guidelines which would be passed on to schools and act as 'blueprints' for the curriculum. They also acted as checklists for inspection: the LEA – the inspecting body for a large number of maintained schools in these pre-Ofsted days – would expect to find a curriculum in place in schools which matched those guidelines. Few had reference to the place of classics in the secondary curriculum and thus a further nail was placed in the coffin of Latin in the maintained sector. Some – like Northamptonshire, where a strong classics lobby existed within the elected membership and amongst the secondary schools themselves – did produce guidelines for classics in the curriculum. But in other LEAs, how many classics teachers knew of Circulars 6/81 and 8/83 and their implications for the future of their subject?

When the Education Reform Bill was unveiled in the House of Commons in 1987, it was clear that it contained many complex issues which were going to affect the education systems of England and Wales for many years to come. Contained in the bill were proposals for open enrolment, the creation of grant-maintained schools and city technology colleges, the introduction of assessment and testing at the ages of 7, 11, 14 and 16 for all pupils, the delegation of financial control to governing bodies of schools, and, of course, the proposals for a National Curriculum. The National Curriculum proposals stated that there would be three 'core subjects' – maths, science and English, and a further list of seven foundation subjects – history, geography, a modern foreign language, technology, music, art and physical education. There was to be no place for classics amongst the foundation subjects.

The discussion document sent out by the DES to clarify certain issues and to stimulate discussion contained any number of laudable aims – to raise standards consistently, to provide a broad and balanced curriculum, to offer access to such a curriculum to pupils of all abilities. However, beyond these general aims, there appeared to be a distinct lack of any coherent educational philosophy. The proposals seemed to have been framed in such a way as to promote only a limited range of subjects, constraining the options open to the pupil. Little regard seemed to have been paid to the possibility of integration of subjects and the development of cross-curricular skills. There seemed to be no recognition of any curricular development that had taken place over the preceding years, such as the Humanities Curriculum Project, work on integrated humanities, nor the contribution of HMI's *Curriculum Matters* series.

Debate centred on the percentage of time that the core and foundation subjects should occupy. Although figures of 80 per cent and above had been bandied around early on in the discussion, the then Secretary of State for Education, Kenneth Baker, made the following statement during the debate on the second reading of the bill on 1 December 1987:

> We do not intend to lay down, either on the face of the Bill or in any secondary legislation, the percentage of time to be spent on different subjects. This will provide an essential flexibility. But it is our belief that it will be difficult, if not impossible, for any school to provide the National Curriculum in less than 70% of the time available. The remaining time will allow schools to offer other subjects – among them home economics, Latin, business education, careers education, and a range of other subjects.

This statement did little to allay the fears of classicists, and a considerable 'classics lobby' was mobilised – thanks in large measure to Dr Peter Jones, then a member of the classics department at the University of Newcastle, and Adrian Spooner, at the time a vociferous Head of Classics at Park View Comprehensive School in Chester-le-Street, as well as organisations such as JACT. Representations were made to Kenneth Baker, in an effort to change the proposals and to allow for the inclusion of some elements of classics within the list of foundation subjects. A flood of articles and letters appeared in the 'quality' newspapers, even one in Latin from Frances Morrell, at the time Leader of the Inner London Education Authority. One article [7] detailed the great and good enlisted to help in the campaign to 'save the classics': Sir Jeremy Morse (Chairman, Lloyds Bank), Jeremy Isaacs (Chief Executive, Channel 4), Dr Anthony Kenny (Master of Balliol College, Oxford) and many other names. There was even an adjournment debate in the House of Commons devoted to Latin, moved by Michael Fallon, MP. It was in this debate that Angela Rumbold made the following statement, justifying the absence of classics from the list of foundation subjects:

> I have discovered that in the maintained schools some form of classics is taught in about 30% of comprehensive schools and about 50% of our grammar schools ... In 1985, there were 33,000 entries for CSE or O level in classical subjects, about 0.5% of entries in all subjects. At A level, there were more than 6,000 in classical subjects – about 1% of the total entry. Although I warm to the notion that nothing should be done to further reduce the teaching of classics, those figures I think show that classics are not on offer to all pupils and may reflect some schools' judgement on whether to offer the subjects at all.

---

[7] 'Caveat Mr Baker, top people rally to defend Latin', *Sunday Telegraph* (27 September 1987).

The debate reinforced many old prejudices and Latin became a political football, as Messrs Fallon and Straw exchanged words over the axing of Latin by some Labour-controlled authorities. If it had not already been lost, the campaign to have classics included in the list of foundation subjects was lost in this debate. Many of the MPs in the chamber had no idea of the changes that had come over education as a whole since they were at school, let alone those that had occurred in the teaching of classics. Michael Fallon conspicuously failed to bring that point home.

The Joint Association of Classical Teachers, of course, had made strenuous efforts to combat the inevitable omission of any form of classics from the list of foundation subjects. Evidence of their argument can be found in Julian Haviland's excellent *Take Care, Mr Baker!* This book represented 'a selection of the advice on the Government's Education Reform Bill which the Secretary of State for Education invited but decided not to publish'.[8] As well as arguments concerned with the National Curriculum from such organisations as JACT, the book contained essays on other aspects of the bill – opting out, local financial management, open enrolment, and testing and assessment – all of which are now with us. JACT's submission is quoted as follows:

> These curriculum proposals, if implemented as they stand, will mean the end of any teaching and learning of classics in maintained secondary schools in the very near future … These are tried and tested subjects and must not be abandoned until it has been demonstrated that they are to be replaced by something clearly superior to them. If they were lost, the damage to the study of English, medieval history, theology, philosophy and a number of other subjects would be enormous. The fact that we would be cut off from the core of western civilisation and the basis of much of our own culture is frightening.

The stated purpose of Haviland's book was to highlight the advice which Kenneth Baker and his colleagues had received, but ignored. So, like the other submissions he quotes, these arguments fell on deaf ears. In the concluding paragraph of an article in *Perspectives* 32,[9] Wiseman summed up the feelings of classicists – and many other supporters of classics:

> In effect, whether deliberately or by inadvertence, the exclusion of classical studies from the foundation curriculum is an announcement that the subject is not important enough to protect. It will have to take

---

8 Julian Haviland, *Take Care, Mr Baker!* (Fourth Estate, 1988).
9 T.P. Wiseman, 'On the absence of classical subjects from the foundation curriculum, Perspectives on the National Curriculum', *Perspectives* 32 (University of Exeter, 1987), 82–6.

its chance with the inessentials, competing for scarce resources of time and support without being able to show the customers why it is worth spending time on. That, it seems to me, is either a gross blunder or an abdication of educational responsibility.

Her Majesty's Inspectors made their own contribution to this debate and had been doing so almost since Callaghan's Ruskin speech of 1976 (see p. 21). Spurred on by this speech, HMI, led by Sheila Browne, initiated an enquiry into the curricular practice of five LEAs, beginning in 1977. This enquiry led to the publication of the three 'red books' in 1978, 1981 and 1983. So, as well as heralding the dawn of the National Curriculum, the eighties also saw the publication of the series of booklets entitled *Curriculum Matters*. The second of these booklets – apparently known amongst HMI as the 'raspberry ripples' – set out the aim of the whole series:

> ...to stimulate the professional discussion about the whole curriculum, about the possible basis for agreement, about the broad purposes of primary and secondary education in England and Wales, and about the ways in which teachers working in schools might give them expression.[10]

The booklets were based on the findings of inspection reports and a good deal of research – some of which had been reported in *Curriculum 11–16*,[11] published by HMI in 1983. In the explanatory and introductory booklet HMI covered elements such as the demands on schools, the nature and scope of the curriculum, the overall design of the curriculum, and the need for assessment. Perhaps the most interesting aspect of this booklet was that HMI spoke of the 'areas of learning and experience': aesthetic and creative, human and social, linguistic and literary, mathematical, moral, physical, scientific, spiritual, and technological. They also spoke of 'elements of learning': knowledge, concepts, skills, and attitudes. Those who read these booklets hoped that the well-founded scholarship and common sense to be found in them would inform the debate about the National Curriculum. Sadly, that was not to be the case.

In 1988, *Curriculum Matters 12*[12] was published – in the chronology of the genesis of the National Curriculum, too late to have any serious impact on deliberations. It contained the following statement which sadly would turn out to be less than prophetic:

> Although the Education Reform Act 1988 does not designate classics as a foundation subject of the National Curriculum, many secondary

---

10 *The Curriculum from 5 to 16, Curriculum Matters 2* (HMSO, 1985).
11 *Curriculum 11–16, Towards a Statement of Entitlement. Curricular Reappraisal in Action* (HMSO, 1983).
12 *Classics from 5 to 16, Curriculum Matters 12* (HMSO, 1988).

schools will nevertheless want to include it in the time available for 'non-foundation' subjects.

The booklet covered such elements as the nature and scope of the subject, the aims of classics teaching, linguistic and non-linguistic courses, objectives for all stages from 5 to 16 and principles of teaching and learning, and even the delicate subject of differentiation. The influence of this slim volume could be seen in the development of the National Criteria for Classical Subjects and in the new GCSE examinations and it contained much that was helpful for classics teachers about the development of classical courses. It addressed two questions in particular, the answers to which it hoped would be of interest not only to specialist teachers of classics, but to other secondary school teachers, to teachers in primary and middle schools, as well as to heads, LEAs, governors, and parents:

- what contact with the classical world is it appropriate to provide for all pupils, and what benefits might they be expected to derive from it?
- what, in addition, is it reasonable to expect of those pupils whose study of a classical subject has been more extensive or more specialised?[13]

The soundly based, rational arguments in *Curriculum Matters 12* may well have been of *interest* to such parties, but they did little to halt the slow but steady decline in numbers taking classical subjects in maintained schools.

In June 1984, the Secretary of State for Education announced to the House of Commons that a new, single system of examinations at 16+, the General Certificate of Secondary Education (GCSE), would replace the GCE O level, CSE and any joint 16+ examinations in England and Wales, with effect from the summer of 1988. The announcement heralded the biggest change in the examinations system since the inception of CSE, but more importantly, perhaps, it was to initiate changes in teaching methods and strategies. Like many other subjects, classics had been preparing for these changes and, indeed, some would say that the work already accomplished by the Cambridge Schools Classics Project and the examination boards (most notably the Southern Universities Joint Board and a northern consortium of examination boards) had paved the way admirably for the changes that were to come. The northern consortium, for example, had been offering examinations in classical studies at 16+ for some ten years and had offered a coursework option as part of the assessment programme for most of that time.

---

[13] Ibid.

National criteria were issued for twenty subjects, among them 'classical subjects', the umbrella title favoured by the Secondary Examinations Council, in view of the plethora of syllabus options already available: Latin, Greek, Roman civilisation, Greek civilisation, Latin and Roman civilisation, Greek and Greek civilisation, and classical civilisation (Greek and Roman). This large number of syllabus options was a testament to the fact that – outside the independent schools – classics teachers were striving to keep the subject alive. However, an analysis of the numbers of pupils taking some of these options reveals that rationalisation was required. The very fact that national criteria were prepared for classical subjects could be taken as an indication that the position which the range of subjects occupied in the secondary curriculum was an important one, and that the classics 'revolution' had prepared the subject area well for the inception of GCSE. Whatever the reason for the inclusion in the list of twenty subjects, the criteria were prepared and published in 1985 and were generally accepted by teachers as meeting their needs, particularly in respect of non-linguistic subjects, in which a wide range of ability was already being examined. There had been CSE and O level and joint 16+ examinations in classical studies. In Latin, however, though there had been CSE syllabuses, by far the majority of candidates had been examined at O level. The national criteria for Latin (and Greek), therefore, were couched very much in the terms that had been applicable to O level examination. GCSE was intended to cater for a much wider ability spectrum. Many classicists asked at the time whether this was a realistic aim for Latin. Latin teachers may have wanted to shed the tag of 'élitism', and CLC may have been designed to help them do this. However, in schools where Latin did survive, it was usually only offered to pupils of higher ability – likely to achieve a grade C or above, the equivalent of an old O level pass. In the event, the restructuring of the examination boards did little to widen the range of candidates able to tackle the examinations and the examinations differed very little from those that had been available before.

The first GCSE examinations were taken in the summer of 1988 and they met with a generally favourable reception from teachers, pupils, parents and even Her Majesty's Inspectorate. However, the numbers of pupils actually sitting the examinations did not look very healthy – even at this early stage. The table on page 17 shows the subject entries for the various syllabus options with the four main English examination boards in 1988.

GCSE Subject Entries By Syllabus Option – 1988

	MEG	NEA	SEG	LEAG	Totals
Latin	4437	2473	420	1509	8839
Latin (SCP)	5538	1158	-	-	6696
Latin & Roman Civ.	365	289	-	57	711
Greek	771	290	22	217	1300
Greek & Greek Civ.	2	6	-	3	11
Classical Civ.	1600	1794	419	414	4227
Roman Civ.	265	114	-	18	397
Greek Civ.	960	236	-	259	1455
	13938	6360	861	2477	23636

The figures revealed a great deal and presented the examination boards with a challenge. Some of the options were clearly not viable and moves were made very quickly to rationalise them. Since that time, of course, the examination boards themselves have 'rationalised' into just three (OCR, AQA and Edexcel) and now only AQA and OCR offer syllabuses in classical subjects.

What happened in the maintained sector throughout the nineties? The story remained much the same – a steady decline, but with Latin and classical civilisation clinging on where the head teacher showed encouragement for it, or where there were teachers available. The tables below show the entries for Latin and classical civilisation since the inception of GCSE in 1988 and the A level entry figures for both Latin and classical civilisation.

GCSE Inter-Group Statistics – All Examining Groups –
UK Candidates Only

	1988	1989	1990	1991	1992	1993	1994
Latin	16236	15805	14509	13821	13408	12630	12844
Classical Civilisation	4227	2624	2416	2532	2536	2564	2448

	1995	1996	1997	1998	1999	2000	2001
Latin	12958	12659	11860	10908	10451	10561	10365
Classical Civilisation	2471	4040	4038	3543	3533	3870	3904

The GCSE entries for Latin show a steady decline from 1988 to 2001 – but, viewed optimistically, they appear to have reached a plateau from 1999 onwards. Unfortunately, these figures are not broken down by type of school. Obviously, there will be a substantial number of independent schools included in these totals, as well as some grammar schools – in fact, they almost certainly represent the vast majority of the entries. For classical civilisation, the picture is even less optimistic. With numbers regularly below 4,000, the examination boards might at some time consider the viability of offering the syllabuses – in terms of cost effectiveness. However, there are positive signs, such as the significant rise in entries in 1996 and the relatively stable position from that point onwards.

A Level Inter-Board Statistics – All Examining Groups –
UK Candidates Only

	1988	1989	1990	1991	1992	1993	1994
Latin	1645	2024	1921	1910	1834	1772	1690
Classical Civilisation	N/A	N/A	1708	2174	2334	1506	1407

	1995	1996	1997	1998	1999	2000	2001
Latin	1625	1589	1539	1540	1321	1309	1264
Classical Civilisation	1365	1740	1691	1570	3373	3214	3188

The A level statistics for Latin show a less regular, but still downward trend. It could be argued that they have remained relatively stable over the whole period since the inception of GCSE. However, though it is not possible to break these figures down further, very few of the entries come from the maintained sector and that position is unlikely to change. Classical civilisation is, on the other hand, a success story. There can be no doubt that classical civilisation is now a popular choice in schools where it is available. The substantial rise in entries in 1999 – maintained since then – made it one of the fastest-growing subjects in percentage terms available to sixth-form students. It will be interesting to see the longer-term implications of the introduction of AS levels for examination entries – in both Latin and classical civilisation.

The path from the sixties to the nineties has not been an easy one for classical subjects in the maintained sector – nor for those who have attempted to keep them alive. Many factors have militated against their survival – the abolition of O level Latin as an Oxbridge requirement, the change to a largely comprehensive system, the introduction of a National Curriculum which recognised no place for Latin or classics in general, the introduction of GCSEs, and the move towards a more vocational curriculum pre- and post-16. Nevertheless, there are still some maintained schools which, thanks to the enthusiasm and dedication of their teachers, keep the classical tradition alive against all the odds, and we enter the twenty-first century with some grounds for optimism.

3 | Classics teaching and the National Curriculum

Brenda Gay

Two books published towards the end of the twentieth century, Stray, *Classics Transformed* and Forrest, *Modernising the Classics*,[1] when read together provide a very comprehensive view of classics teaching from the nineteenth century to 1990. Both show how classics moved from its dominant position in the nineteenth-century public and grammar schools and universities, and how the definition of what counts as classical learning has been broadened. The range of topics and authors on offer in current linguistic and non-linguistic courses in both schools and universities would appear an anathema to the scholarly gentleman of the Victorian era for whom Latin and Greek prose and verse composition was the peak of achievement and a mark of his gentlemanly status and who viewed archaeology with the deepest suspicion.

Like all teachers, classics teachers have had to adapt to a number of significant changes in education since the Education Act of 1944, which marked a major reorganisation of secondary schooling. The position of classics in the selective system of state education was relatively secure, particularly as long as Latin remained a requirement for entry to Oxbridge. However, the abolition of this requirement in the 1950s and 1960s, coupled with the reorganisation of secondary education on comprehensive lines, meant that classics teachers were faced with a new set of demands – namely how to make their subject attractive to a wider ability range of pupils and to adapt their pedagogy to the more child-centred approaches to learning that were being advocated. Forrest described the way in which these two crises acted as a catalyst for the Cambridge Classics Project and other innovative approaches to teaching classics. What Forrest described as the 'third crisis' came in the late 1970s and 1980s, culminating in 1988 with the provision under the Education Reform Act for a National Curriculum for maintained schools.[2]

---

1 C. Stray, *Classics Transformed* (Oxford University Press, 1998); M. Forrest, *Modernising the Classics* (University of Exeter Press, 1996).
2 Forrest, *Modernising the Classics*, p. 138.

Central control over the curriculum

Before examining the effects of the 1988 Act on classics, we must first explore how successive governments sought to gain greater control over what used to be seen as the 'secret garden' of the curriculum. In 1976 James Callaghan, the then Prime Minister, outlined in a speech at Ruskin College, Oxford, some of his government's concerns about the perceived failings in the education system, such as high rates of truancy, declining standards of behaviour and discipline in schools, and the poor performance of pupils in the UK in literacy and numeracy. Education was seen as failing to produce people equipped for the demands of a modern workforce, thus reducing our international competitiveness. Callaghan therefore called for the education system to become more accountable.[3]

In the 1980s successive Tory governments continued to express mounting concern about standards in education and the need to ensure that all pupils were given opportunities to maximise their potential. So began the move for increased central control over the curriculum. From 1984 HMI published a series of *Curriculum Matters* papers, which looked at the principles behind the curriculum as a whole[4] and individual subjects. The twelfth in the series, which was published in 1988, was on classics.[5] One of the features of these documents is the emphasis on the all-round development of pupils and the potential contribution of each subject in the curriculum to this. Contrary to popular belief, central control over the curriculum in this country is not a new phenomenon. In the nineteenth century and first decades of the twentieth century the curriculum in the elementary schools, but not the state grammar schools, was heavily prescribed and regulated. By contrast, the 1994 Education Act did not contain any requirements for the curriculum apart from the inclusion of religious instruction and physical education. Individual schools and teachers therefore to some extent enjoyed considerable autonomy over both curriculum content and pedagogy. Yet in reality secondary schools operated within the constraints of the syllabuses for public examinations, although the choice of examination board for each subject lay with the school.

The 1988 Act and the National Curriculum

The 1988 Education Reform Act, with its shift towards state control over the curriculum, reflected the importance placed on education as

---

[3] J. Callaghan, Speech delivered at Ruskin College, Oxford, reported in *Times Educational Supplement*, October 1976.
[4] DES, *The Curriculum from 5–16, Curriculum Matters 2* (HMSO, 1985).
[5] DES, *Classics from 5–16, Curriculum Matters 12* (HMSO, 1988).

a means of meeting the political, social and economic needs of society, as well as contributing to the development of each individual. Behind the Act lay a concern to raise standards, to give all children the right of access to a worthwhile curriculum (an entitlement curriculum); to give equality of access to educational chances on a national basis and to minimise local differences in the quality of education. The National Curriculum Orders reinforced this by requiring schools to implement an equal opportunities 'policy to which the whole school subscribes and in which positive attitudes to gender, equality, cultural needs and special needs of all kinds are actively promoted'.[6]

The Act established general curriculum principles which must be reflected in the education of all pupils aged 5–16. This is an entitlement curriculum which, as well as being broad and balanced, must:

a) promote the spiritual, moral, cultural, mental and physical development of pupils at the school and of society;

b) prepare pupils for the opportunities, responsibilities and experiences of adult life.[7]

The National Curriculum consisted of three Core subjects – English, mathematics and science – and seven Foundation subjects – technology, modern foreign languages, history, geography, art, music, and physical education. Religious education remained a statutory requirement, as it always had been, but was tackled differently through locally constituted Standing Advisory Councils on Religious Education (SACREs). The National Curriculum was subject based rather than integrated, although some acknowledgement of the importance of cross-curricular work was made in the inclusion of three non-statutory cross-curricular dimensions and five cross-curricular themes. This commitment to the all-round development is reflected in the statement that the

> basic curriculum as prescribed in law – the ten cores and the other foundation subjects plus Religious Education – is not intended to be the whole curriculum. The whole curriculum of a school, of course, goes beyond the formal timetable. It involves a range of policies and practices to promote the personal and social development of the pupils, to accommodate different teaching and learning styles, to develop positive attitudes and values, and to forge an effective partnership with the local community.[8]

[6] National Curriculum Council, *Curriculum Guidance 3: The Whole Curriculum* (HMSO, 1990).
[7] 1988 Education Reform Act, Section 1(2).
[8] The National Curriculum Council, *National Curriculum and Whole Curriculum Planning: Preliminary Guidance* (HMSO, 1989).

The 1988 Education Reform Act did not designate classics as either a core or foundation subject and very little space seemed to be left in the curriculum for teaching subjects other than those prescribed. As a result 'optional subjects such as classics, drama, media studies and social studies began to struggle for survival and many cross-curricular programmes were discarded'.[9] Some schools did manage to retain their usual allocation for classics within the timetable; others closed their classics departments down. In some schools where it was no longer possible to retain classics on the timetable, Latin and in some cases Greek were taught in 'twilight' sessions to selected groups of pupils.

Despite the fact that classics as a distinctive subject was excluded from the National Curriculum, one positive development was the inclusion, in the history programmes of study for English schools, of core units on ancient Greece at Key Stage 2 and the Roman empire at Key Stage 3. This did ensure that for the first time, all pupils in schools in England gained some knowledge and understanding of the history and culture of the ancient world, if not of the languages.

The 1988 Act introduced Local Management of Schools (LMS) with per capita funding and greater responsibility for their budgets being devolved to schools. It also allowed greater parental choice of school. This has led to what Ball has called a quasi-market in education.[10] Publication of league tables has meant that secondary schools, in particular, have been attempting to attract those pupils who are likely to achieve high results in public examinations. Classics, particularly Latin and Greek, carries connotations of élite academic and social status and some schools have not only retained but expanded their classics departments and others have added or are currently in the process of adding Latin to the timetable.

The National Curriculum 2000

Complaints from parents, school governors and teachers about the overcrowding of the curriculum led to the government's appointment of Sir Ronald Dearing to review the curriculum and assessment systems. Following the publication of his report, revised orders for each subject were issued in 1994–95, accompanied by a moratorium on any further change until 2000.

The revised National Curriculum was published in 1999 to take effect from September 2000 and reflected some of the concerns raised by the Dearing Report. It included three core subjects – English,

[9] J. Head, M. Maguire, J. Dillon, 'Teaching in a new ERA', in J. Dillon and M. Maguire (eds.), *Becoming a Teacher: Issues in Secondary Teaching* (Open University Press, 1997), 12.
[10] S.J. Ball, *Education Reform: A Critical and Post-Structural Approach* (Open University Press, 1994).

mathematics, science, which are statutory in all key stages – and nine non-core foundation subjects – design and technology, ICT (statutory in all key stages); history, geography (statutory in KS 1–3); an MFL (statutory in KS 3 and 4 from 2001); art and design (statutory KS 1–3); music, physical education (statutory KS 1–3); and citizenship (statutory from 2002). Again religious education was treated separately. Requirements were also laid down for careers and sex education. The promotion of spiritual, moral, social and cultural development across the National Curriculum was reinforced and ways in which each subject might contribute suggested.

Like its predecessor, the revised National Curriculum did not include classics as a core or non-core foundation subject. However, it has established a more favourable climate for classics. For a start there has been a shift from the principle of equality as meaning that all pupils are entitled to the same curriculum, towards the principle of equality of concern for individual needs and differences. This is seen in the provision that schools may now disapply up to two National Curriculum subjects

> to allow pupils making significantly less progress than their peers to study fewer National Curriculum subjects in order to consolidate their learning across the curriculum … or to respond to pupils' individual strengths and talents by allowing them to emphasise a particular curriculum area by exchanging a statutory subject for a further course in that curriculum area.[11]

This move clearly offers schools the opportunity to free up time which may be, and in some schools already has been, allocated to teaching classics.

Classics within programmes of study for core and foundation subjects

A significant way in which the value of understanding about the classical world has been acknowledged in the revised National Curriculum is the increased opportunity for classics to be taught within the programmes for English and history at all key stages, with the result that the subject is being made more accessible to more pupils. This is a welcome recognition of the importance of classics in our own cultural heritage. For, as Tate argued, classical learning in schools is central to an understanding of our historic culture and awareness of our identity. To deprive children of it is to disinherit them.[12]

---

11 Department for Education and Employment (DfEE) and Qualification and Curriculum Authority (QCA), *The National Curriculum: Handbook for Secondary Teachers in England and Wales* (HMSO, 1999), 17.
12 N. Tate, Speech to the Secondary Heads Association (1995).

Programmes of study for history

The programme for Key Stage 2 history contains a number of areas of study which offer topics on the Greeks and Romans.

> In their study of British history, pupils should be taught about: the Romans, Anglo-Saxons and Vikings; Britain and the wider world in Tudor times; and *either* Victorian Britain *or* Britain since 1930. They should gain an overview of how British society was shaped by the movement and settlement of different peoples in the period before the Norman Conquest and an in-depth study of how British society was affected by Roman or Anglo-Saxon or Viking settlement.[13]

The importance of understanding how the cultural heritage of ancient Greece has influenced European history is stressed in the inclusion of the 'study of the way of life, beliefs and achievements of the people living in Ancient Greece and the influence of their civilisation on the world today'.[14]

The topics suggested under these areas are concerned with both the public and domestic arenas of Greek and Roman life: the high culture and the everyday culture. Thus a European study of ancient Greece might cover:

> *Aspects of the way of life:* arts and architecture; houses, cities and public buildings; citizens and slaves; education for girls and boys; language; medicine, health and hygiene; games and leisure including the Olympic Games; plays and the theatre; ships and trading; soldiers and warfare.
>
> *Beliefs and achievement:* the city states of Athens and Sparta; gods and goddesses, myths, legends, beliefs and customs; Pheidippides and the battle of Marathon; Pericles and the building of the Parthenon; the conquests of Philip of Macedon and Alexander the Great; great scholars and discoverers.[15]

The study of the ancient world within the framework of the National Curriculum at Key Stage 2 is complementary to the introduction in a growing number of primary schools of *Minimus*, the course written to introduce pupils to the classical world and the Latin language, which takes as its starting point the Vindolanda manuscripts (see p. 63). There are various reasons why primary schools have adopted the *Minimus* project with such enthusiasm. First there is the intrinsic value of the course; secondly, it complements work done in Key Stage 2 history and English; thirdly, it provides an enhanced learning experience. In addition it can serve to make a statement about the academic standing of the school.

---

[13] DfEE / QCA, *The National Curriculum for England: History* (HMSO, 1999), 18.
[14] DfEE / QCA, *The National Curriculum for England: History*, p. 18.
[15] DfEE / QCA, *The National Curriculum for England: History*, p. 19.

Although there is less emphasis in the Key Stage 3 history programme on the ancient world, the opportunity exists within a European Study before 1914 to make a study of a significant period or event in the pre-history or history of Europe, one of which might be the Roman empire.

Programmes of study in English

The National Curriculum for English contains programmes of study for three aspects: Speaking and Listening, Reading, and Writing. In the programmes for Reading there are opportunities in all key stages for introducing classical literature.

At Key Stage 1 the range of literature should include the re-tellings of traditional folk and fairy stories; stories and poems from a range of cultures; stories, plays and poems with patterned and predictable language and stories and poems that are challenging in terms of length or vocabulary. This opens up the possibility of introducing pupils to Greek and Roman mythology and could continue in Key Stage 2: literature where 'the range should include: texts drawn from a variety of cultures and traditions and myths, legends and traditional stories'.[16]

Cultural heritage forms an important part of the English literature programme in Key Stage 3: English Reading, where explicit reference is made to literature from the ancient world and to the need for pupils to critically examine its influence on English literature. Thus pupils should be taught 'how and why texts have been influential and significant (for example, the influence of Greek myths, the Authorised Version of the Bible, the Arthurian legends) and the characteristics of texts that are considered to be of high quality'.[17] Here translations of classical texts would provide a rich source of material for literary appreciation in terms of content, language and form.

As far as writing and speaking and listening are concerned there is a welcome emphasis on understanding the grammatical features of written Standard English in all key stages. In Key Stage 3: Speaking and Listening there is an acknowledgement of the importance of looking at the development of English, 'including changes over time, borrowings from other languages, origins of words, and the impact of electronic communication on written language'.[18] This offers an opportunity for looking at the influence of Greek and Latin on the English language through work on derivations and through looking at the structure of language and the way in which classical styles and literary devices have been used in spoken and written English.

---

[16] DfEE / QCA, *The National Curriculum for England: English* (HMSO, 1999), 26.
[17] DfEE / QCA, *The National Curriculum for England: English*, p. 34.
[18] DfEE / QCA, *The National Curriculum for England: English*, p. 32.

Promoting pupils' spiritual, moral, social and cultural development

Another way of looking at the place of classics in the National Curriculum is in its contribution to those areas of the curriculum that lie beyond subject boundaries. As we have already seen, the revised National Curriculum re-emphasised the responsibility of schools for pupils' all-round development. Although the 1988 Act stipulated that the curriculum for a maintained school should 'promote the spiritual, moral, mental and physical development of pupils at the school and of society',[19] no attempt was made in the legislation to define the meaning of the terms 'spiritual' and 'moral'. Thus schools were left with some sense of uncertainty about their meaning. It was not until 1994 that Ofsted issued guidance on spiritual, moral, social and cultural development.

Attempts were made by theologians, academics, teachers and the National Curriculum Council (NCC) to define the meaning of these terms. A series of discussion papers on spiritual and moral development was published from 1993 onwards by the National Curriculum Council, which became the Schools Curriculum and Assessment Authority (SCAA) and is now the Qualifications and Curriculum Authority. The SCAA *Discussion Paper 3* identified eight aspects of spiritual development: the development of personal beliefs, including religious beliefs, and a developing understanding of how beliefs contribute to personal identity; a sense of awe, wonder and mystery; experiencing feelings of transcendence; the search for meaning and purpose; self-knowledge; the ability to build up relationships with others and develop a sense of community; creativity – which involves 'exercising the imagination, inspiration, intuition and insight and feelings and emotions'.[20] Gay, examining the various definitions that came from both official documents and theological debate, concluded that, although spiritual development might seem a rather nebulous concept, an appropriate working definition appeared to be that it encompasses the development of beliefs, values, self-knowledge, awareness of others and a perspective on life; the capacity for reflection on oneself and the world; the capacity to ask the ultimate questions in life; an awareness of something beyond and above everyday existence and the development of the skills of worship.[21]

The National Curriculum for 2000 went further than its predecessor in that it not only stated that the curriculum should

---

[19] Education Reform Act, Section 1, p. 2.

[20] SCAA, *Spiritual and Moral Development. Discussion Paper 3* (SCAA Publications, 1995).

[21] B. Gay, 'Fostering spiritual development through the religious dimension of schools: the report of a pilot study in 17 independent schools', *International Journal of Children's Spirituality,* vol. 5, no. 1 (2000), 61–73, p. 62.

promote spiritual, moral, social and cultural development but actually attempted to define what is meant by each of these terms. Whilst it recognised that explicit opportunities to promote pupils' development in these areas are provided in religious education, citizenship and the non-statutory framework for personal, social and health education (PSHE) at Key Stages 3 and 4, it also acknowledged 'the significant contribution that can be made by school ethos, effective relationships throughout the school, collective worship and other curriculum activities'.[22] Furthermore the programmes of study for each of the core and non-core foundation subjects indicate how they can contribute to these aspects of pupil development.

To understand the part classics can play in promoting spiritual, moral, social and cultural development, we should first look at the way these terms are defined in the National Curriculum and then at the ways in which two subjects which have some similar features to classics – history and English – are seen to contribute to these aspects of pupils' development. If we look first at the general definitions in the National Curriculum we find that spiritual development:

> involves the growth of their sense of self, their unique potential, their understanding of their strengths and weaknesses, and their will to achieve. As their curiosity about themselves and their place in the world increases, they try to answer for themselves some of life's fundamental questions. They develop the knowledge, skills, understanding, qualities and attitudes they need to foster their own inner lives and non-material well being.[23]

Moral development involves pupils:

> acquiring an understanding of the difference between right and wrong and of moral conflict, a concern for others and the will to do what is right. They are able and willing to reflect on the consequences of their actions and learn how to forgive themselves and others. They develop the knowledge, skills, and understanding, qualities and attitudes they need in order to make responsible moral decisions and to act on them.[24]

Social development involves:

> pupils acquiring an understanding of the responsibilities and rights of being members of families and communities (local, national and global), and an ability to relate to others and to work with others for the common good. They display a sense of belonging and an increasing willingness to participate. They develop the knowledge,

---

[22] DfEE / QCA, *The National Curriculum Handbook*, p. 21.
[23] DfEE / QCA, *The National Curriculum Handbook*, p. 21.
[24] DfEE / QCA, *The National Curriculum: History*, p. 8.

skills, understanding, qualities and attitudes they need to make an active contribution to the democratic process in each of their communities.[25]

Cultural development involves:

pupils acquiring an understanding of cultural traditions and an ability to appreciate and respond to a variety of aesthetic experiences. They acquire a respect for their own culture and that of others, an interest in others' ways of doing things and curiosity about differences. They develop the knowledge, skills, understanding qualities and attitudes they need to understand appreciate and contribute to culture.[26]

Aspects of spiritual development discussed earlier in this chapter included a sense of awe and wonder; an awareness of self and others and the development of a perspective on life. The National Curriculum suggests ways in which these aspects might be operationalised through history and English. Thus history may promote spiritual development, 'through helping pupils to appreciate the achievements of past societies and to understand the motivation of individuals who made sacrifices for a particular cause'.[27] Whilst English may do so 'through helping pupils represent, explore and reflect on their own and others' inner life in drama and the discussion of texts and ideas'.[28]

Moral development includes the capacity to understand the motivations of others, the reasons behind the choices made by individuals and societies and to appreciate the consequences of actions. Thus history may enable pupils 'to recognise that actions have consequences by considering the results of events and decisions, and to explore how different interpretations of the past reflect different viewpoints and values'.[29] Similarly, English explores 'questions of right and wrong, values and conflict between values in their reading of fiction and non-fiction, in discussions and in drama'.[30]

The definition of social development involves an awareness of the macro and micro levels of society from both a contemporary and historic perspective. The contribution of history to social development lies in promoting an understanding of the macro level, through 'identifying how different societies were organised in the past and considering different political structures, for example democratic, autocratic, hierarchical'.[31] English on the other hand is seen as being concerned more with the micro level through:

---

[25] DfEE / QCA, *The National Curriculum Handbook*, p. 21.
[26] DfEE / QCA, *The National Curriculum Handbook*, p. 21.
[27] DfEE / QCA, *The National Curriculum: History*, p. 8.
[28] DfEE / QCA, *The National Curriculum: English*, p. 8.
[29] DfEE / QCA, *The National Curriculum: History*, p. 8.
[30] DfEE / QCA, *The National Curriculum: English*, p. 8.
[31] DfEE / QCA, *The National Curriculum: History*, p. 8.

helping pupils collaborate with others to create or present devised or scripted drama and to take account of the needs of audience and the effects they wish to achieve when adapting their speech and writing, and through reading, reviewing and discussing texts that present issues and relationships between groups and between the individual and society in different historical periods and cultures.[32]

Cultural development is concerned with understanding cultural development and transmission and having respect for cultural difference and diversity. This may be promoted in history through 'helping pupils recognise differences between cultures and within cultures over time, and explore a range of sources and different interpretations of what constitutes culture and cultural development'.[33]

Similarly English offers opportunities for cultural development through:

helping pupils explore and reflect on the way that cultures are represented in their stories and poems, through introducing pupils to the English literary heritage, and through learning about language in English and how language relates to national, regional and cultural identities.[34]

There are clear parallels between the ways in which history and English, and classics can contribute to spiritual, moral, social and cultural development. The art and architecture of Greece and Rome, the scale of the military and engineering feats of the Roman empire, the writings of Greek and Roman philosophers, poets and orators are among mankind's greatest achievements, and should provide sources for inspiring awe and wonder. The tales of the epic adventures of Aeneas and his commitment to his destiny, the struggles of the Greek heroes against human and divine enemies make useful starting points for understanding what inspires and motivates people. The Greeks asked and tried to answer some of the ultimate questions about the meaning of life, the origin of the universe and the relationship of the divine and human, all of which are fundamentally spiritual questions. In looking at the ways philosophers, historians, playwrights and poets explored these issues, pupils are being asked to engage in an activity that can contribute to their spiritual development. Through reading plays, poetry and prose from Greece and Rome pupils are imaginatively exploring the emotions, thoughts and feelings of men and women who, though removed in time, experienced the whole gamut of

---

[32] DfEE / QCA, *The National Curriculum: English*, p. 8.
[33] DfEE / QCA, *The National Curriculum: History*, p. 8.
[34] DfEE / QCA, *The National Curriculum: English*, p. 8.

human emotions, such as love, anger, grief, jealousy.

Like history and English, classics provides ample opportunities for looking at questions of right and wrong and the consequences of actions on oneself, family and friends and the wider society. For example, the idealism of Antigone as she sacrifices her life for a religious principle, in stark contrast to the *realpolitik* of Creon and the accommodation of Ismene, and the consequences of both stances for their family and the state of Thebes, raise in a dramatic form the dilemmas surrounding moral choice. The effects of war seen through the eyes of Homer and Virgil, the consequences of the destruction of Troy; the morality of Greek and Roman imperial rule; the status of non-Greeks or non-Romans, of women and of slaves all invite pupils to explore the sort of moral issues mankind has had to address throughout history. A look at ways in which these issues were dealt with in the ancient world can open up an examination of major moral dilemmas, such as the justification for going to war; the treatment of the vanquished; dominance and subordination of different groups within and among nations and societies. This makes it possible to contextualise contemporary moral choices within a broader, historic framework. This, in turn, should enable pupils to develop a wider perspective on moral choice at both a personal and macro level.

Opportunities abound within the classics classroom for social development in terms of content and pedagogy. Both Greece and Rome represent societies whose political structures developed and changed over time. In each society we can see the emergence of different groups as wielders of power and can see the relationships of subordination and domination between different groups, such as citizens and slaves, or Greeks and barbarians. The *Odyssey* and the *Iliad*, for example, present a myriad of opportunities for looking at a whole range of social relationships in different contexts, with the consequences of breaking social conventions or being constrained by them vividly represented. Enacting Greek plays, improvising role-plays, discussing Latin and Greek texts, in the original or in translation, all contribute to pupils' social development.

Classics has a vital role to play in understanding our cultural heritage. The legacy of the political institutions of Greece and Rome, the influence of Platonic thought, the continuity of the classical tradition in Western literature, the effects of Roman colonisation on our history, legal and political systems, culture and religion – all are essential parts of pupils' cultural heritage of which they need to be aware.

Classics and citizenship

The revised National Curriculum introduced a new subject to be taught in schools from 2002 – citizenship. This was in part a response to the perceived need of education to act as a means of helping provide and maintain social order. Announcing plans for the inclusion of citizenship in the National Curriculum, David Blunkett, the then Secretary of State for Education, said:

> The Lawrence inquiry has placed a particular emphasis on the role of the curriculum in encouraging children to value cultural diversity and in combating the development of racism. Our proposals for education for citizenship, which reflect the best work done by schools, will play a vital role in promoting a greater understanding of the rights and responsibilities that underpin a democratic society.[35]

It is clear from the previous discussions that the classical world offers a microcosm for the discussion of the very issues which Blunkett raised as being the responsibility of the school to tackle.

Furthermore, the revised National Curriculum draws attention to the fact that an important dimension of citizenship is helping pupils see the 'world as part of a global community'.[36] I have argued elsewhere that globalisation has tended to be described primarily in terms of its economic aspects, the spread of mass popular culture and the emergence of English as the dominant language of international communication and that, by focusing on these aspects, we are in danger of neglecting the whole area of our common cultural heritage.[37] Here classics has a distinctive role, for not only does classics constitute an essential common part of our European cultural heritage, but there is also a rich global dimension to this heritage.

> The language and culture of both Greece and Rome spread beyond Europe into Asia Minor, Africa and India. Grammar books drawn up by the Romans for use throughout the empire testify to the importance of language as a unifying factor in a multi-ethnic empire. In turn, both pre-classical and classical Greece and Rome were receptive to influences from other European and non-European cultures, partly through global trade and the resultant exchange of artifacts and commodities. Oriental influences on classical religion, art and philosophy are discernible and comparative mythology suggests strong communality of symbols and search for meaning.[38]

---

[35] David Blunkett, quoted in the *Times Educational Supplement*, 26 March 1999.

[36] DfEE / QCA, *The National Curriculum for England: Citizenship* (HMSO, 1999), 14.

[37] B. Gay and J. Jones, 'Classics and MFL: their part in educating pupils in a world of increasing globalisation from a PGCE student perspective', *Westminster Studies in Education*, vol. 25 (2002), 137–46.

[38] Gay and Jones, 'Classics and MFL', p. 138.

Promoting skills across the National Curriculum

A cross-curricular element in the revised National Curriculum is the inclusion of six Key Skills to be developed through all subjects – communication, application of number, information technology, working with others, problem solving and thinking skills. These relate to both content and pedagogy. Whilst it is self-evident how the skills of communication, information technology, working with others, problem solving and thinking skills may be developed in the classics classroom, it is, at first sight, more difficult to see how opportunities for developing the key skill of application of number might be created. Yet, faced with this challenge, trainees on the PGCE course at King's College London and classics teachers on INSET courses have come up with some very interesting ideas, such as trade, the calendar, the monetary system, the mathematical basis of Greek architecture, to name just a few topics which arise naturally in the course of their schemes of work.

Conclusion

Classics *per se* was not included as a core or foundation subject in either the National Curriculum of 1988 or its successor. However, there are, as we have seen, a number of opportunities within other subjects, such as history and English, for pupils to be introduced to the heritage of the Greek and Roman world. Thus, as well as being able to teach Latin, classical civilisation and in some cases Greek, classics teachers are uniquely placed to engage in cross-curricular schemes of work with colleagues in other departments. At the same time it is important that classics teachers highlight the ways in which linguistic and non-linguistic classics can be made available to a wide range of pupils within their subject specialism.

The National Curriculum rightly emphasises a paramount concern for the all-round development of pupils. In practice, classics departments have been at the forefront of extending pupils' knowledge beyond the boundaries of the classroom, with a whole range of activities such as visits to classical sites in this country and abroad, and trips to museums and Greek plays. Such activities complement the manifold opportunities within the classics classroom for contributing to spiritual, moral, social and cultural development, which are and should be acknowledged both implicitly and explicitly in schemes of work and programmes of study.

The future of classics in our schools of the twenty-first century rests on the recognition of the subject's importance in promoting an awareness of a shared global cultural heritage; its intrinsic value as an academic subject; its humanising role in helping pupils engage with questions of a moral and spiritual nature, in short on the rich variety of cognitive and affective experiences to which it gives access.

References and further reading

Ball, S.J. (1994) *Education Reform: a critical and Post-Structural Approach.* Open University Press

Callaghan, J. (1976) Speech delivered at Ruskin College, Oxford reported in *Times Educational Supplement* October 1976

Department for Education and Employment (DfEE) and Qualification and Curriculum Authority (QCA) (1999a) *The National Curriculum: Handbook for Secondary Teachers in England and Wales.* HMSO

Department for Education and Employment (DfEE) and Qualification and Curriculum Authority (QCA) (1999b) *The National Curriculum for England: History.* HMSO

Department for Education and Employment (DfEE) and Qualification and Curriculum Authority (QCA) (1999c) *The National Curriculum for England: English.* HMSO

Department for Education and Employment (DfEE) and Qualification and Curriculum Authority (QCA) (1999d) *The National Curriculum for England: Citizenship.* HMSO

Department for Education and Science (DES) (1985) *The Curriculum from 5–16, Curriculum Matters 2.* HMSO

Department for Education and Science (DES) (1988) *Classics from 5–16, Curriculum Matters 12.* HMSO

Forrest, M. (1996) *Modernising the Classics.* University of Exeter Press

Gay, B. (2000) 'Fostering spiritual development through the religious dimension of schools: the report of a pilot study in 17 independent schools', *International Journal of Children's Spirituality,* vol. 5, no. 1: 61–73

Gay, B. and Jones, J. (2002) 'Classics and MFL: their part in educating pupils in a world of increasing globalisation from a PGCE student perspective', *Westminster Studies in Education,* vol. 25: 137–46

Head, J., Maguire, M. and Dillon, J. (1997) 'Teaching in a new ERA', in J. Dillon and M. Maguire, eds., *Becoming a Teacher: Issues in Secondary Teaching.* Open University Press

McClure, S. (1988) *Education Reformed.* Hodder and Stoughton

National Curriculum Council (1989) *National Curriculum and Whole Curriculum Planning: Preliminary Guidance.* HMSO

National Curriculum Council (1990) *Curriculum Guidance 3: The Whole Curriculum*. HMSO

SCAA (1995) *Spiritual and Moral Development. Discussion Paper 3*. SCAA Publications

Stray, C. (1998) *Classics Transformed*. Oxford University Press

Tate, N. (1995) Speech to the Secondary Heads Association.

4 | The place of classics in the curriculum of the future

Marion Gibbs

At the time of writing the omens are apparently more auspicious for classics than during recent decades. The government has declared a wish to see an end to the 'bog-standard comprehensive'. More state-maintained schools are to be encouraged to become specialist schools and to develop their own individual strengths and identities. Indeed the education legislation which is currently before Parliament proposes that the highest-achieving state schools should be able to opt out of the National Curriculum and become more independent in other ways. However, will such additional independence guarantee a brighter future for the teaching of classics in schools? If state schools embrace diversity, will the independent schools respond by strengthening their provision of less common subjects such as classics?

The recent 14–19 Education Green Paper, *Extending Opportunities, Raising Standards* (DfES, 2002), while making no explicit references to the existence of classics, nonetheless signalled a further retreat from the National Curriculum monolith. It suggested that only English, mathematics, science and information and communications technology (ICT) would be compulsory at Key Stage 4, although adding, 'alongside citizenship, religious education, careers education, sex and health education, physical education and work-related learning' – a relatively substantial list of time-consuming additions! This Green Paper also postulated a 'new statutory entitlement for all young people to access a subject within each of modern foreign languages, design and technology, the arts and the humanities during Key Stage 4'. Thus every student would have the entitlement to study one modern foreign language, design and technology, something from the arts field and one subject from the humanities, if they chose to exercise their right, in addition to the four core subjects and the six other curriculum areas already listed above. Classical civilisation would qualify as a humanity, but where would Latin and Greek fit in? Moreover, will schools offer the full range of subjects in each of these areas or will they impose restrictions? Will modern foreign languages amount to a choice between two or three languages or perhaps just one? Will the humanity option be restricted to history, geography and religious studies? When making decisions about the curriculum, head teachers and governors have always been influenced by which subjects their existing teaching staff can offer. If subjects such as French, history or religious studies are compulsory within Key Stage 3 and staff are employed to teach them, it makes economic sense to fill up those teachers' timetables by offering the same subjects for GCSE. Therefore if the proposed new Key Stage 4 model is adopted there may perhaps be more opportunities for the teaching of classics, but it is also possible that in many schools there may still be little scope for such an option.

Another government Green Paper proposal is that students should be able to study subjects which are not offered in their own institution either by attending a neighbouring institution for some lessons or by the use of 'online learning'. Classicists have long been pioneers in such schemes. For many years now it has not been uncommon for students from neighbouring schools to share an A level Latin class. In some areas groups of students from different schools have come together for GCSE Latin or Greek lessons with a single teacher, and often these classes have been held immediately after the end of the normal school day. In other areas a peripatetic Latin teacher has moved between a number of schools. There is an increasing tendency for state schools to offer an extended school day with a compulsory 'enrichment hour' at the end, during which all students have to choose an additional activity. If classics cannot be fitted into the mainstream curriculum, perhaps there will be a chance for it to feature within this special activity time.

Already Latin is being taught to 'high-flying' students in some areas within the extension and enrichment programmes provided under the auspices of the government's scheme for the 'gifted and talented', part of its Excellence in the Cities initiative. This involves each and every secondary school in a particular local area identifying the top 10 per cent of its pupils, who will then take part in specially funded extension and enrichment activities. In an area where there are grammar schools and the equivalent of the old secondary modern schools, or comprehensive schools of widely differing standards, the top 10 per cent of each school will be chosen, regardless of students' absolute ability. This 10 per cent must also reflect the gender and ethnic mix of the school and include those who are talented in sports, music and arts as well as those who are academically gifted. The government hopes to attract more middle-class parents to less successful state schools with the enticement that their children may be identified as being within the top 10 per cent in those schools and will receive all the extras that come with participation in the 'gifted and talented' programme. Classics is certainly finding a place as part of this offering, although this may reinforce the stereotype of classics as a particularly élitist subject.

Latin was chosen, along with Japanese and mathematics, for the government-sponsored pilot Key Stage 3 'online learning' project. The Latin scheme involved studying an audio-visual version of part of the Cambridge Latin Course. Many useful lessons were learnt from this pilot scheme, most of them not entirely unpredicted. It was difficult to deliver proper on-line learning in schools because of the unreliability of their IT systems: overloading of the schools' network led to breakdowns, unreliable internet connections caused additional problems and all this was compounded by a shortage of technical support. It was possible to deliver the course with much greater reliability by using the CD-ROM format, but the full range of material was not initially available. The students involved in the pilot schemes particularly appreciated the opportunity to have interactions with a teacher; video conferencing was preferred to exchanges by e-mail, but what students especially enjoyed was a personal visit from a tutor. Whatever is preached about the value of ICT, it is just a tool; human beings do not want to learn exclusively from a machine – they relish personal contact and a real person whom they can question and who can inspire and enthuse them. Much has been spoken and written about the power of the internet and how all education's problems and specialist teacher shortages will be solved by beaming eminent professors or 'super-teachers' delivering brilliant lectures or demonstration lessons onto the latest interactive whiteboards in classrooms around the country. However, students do not enjoy being passive learners, and sitting watching such lectures soon loses its fascination. In theory, students might also be able to use the internet to question these experts immediately, but the technical problems involved are substantial, even if all schools were to be equipped with the latest broadband connections. I believe that there will always be a vital role for the gifted teacher in the curriculum of the future.

The Green Paper also referred to encouraging students to take examinations such as GCSE early. Indeed, some able Year 6 primary school pupils are already being prepared for GCSE mathematics and ICT. Moreover, in some areas secondary schools are being offered financial incentives to enter students for examinations ahead of their age cohort. Leaving aside the debate about whether schools should be involved in education, providing breadth, depth and enrichment, rather than mere 'stamp collecting' and ignoring questions about the standard of GCSE if it can be easily achieved by younger students, this policy may create greater opportunities for the study of subjects such as classics. If students have already amassed GCSE certificates in mathematics, English, French, ICT and such subjects earlier in their secondary schooling they will obviously have more time for undertaking something new such as classics.

This may be an apposite moment to study the entrails of our present system of assessment and examinations. With the advent of AS and A2 we now have more public examinations than ever before, an acute shortage of examination accommodation, invigilators and markers and a loss of confidence in the accuracy (never mind the quality of the content or the standard) of both the question papers and the marking. One possibility is that all public examinations will be reduced to a series of bite-size modules which will be taken on a computer in the manner of the current theory driving test and the numeracy test for trainee teachers. In future we may have 'anytime, anywhere' assessment: when students are ready they will log on to the system, complete the modular test within the specified time limit and if they are successful the computer will print out a certificate for them. This also fits neatly into one vision for education in the future, where schools as we know them will no longer exist, but students will learn almost everything from computers, either at home (supervised by their parents who will no longer be going out to work?) or in community learning centres open twenty-four hours each day and staffed mainly by technicians and learning facilitators rather than teachers. If this scenario were ever to be enacted (bearing in mind my earlier comments about students' desire for human contact and inspiration rather than machines), could the study of classics be accommodated? In many ways, languages such as Latin and Greek are ideally suited for such modular tests. The Cambridge Latin Course developed unit tests years ago to motivate and reward students who were studying Latin but perhaps not continuing to GCSE. Classical civilisation could possibly also be assessed in this way, with identification of artefacts and short questions on literary extracts, but machine testing and machine marking entirely precludes even the briefest of essays and is at its most efficient when dealing with simple multiple choice questions. Clearly, students' deeper understanding, powers of analysis and ability to construct a cogent argument would have to be tested through coursework assignments assessed by their teachers, who would thus not be altogether redundant!

Fitting classics into the school timetable has not been easy since the introduction of the National Curriculum, but the trend of the past few years towards timetabling in blocks of fifty minutes or an hour has made things even more difficult. When there are only 25 or 30 slots available in the week they can rapidly be filled with English, mathematics, science, technology, modern foreign languages, history, geography, religious studies, physical education and personal, social and health education (PSHE). The older-style 40- or 45-period week is far more flexible. However, there is now an interest in devoting whole days or half days to the same subject. Researchers have been asked to investigate the apparent decline or stagnation in pupils' levels of achievement in Years 7 and 8. Some educationists have suggested that it reflects primary school teachers' ability to teach successfully to the test and to maximise their pupils' performance at the end of Key Stage 2. Certainly most secondary schools which test their new pupils in English and mathematics on entry to Year 7 find that they are less competent than their National Curriculum standardised test results might indicate. However, another suggestion which is attracting some support from the DfES is that the constant changing of subjects and teachers as pupils move from lesson to lesson in secondary schools is disruptive to pupils' learning. One may have much sympathy with this: it is after all rather odd that whatever one is doing, however interesting it may be, whatever crucial point has been reached, the lesson has to end when the bell sounds and teacher and pupils move on to something else. Would moving away from a traditional lesson structure be beneficial for the teaching of classics? Certainly all past research seems to indicate that the best way to learn a language is little and often, but perhaps for a Year 7 cohort in a school where Latin was not offered at that stage, to have a block of time where one could explore an aspect of classical civilisation might inspire the pupils with a genuine thirst to learn more about the language or culture of the Romans or Greeks. Whether such a style of timetable will become widespread is hard to predict; it would make staffing very difficult, but it could also provide a block of time for study of a classical topic in some depth.

This year the University of Cambridge announced that it was to offer a classics degree to students who had not taken Latin (or Greek) at GCSE, following in the footsteps of Oxford and the other universities which have been offering such degrees for some time. What effect will this lack of a requirement for any qualification in classics have on the place of classics in the school curriculum of the future? Will this be another threat to the existence of classics in schools? Two separate issues arise. Firstly, will school head teachers and governors see the need to offer classics courses if they are not a requirement for entry to a classics degree course and secondly, if students are acquiring classics degrees after very short periods of study of the classical languages, how well will they be equipped to teach the next generation of classicists? To address the first point: for many years it has been possible to study Spanish, for example, for a university degree without any prior knowledge of the language, but numbers taking Spanish courses in schools have been steadily increasing in recent years. Why is this? Students have become more interested in Spanish culture, apparently because of the popular music scene and because many of them have visited Spain or plan to visit South America. Whatever the precise reasons, it is clear that it is possible to capture students' imagination and for there to be a demand for a subject at school level even when it is also possible to begin that subject at university. The second issue is not new: there are already classics teachers emerging from PGCE courses who have not studied Latin or Greek to A level, but have taken accelerated courses in the languages as part of a classical studies degree. The classical organisations which offer INSET courses and other support will have an increasingly important role to play in ensuring that teachers continue to develop their expertise and that they have opportunities to learn from and with one another.

Classics is one of the broadest subjects available: it encompasses two different languages and cultures, a wealth of literature, poetry, drama, history and philosophy, a rich feast of art and architecture and the study of every aspect of complex societies. Very young children are often introduced to the classics through stories from classical mythology and now, thanks to Barbara Bell, we have a new introductory Latin course, *Minimus*, specifically aimed at the primary school pupil. Classics is also blossoming in the Open University, with students of all ages eagerly embracing the study of the Greeks and Romans and Latin and Greek language courses, too. Children who are introduced to Latin through *Minimus* at primary school want to be able to continue with it at secondary school and parents and grandparents who have discovered the joys of classics through the Open University are demanding that their children and grandchildren should be able to enjoy the richness of the subject at school. Public perception may at last be changing and classics may no longer be seen as a relic from the days of the British empire, inextricably linked to a privileged élite.

The key to the future of classics lies with its teachers: it is they who can inspire students with a passion for the subject, with a desire to know more about the classical world and to understand its languages and culture. Students' initial curiosity may be aroused by something on the internet or a CD-ROM or a television or radio programme or a visit to a classical site while on holiday, but it is the classics teacher who will be able to foster and develop that interest.

Enthusiasm and passion are infectious: we are at our best when talking about the things we love and which excite us. Teachers need to kindle this passion for the classics in students and ensure that the ability to understand, appreciate and possibly even learn from the past is not lost to future generations. Where there are such teachers, classics will have a greater chance of survival in tomorrow's curriculum, whatever form that may take.

5 | Effective teaching and good practice in classics

Richard Shannon

The quality of teaching

Good teachers are successful in bringing classical subjects to life by showing the timeless elements of human character and circumstance and encouraging comparisons and contrasts with the modern world and its languages, particularly English. They bring out the richness of Latin or Greek by treating the language, literature and cultural or historical context as parts of a single whole. The best teachers of classics have a high level of subject expertise, with thorough knowledge of the relevant aspects. These include the writings, intentions and styles of classical authors, detailed features of classical culture and civilisation and (for the languages) the niceties of grammar, vocabulary and idiom. They are scrupulously accurate in their knowledge and understanding of the classical world and do justice to the rhetorical nature of the language through their representation of its sound and rhythm. Their own interest and enthusiasm are palpable and include making links with other subjects. They relate well to the pupils as learners and build on their existing knowledge to help them understand new classical work.

In a mixed comprehensive school, the teacher closely questioned a Year 8 class to see what they had learnt about Roman theatres from their homework reading. His genuine interest in the pupils' ideas prompted a very good response from volunteers, who pursued interesting similarities and differences between the theatres in their own town and the one in Pompeii. The notion of 'hearing a pin drop' in the Roman theatre was paralleled in the pupils' own rapt attention.

In working on the associated Latin text, the teacher cleverly reinforced the concept of singular and plural through English usage and made selective use of a worksheet with references to French. The pupils volunteered answers to his questions, with a forest of raised hands. In these ways, they gained a firm grasp of the Latin vocabulary and grammar.

The teacher's reading of Latin was excellent, with complete accuracy and Italianate value for double consonants. The pupils picked up the rhythms and read very well in chorus (clearly something familiar to them).

Good teachers have a strong sense of purpose, based on a clear appreciation of the learning needed and the methods suited to the linguistic, literary or cultural objective in mind. They have ways of maintaining interest. For example, they may pose an intriguing question for the pupils to answer in the course of the lesson, or ask them to support their work with dramatic or visual representations. They vary the ways of working, including written and oral activities for the class, individuals or pairs.

> A Year 9 class in a selective school was working on translation, comprehension and rehearsal of the new grammatical item, the genitive case. The teacher called on pupils to translate and interjected quick comments and questions on the grammar, without disturbing the flow of meaning and interpretation. She introduced variety and extended the work by asking the pupils to read the information on the religion of Isis in the course book. They consulted together very productively to identify reasons for the popularity of Isis – for example, the hope of an after-life for the worshipper.
>
> Throughout the lesson, the pupils had very good concentration and attitudes to the work. They demonstrated considerable interest, which the teaching had accentuated by requiring the use of illustrations – in the course book, on the wall display, and drawn by the pupils themselves.

One of the most significant features of good teaching lies in the high expectations which the teachers have of their pupils. These may involve careful preparatory homework, so that progress is rapid in class. The demands for accuracy and idiom are considerable, to emphasise differences between English and Latin or Greek. There is an insistence that pupils relate current work to previous knowledge and consolidate their learning, so that it is coherent and applicable to new contexts. Homework includes extension activities in addition to learning and preparation.

> In a Year 11 class, the pupils revised earlier work before reading a new Latin passage. Their understanding was good and they recalled a class visit to Aquae Sulis, the scene of the earlier narrative. The teacher read the Latin accurately and helped to bring out the sense through careful phrasing. The pupils had prepared well, and they rose to the challenge of idiomatic translation. For example, in chiastic and parallel word order, they translated the commas as 'and'. They also showed a precise understanding of previously learnt grammar – including participles and indirect statements.
>
> The teacher emphasised grammar, legal background and the relationship between the emperor and his minister, expecting the pupils to understand all aspects thoroughly. She used the board well in exposition and issued an interesting challenge in the form of a translated extract from Juvenal. This was to illustrate the historical

parallel with Tiberius' minister Sejanus, as part of an investigative homework. Later in the day, some pupils in the computer room had pursued the task and were using an internet site with relevant information.

In classical civilisation, the highest-performing departments realise their expectations by giving the pupils sufficient guidance and also providing good scope for their own ideas. In the study of source material, including literature, there is a strong emphasis on the use and interpretation of evidence, which leads to high attainment.

Year 12 students were working on a section of Euripides' *Electra*. They read aloud from the translation, bringing out the meaning well. The teacher helpfully asked for the identification of quotations which might raise interesting questions of character and motivation. The division of the class into three groups made for good variety of working, to pick up the questions and reach conclusions about the respective characters of Electra, Orestes and the chorus. The report back to the class revealed interesting appraisals. Electra was self-pitying, romantic and even unbalanced. Orestes was reflective and reluctant. The third group touched on several of the features characteristic of the chorus. The students identified good quotations to support their views.

Similarly in ancient history, good teaching challenges pupils by requiring individual interpretation in the use of sources.

Students in Year 13 studied well-chosen material illustrating Greek and Roman historical topics. The teaching challenged them to form their own judgements. They had good ideas for the interpretation of the sources – for example, the likelihood that 6,400 Persians were killed at Marathon, as compared with 192 Athenians. They contributed well in identifying the use of innuendo in Tacitus through the clues presented by 'some say that' and the citing of an individual opinion.

Assessment has an important part to play in effective teaching. Pupils enhance their achievement when they can see clearly the work to be covered, and can measure their progress in easy stages. In several of the departments visited, new work had resulted from relative weaknesses identified in trial examinations. During lessons, and in tests, good teachers take care to weigh the effect of easier and harder questions to suit different pupils, to boost confidence and to challenge fuller understanding. For example, in a mixed selective school, a written test on Virgil, *Aeneid* II was very successful in grading the revision questions for a classical civilisation examination. To challenge the ablest pupils, vocabulary and grammar tests include features such as grammatical manipulation or less obvious word derivations. In several of the best departments, the return of papers was very helpful in showing how to meet higher demands.

The teacher returned examination papers in classical civilisation and ancient history, with marks and annotations. He explained the banding for the various grades and showed how relatively small improvements in quality might lead to higher grades. He gave advice on examination technique and warned against insufficient scope to answers, vagueness and lack of supporting evidence.

Systematic planning and lively teaching are important for effective learning. In the best practice, they not only provide pupils with systematic material for revision but relate closely to assessment, giving evidence of progress in the course. This is an effective way of managing the complex range of work required for examinations.

In a mixed comprehensive school, it was possible during the course of one lesson to see the quality of the teaching, planning and assessment for the Year 11 course. The main part of the lesson was the study of the hunting scene in Virgil, *Aeneid* IV. For this, the excitement of the teacher's presentation ensured pupils' close attention. The many valuable elements in the lesson included the following. There was a thorough discussion of the 'golden line' *aurea purpuream subnectit fibula vestem*. The teaching made very good use of a map for Lycia, Xanthus, Delos, and Cynthus to clarify the significance of the simile. The pupils showed their clear understanding of the propaganda element in the poem: Ascanius = Iulus (connection with Julius Caesar). They contributed well to a consideration of Ascanius' likely age. Reference to English words ('associate' and 'mollify') strengthened language awareness.

Perusal of the pupils' files revealed that such work formed part of a systematic plan leading to a record which supported revision and gave a sense of progress. Apart from the pupils' notes on the text, there were bridge passages, grammatical work, exercises, examination practice, and 'progress tests' on grammar and vocabulary. All marking included encouragement, points for improvement, and evaluation of standards achieved. Achievement showed up clearly in the increasing sophistication of the work and its quality.

Departmental policy and practice

Effective classics departments usually have a well-argued rationale for the teaching of their subjects, whether Latin, classical civilisation, Greek or ancient history. This rationale is related closely to the overall aims of the school. It is likely to stress the contribution to the school aims – such as linguistic, literary, spiritual, moral, social and cultural development – and to show how classical work illuminates the study of many other subjects. It will tend to proclaim the high quality and interest of the subject matter. In some cases, it confronts head on the notion of 'dead' languages. However, it is most important that the pronouncements of the classics handbook are clearly realised in the practical arrangements for the subject.

In a selective school, care was taken to ensure that the course suited the needs of the school and overcame the problem that no curricular time was available within the normal school day. The head of department wrote a two-year Greek course to suit a particular GCSE examination. The vocabulary was carefully chosen to represent the requirements of the examination word list. Since this was a 'twilight' course, pupils arrived at different times, but good use was made of computer programs for the practice of grammar and vocabulary. Thus, the pupils were well employed in demanding work for this preliminary time, until the whole class was present. Given their ability and the purposeful nature of the work, the pupils were enabled to attain very high standards in their GCSE examination.

The balance of classical provision is well judged in successful departments. Language and civilisation are thoroughly integrated. The meaning of what is read is accorded high priority and the relationship between English and the classical language is an important focus of attention.

In a Year 9 class, the teacher gave a clear explanation of the perfect participle passive and its expression in English. As the pupils met the participles in their reading of Latin, she challenged them to choose the best English expression (for example, 'when', 'as', 'since', 'because'). She reinforced their understanding of the grammatical function of a participle – as an adjectival part of the verb. She helped the pupils to relate the participles to relevant principal parts and helpful English derivatives. The work was closely linked with the archaeological content of the reading and the subsequent identification of illustrated artefacts.

The best departments have good planning and administration. Their subject handbooks include not only the content to be covered but also guidance on teaching. This might include matters such as the exploitation of the pupils' existing knowledge, use of resources, class involvement, revision and consolidation, varied ways of working, opportunities for initiative, the interpretation of evidence and the use of technical terminology. Also represented might be differences between English and Latin/Greek idiom, suiting work to the varied capabilities of the pupils, emphasising the sound of Latin and showing the progressive development of skills in understanding word derivation. The assessment policy will include marking and reporting, to give credit for good work and to promote improvement. Departmental policies will be well implemented in practice.

In a Year 10 class, the teacher had clear objectives. He went over the main strengths and weaknesses in a recent test and proceeded to lead a related revision activity on verb forms. This involved the pupils in a question and answer session conducted at a brisk pace and in a purposeful atmosphere. He introduced the subsequent piece of translation with an over-arching question which set the pupils wondering what the passage would reveal. He delivered a fluent and expressive Latin reading of the opening section. In the pupils' translation, he expected accuracy of English expression (for example, 'began to' for an imperfect tense and a suitable English abstract noun for *res*). There was a variety of working, with paired translation, classwork, reading, discussion and writing.

In a Year 12 literature lesson, the students were challenged to use their initiative in reviewing the text they were studying, so as to find quotations illustrating a main character. They then analysed the literary qualities apparent in their quotations, using terms such as 'anaphora', 'assonance', 'alliteration' and 'enjambement'. This work was to be used in an essay – part of a planned series which had started early in the course.

In effective classics departments, there is considerable investment in resources, both to celebrate the interest of classical subject matter and to enhance the effectiveness of pupils' learning. They engage in a wide range of extra-curricular activity. This may well include participation in reading or other competitions and visits to museums, lectures, plays and archaeological sites. The departments often organise visits to Italy, Greece and other countries of classical interest. Displays of published material and pupils' work are conspicuous in classrooms and corridors and there are readily available maps and reference books.

In a preparatory school, the classics room had displays of scenes from Roman life, including descriptions of a Roman dinner party and its associated menus. There were several large maps so that mythological or historical references could be given a ready location. The walls and ceiling had colour-coded paradigms of nouns and verbs. There were class sets of books on Roman life, mythology and history and a good selection of videos.

In a comprehensive school, a long corridor wall outside the classics room had photographs of the recent school party to Rome and the Bay of Naples, with short articles written by the pupils.

The heads of successful classics departments usually plan their courses with particular care to maximise the effectiveness of the available teaching time, which is rarely generous. Thus, in planning the use of a course book, there are clear suggestions of parts which may be omitted and supplements which may be beneficial. In practice, the good use of time applies not only to the way in which the course is provided but also to the use of time within individual lessons.

> In a well-planned extra-curricular Greek class, after revision of current grammar and vocabulary, the teacher introduced the pupils to a new item of grammar, neatly related to their recent reading. The pupils then worked quickly and productively in pairs to translate from a continuous passage of Greek. There followed an efficient review of the translation and a brief discussion of the social conventions implicit in the subject matter. This provoked lively and perceptive contributions. The amount of work covered in the lesson represented an excellent use of time, since both teacher and pupils had very clear objectives and pursued them purposefully.

There is particular care to draw on the strengths of the various members of the department. For example, the head of department may produce much of the teaching material but leave the production of related computer programs to a colleague with advanced skills in information and communication technology (ICT). Whoever it is who takes the lead in ICT, this resource can be helpful in showing that classics is an up-to-date subject. It can enable rigorous practice of the language, interesting research through internet sites and clear presentation of material.

> Pupils in a preparatory school were given sufficient preliminary information on internet sites to allow them to find further details of familiar myths. They were able to print out illustrations as found on vase paintings and describe the details depicted.
>
> Students in Year 12 were shown computer-projected and colour-coded text taken from their set book. They used this to identify, translate, scan and comment on verse forms and points of psychological interest in the narrative.

A successful department keeps its curriculum and teaching under constant review and judges its success by the available indicators, such as the take-up for option groups and year-on-year trends in examination results. Any new development, such as the introduction of sixth-form classical civilisation, is approached carefully and after proper research and training. The members of the department belong to a professional association for classics and take opportunities for their own in-service education and training. The head of department maintains contact with other departments and promotes liaison where possible. If there are several members of the classics department, there are formalised arrangements for observing and discussing one another's lessons. In particular, the teaching of the head of department needs to be of a high quality, to provide guidance and inspiration for the other teachers of classics.

Formal meetings are held to discuss particular topics and their assessment and to consider national developments, examination specifications, inspection reports and national guidance on the inspection and self-evaluation of classics.[1] There are arrangements to see that any part-time or non-specialist members of the department are sufficiently involved and supported. The aim to share good practice is strongly realised in practice.

---

[1] www.ofsted.gov.uk/publications: *Inspecting Classics 11–16* and *Inspecting Post-16 Classics.*

6 | Special needs in classics

Tony Hubbard

Background

The teaching and emphasis of the classical subjects have changed over time in dramatic ways, welcomed by some, lamented by others, that have implications for the teaching of both the most and the least able. Teachers of classics can no longer afford, if they ever did or could, to dismiss the less able or take for granted the brilliant.

Mastery of the language is seen now not as the principal end of classical study but essentially as a means to the end of the reading of classical texts, authentic for the older, made up for the younger and less experienced. In addition, the development of more literature-based approaches to ancient history within the General Certificate of Education and the emergence of classical civilisation have broadened the range both of coverage and of the ability of students catered for.

This essay deals with ways in which classics teachers can extend and support pupils at both ends of the ability spectrum. It does not attempt to cover ground on provision for gifted and talented pupils that is dealt with in greater detail in publications by Ofsted, QCA and other bodies.[1] Nor does it attempt to cover general matters of Special Educational Needs, which are the province of whole-school policies in relation both to learning difficulties and to the gifted and talented. All maintained schools must now have a policy for both ends of the spectrum, as well as a special needs coordinator (SENCO). This essay is particular to classics.

Ability and the character of classics

Much testing for ability is related to specific skills in the development of language, and of logical and mathematical reasoning. Despite the widening acceptance of Howard Gardiner's idea that ability is complex and that there are many intelligences, many teachers still operate on the basis that ability is a single thing. Indeed in recent years, influential voices, full of enthusiasm to return to traditional basics, decried such ideas as woolly liberalism. However, it is well established that few pupils perform uniformly well across all subjects and most show

---

[1] I am thinking mainly of the National Association for Able Children in Education (NACE), and the National Association for Gifted Children (NAGC).

more aptitude for some aspects of a given subject than for others.

A second false belief is that ability is fixed for life. It is not. Children develop at different rates. Moreover, there is evidence that effective teaching of, for example, thinking skills can enhance children's performance on many of the standard tests of 'ability'.[2]

It follows that we must be attentive to the diverse nature of our subject and the demands it makes on youngsters and to the character of each pupil's strengths, weaknesses, needs and potential. In particular, we should keep in mind the following four points.

Classics is not one subject but many

There are two languages, literature, history, art, social studies and philosophy. They call upon a wide range of capacities. To name only the most obvious: linguistic ability, including the capacity to memorise vocabulary and rules of accidence and syntax, the ability to analyse and discern idiomatic and special usages and to perceive nuance of meaning and style; literary knowledge and understanding, including the ability to understand plot, motivation and character, to perceive symbol and metaphor and to analyse structure; social and historical knowledge and understanding, including matters not only of chronology, fact and evidence, but of pattern and cause; philosophy and the history of science, including inductive and deductive reasoning and the history of ideas; art and literature, including the historical analysis and aesthetic appreciation of visual forms and structures.

Not even the most gifted will be equally good at all this. The weakest will have ability in some aspect, if only it can be recognised and drawn out. The broad aims and objectives that feature in schemes of work are important not only to underpin the full coverage of the subject but also to ensure that each pupil has the opportunity to do well in at least one significant area: they will help teachers to identify potential.

Lack of interest and lack of ability are not the same

At any stage, pupils may have a stronger inclination to the philological over the literary or towards drama over poetry or political over social history. For that reason, the good teacher of classics has to assume that in a course of Greek, Latin or classical studies the full range of the subject is given a proper airing and not just that in which s/he

---

2 Examples of this are found in schemes such as the Philosophy for Children, developed by Matthew Lipman and operated from the Institute for the Advancement of Philosophy for Children (IAPC) www.montclair.edu/pages/iapc/index.html; Reuven Feuerstein's programme of Instrumental Enrichment, based at the International Centre for the Enhancement of Learning Potential (ICELP) www.icelp.org. Both have been operated in the United Kingdom and in both there is evidence of improvement not just in thinking skills but in the skills of literacy and numeracy.

happens to be interested. That is one reason why it is so important that teachers interest their pupils. There is nothing more inimical to interest than the replacement of personal responsibility for study and thought by routine drill and exposition, necessary as these are in their proper place.

The starting points and organisation differ widely

Teachers of classics may be teaching Latin or Greek to pupils starting at almost any age from seven or eight years old to adults of over sixty, who have come to this subject late in life. They may be inheriting pupils from different schools, in some of which they have studied Latin for several years, while in others they have only recently started or are absolute beginners. Or their pupils may have studied different courses, some more traditional and others more progressive.

Latin may be compulsory for pupils of every ability or motivation or only for the most able linguists. Some pupils may be entering their first year of secondary school perfectly grounded, while others, though effectively coached for entrance, may have gaps and insecurities. They may be taught in sets by ability or all together. All these will affect the complexity of the teacher's task, but awareness of the problem is a good beginning.

In relation to ancient history and civilisation, the case is less complicated and more similar to that which applies to humanities in general. It is not uncommon to find pupils opting for classical civilisation at GCSE or at AS and A2 level who think of the subject as 'easier' than the other alternatives. So the range of abilities is often wide and sometimes weighted to the less able end of the range. Classics, including works of ancient authors studied in translation, is a subject in which pupils who have previously struggled or been unsuccessful can excel.

This is not because the subject is easier but because the thought, forms and structure of the ancient world, being early precursors of our own, embody them in their most direct and simple form: this can be said of their political organisation, philosophical ideas and of their literary, dramatic and artistic forms and feelings. Less able sixth formers can understand a Sophocles or a Plato, where they might flounder with a Karl Marx or a Samuel Beckett. The alert and sensitive classics teacher may need to concentrate on the clarity of weaker pupils' organisation and expression but will never underestimate their potential for intellectual and aesthetic development, however limited their previous attainments or weak their writing skills.

No matter what the level of ability, solid foundations are essential

This obvious truth can easily be overlooked. Without a sufficient vocabulary, both the most and the least able are seriously handicapped, just as without a sufficient base of information about literature, civilisation and history, perception and judgement degenerate into jejune opinion.

Differentiation for the most and least able

Differentiation is a term widely used and less widely understood. In part because of its more recent association with inspection, it can misleadingly be thought of as a visible difference in documentation or provision, easily notable by an observer (inspector). What really matters, however, is that in planning work, we give thought not just to the work in general but to how to cater for the difficulties and potential of individual pupils. The key word here is *anticipation*: anticipating the general potential and difficulties, and anticipating the ways in which the work will extend or be difficult for our individual pupils as we know them. More will be said of this under the heading of assessment. For now, there are five standard approaches to differentiation: differentiation by outcome, by acceleration, by enrichment, by setting and by underlying planning.

Differentiation by outcome

Differentiation by outcome involves giving the same task to all pupils in such a way that each performs at her/his appropriate level. The question 'Discuss the role of women in ancient Athens' can be answered at a relatively simple level or to the highest degree of scholarship. Similarly, most pupils can deal at their appropriate level with 'Did Aeneas wrong Dido?' In Latin or Greek language, the case is more difficult. After the early stages, there is no passage which stretches the ablest without overwhelming the least able.

For that reason, differentiation by outcome is at its best as a differentiated way of assessing attainment, and indeed first gained its general currency in the context of the introduction of GCSE in the early 1980s. It tells us nothing about how to teach in the first place. Moreover, even in the setting of tasks, naming the same essay title is not differentiation unless we have also made differentiated expectations explicit to the different pupils. That involves differentiated input.

Differentiation by acceleration

Differentiation by acceleration is a notion that applies best to the learning of languages. In history, for example, it would be folly to have one or two pupils studying the rise of the principate, while the others were still on the civil war. Even in the case of languages, acceleration is likely to pose more problems than it solves. For one thing, the majority of Latin and Greek courses are developed through story lines and so require the whole class to work together for significant periods of time. For another, the brightest and most gifted progress and work at faster rates, so that the gap between them and the others and the pedagogical problem this poses will relentlessly grow. The most common solution to this, allowing each pupil to progress at his/her own pace, works only with the very best teaching and with the smallest classes. Otherwise, it leads to drift and loss of motivation. Acceleration really works only where a decision is taken by the school, having weighed all the considerations, to move the pupil forward a full year. Even here, careful and time-consuming steps are needed to effect the necessary transition.

Even though acceleration does not apply to the less able, it is important to be aware of those who naturally work at a slower pace than others or who develop or mature more slowly. There are some, of course, who work slowly out of laziness and need the pressure of high expectations. Some, however, may be inherently slow readers or writers. For such pupils, the quantity and rate of work demanded should be within their ability to complete with their best effort. Unfinished exercises and rushed, error-ridden work serve only to discourage. A good teacher will always be careful to ensure that the expectations stretch but are in reach, and will never cease to be on the look-out for delayed or hidden potential.

Differentiation by extension or enhancement

Differentiation by extension or enhancement has many possibilities, provided it does not serve as a 'bolt on' to keep the most able busy while others catch up.

To take the languages first, there are many ways to enhance the level of demand within the framework of most of the standard courses. A talented linguist may well have an appetite for the finer points of grammar and syntax and be willing and able to pursue these further than the majority. The teacher may start early on to assess not only the accuracy of a translation but also its quality as a rendering of the spirit of the original.

The translation into a classical language from English is less emphasised than it used to be, though it is making a bit of a comeback in some more 'revisionist' courses. Abler pupils can develop this important skill, especially if it is used to deepen their understanding of meaning, nuance and style, particularly in translation of continuous prose. Continuous prose survives as an option in one A level syllabus and verse composition has disappeared. Both verse and prose composition are, nevertheless, powerful tools for extending the understanding of ancient thought and style, provided they are pursued continuously and systematically and are not one-off exercises.

Extension is ready to hand also in the study of history, society, culture, literature and civilisation. In this context, the extension is often of the student's reading of primary literature, either to give a wider field of context for comparison or to introduce more difficult authors or passages in the original or in translation. For the brightest pupils studying history or civilisation in translation, the possibility exists to introduce them to some Latin or Greek.

History and civilisation courses can be enriched by the wider reading of the ancient historians and other sources in the original or by introduction to more challenging secondary literature, which raises the level of scholarship or introduces a more complex level of theory to the study. Indeed, the choice and use of secondary literature at the appropriate demand and level are fundamental. So, for example, we can range in the study of Homer from Jasper Griffin's short and general book *Homer* in the Oxford Past Masters series to the more argumentative and challenging *Homeric Soundings* of Oliver Taplin.

That, in turn, illustrates some key requirements for successful differentiation. One is depth and range in the teacher's own subject knowledge. A second is an up-to-date familiarity with the full range of resources and media available, including the bewildering range of material and possibilities available on the internet.

These apply to teaching in primary and preparatory schools just as to sixth form teaching. Bright and motivated pupils of 11 or 12 can deal with and respond to features of poetic and rhetorical style or to more complex political or philosophical ideas.

In addition, the resources of the wider community can be exploited. Where available, university libraries can be a valuable resource for interested and able youngsters. Inviting speakers from nearby universities is a common practice. In one or two cases, it has been possible to set up a link with such a university department, which allows an exceptional student to study a topic of interest under a lecturer.

Differentiation by setting

Differentiation by setting is possible, of course, only where sufficient numbers are studying classical subjects. It is bound to simplify the task of differentiation, but does not eliminate it. A gifted pupil will often be further ahead of a top set than the top set is itself ahead of the set below. Moreover, there may be pupils struggling at the bottom of the top set who need special attention. Above all, it is essential that we have clear criteria for any such grouping, related specifically to the demands of the subject, and a flexible way of reviewing and adjusting sets in the light of pupils' actual progress.

Some teachers may find themselves teaching sets which have been determined for reasons other than ability at the subject being taught. This can often be so in schools that operate some form of streaming, where pupils are taught together for some or all of the time in streams determined by general ability in mathematics and/or English.

Even when there is no setting, it is possible to subdivide a class for some or even all of the time. Such 'two-speed' classes can operate effectively, though it requires particularly efficient planning and effective teaching. In the simplest case, the lesson is divided in half and the pupils in each group are taught for (say) half the time and carry out a task for the other half. The teaching part usually works. However, the work set to the other group(s) has to be such that it will take pupils the exact time allocated and will not require any significant degree of intervention by the teacher. More often, one or two pupils finish early and find themselves with a 'time-filler' while one or two either distract the teacher with persistent appeals for help or drift more and more deeply into uncorrected error. The process operates most successfully with older pupils doing essay and project work.

Differentiation through underlying planning
Differentiation through underlying planning embraces all of the first four. It brings me back to my starting point. In planning each unit of work, each linguistic construction, each set book, period or topic, teachers need to be aware of the features that will prove troublesome to the strugglers or be too easy for the talented. They need to be aware of more demanding linguistic or conceptual levels to which study can proceed and plan strategies for pursuing these. They need to take explicit account of what they know about their individual pupils, their strengths and weaknesses and any gaps or uncertainties in their underlying knowledge, skills or understanding. In short, beyond knowing the subject and possessing a repertoire of methods, teachers need to anticipate and prepare for the different ways in which their pupils will receive and respond to the material. Beyond that, having differentiated their preparation, they need to be alert to the actual responses of different individuals and to respond and adapt their approach accordingly.

Spoon-feeding

At this point, let me say a word about spoon-feeding, against which I inveighed in the ISI's 2000–1 Annual Digest.[3]

Spoon-feeding does have its place. In the learning of a language, repetition, mnemonic and formula can help overcome difficulty. Similarly, clear and structured notes, simplified lists of issues and information, and formulae for the construction of short answers and essays are legitimate aids. Systematic examination preparation is a duty, not a sin.

The problem lies in the total replacement of real study and scholarship with formulaic coaching and drilling, and with the teaching of mixed-ability groups at the level of the least able. If, for example, a teacher goes through virtually every sentence of a passage for translation or every question in a comprehension exercise orally before pupils carry out the task, the subsequent written task becomes perfunctory for the most able. Gone are the days of 'devil take the hindmost', where the weakest were left to sink or swim with the ablest. However, this alternative is no better. Indeed, from the assessment point of view it is worse, since it deprives the bright and even the average pupil of challenge and the teacher of accurate information about what pupils can do for themselves.

The second and widespread case of spoon-feeding is the approach to the study of set books dominated by the writing out and learning of translations. The pupils prepare a passage, which is then translated orally in class and an agreed version written down by pupils or even handed out. In the worst cases, the expectations for advance preparation are vague or non-existent.

In terms of examination success, this approach appears to be successful if, as is usually the case, pupils are suitably diligent in revision. But it holds back the genuine ability to read Latin and Greek and allows able pupils to enter university insufficiently prepared for what they will have to do there.

There is a correspondingly unacceptable version of spoon-feeding in the handing out of pre-written notes. This practice, no less apparently successful, takes away from pupils the opportunity to develop the vital ability to record information in a systematic way and to think and organise for themselves.

The less able

Difficulty with aspects of basic skills or in the ability to organise and

---

[3] *All Round ISC Education 2000–1* (ISI, 2002). The Independent Schools Council (ISC) is the umbrella association covering the major independent schools in the UK, and the Independent Schools Inspectorate (ISI) is its independent inspection arm, recognised by the DfES.

present ideas does not entail inability to understand difficult and challenging ideas and feelings. Indeed, in terms of educational benefit, the expectations of intellectual understanding can rarely be too high. There is much evidence that challenging pupils raises standards at all levels of ability. All abilities benefit from a general understanding, for example, of the rules and regularities that underlie accidence and syntax, even though they may differ in their capacities for memory and induction. They benefit from a thorough understanding of prosody and style. They can thrive on the key ideas of the ancients, even where the quantity of their reading may need to be carefully guided or where care needs to be taken to ensure that they can organise their thoughts and information accurately.

Where pupils have difficulties, the most common features requiring support for strugglers are:

- the capacity to remember and retain;

- the speed and accuracy of reading;

- the ability to set out ideas and information in a clear, coherent and logical way.

In some cases, the roots of the difficulties may lie in a real disability, such as dyslexia (specific learning difficulty), or involve limited auditory or visual memory. (Dyslexia can affect the bright and talented just as much as the less academic.) In such cases, the normal procedures for support and remediation, under guidance from the SENCO, will apply.

Teachers should always adapt their teaching and explaining to the learning needs and potential of all their pupils. It is well known that some learn best by hearing and others by seeing things written or by writing them down themselves. If a teacher relies only on the oral or only on the written, the chances are that some of the pupils will be disadvantaged.

Weaknesses that arise from gaps in concepts, skills or knowledge that should have been acquired previously can be remedied relatively straightforwardly. Others have to be compensated for by providing mnemonics, strategies or formulae that will enable the pupil to cope better. This calls upon the teacher's willingness to look beyond the particular mistake or lack of understanding to the reasons that lie behind, to understand the child, together with the imagination to contrive a strategy to help. This may involve relearning something forgotten or never properly learned; or devising a special routine or mnemonic of which the hoary old subject/verb/object is only the most familiar.

Assessment

The key to proper provision for pupils of all abilities lies in intelligent assessment: assessment that tests what they remember and understand; that checks what they can do for themselves; that identifies and analyses gaps and points of difficulty; that pinpoints potential and opportunity for growth.

This aspect of assessment is not so much a matter of grading and measurement, useful as that may be in its own way. It involves teachers in going beyond the right/wrong or good/satisfactory of correction and marking to ask themselves why the pupil made some particular mistake, or regularly gets this or that construction wrong, and to find a strategy for helping the pupil to move forward. Some mistakes, indeed, may be a sign of high ability. After all, many of Plato's deepest insights involve important error.

For pupils who are promising, good assessment is shown by comments like 'Good, now see if you can express the same thing using a gerund or gerundive'; or 'I see why you said this, and in one way it is true, but…' or 'Yes, this is one common view, but how would you deal with the objection that…?'; or 'This is an interesting idea, why not read…?'; or 'Why did you say this?'

For those pupils who experience difficulty, two features of good assessment and teaching are particularly beneficial. The first is that even where there are many mistakes and imperfections, credit is given for what the pupil does get right, even as error is corrected. The second is that the teacher goes beyond mere correction to explanation of how to avoid error or misunderstanding in the future. This may be recorded in the pupil's marked work, but may with at least as much benefit be done personally and orally.

Conclusion

The nurturing of talent and the support for difficulty require great time and patience. What is required can be summed up in this: that we should remedy and find ways round the weaknesses of the less able, while seeking out and nurturing their strengths; and that we should nurture and challenge the strengths of the talented, while seeking out and remedying any weaknesses.

It is a fortunate thing that teachers of classics are as devoted to their subject and their pupils as they are. It may also appear that catering for the special needs of the gifted or of those who experience difficulty is nothing other than good teaching itself. So it is: good teaching that is, to use an expression which fell for a while foolishly into disfavour, genuinely child-centred.

7 | *Minimus*

Barbara Bell

Those of us who teach classics have surely had the experience of being at a party when someone asks us what we do for a living. When we confess, there is an embarrassed silence; then our interlocutor mutters, 'Oh, how interesting', or, 'Didn't think they still taught those subjects', and rapidly disappears to refill his glass. Imagine a similar scenario when people heard that I was having a term off to write a book.

> 'Oh, how interesting. What's it going to be about?'
> 'Well, I am planning to write a Latin course for 7-year-olds.'

Embarrassed silence writ large. I could see the look of horror and sympathy passing over their faces. I could feel them thinking, 'Poor little things'. This reaction is the result of the not uncommon perception of Latin as a dreary, irrelevant subject that is only taught to the brightest children – and then for no purpose as it won't lead to a job. The reality, as you will see from elsewhere in this book, could not be further from the truth.

Why Latin at 7?

Three factors convinced me that this book needed to be written. Firstly, when I was working for JACT as executive secretary from 1994 to 1998, I received a number of letters, both from primary teachers and from parents, asking if there was a simple introduction to Latin for young children. Although there are some courses on the market, and although many prep school teachers have devised their own material, I couldn't find a British course that had simple, accessible Latin, that seemed right for children in both the independent and state sectors. Secondly, politicians at the time (1994–5) were urging that children should begin to learn languages at a younger age. Dr Nick Tate, then head of the Qualifications and Curriculum Authority (QCA), was quoted on the front page of the *TES* as saying, 'Why should it necessarily be French; why not Latin?' This seemed to make a lot of sense. Thirdly, something happened when I was teaching a class of 11-year-olds. I stressed the importance of looking for the verb in a Latin sentence and met with a sea of glazed expressions. Further enquiries revealed that precious few had any clue what a verb was – and the same went for other parts of speech. Seven years later, with the advent of the National Literacy Strategy (NLS), the situation has changed and children are much more aware of parts of speech. But at that time I was very concerned: how could we expect our pupils to begin at secondary school and take up modern foreign languages when they did not have the basic tools of the trade? At that time I also taught English and I was also concerned by pupils' poor knowledge of English vocabulary. So I decided to try to redress the balance. Like many others, I learnt English grammar through Latin; I wanted young children to have the chance to do the same.

Time, money, expertise

I was wisely advised to take a sabbatical but my school governors refused. They did, however, permit me a term of unpaid leave – which I couldn't afford! So I had to seek sponsorship. The target was £20,000. This was to cover a replacement teacher, fund necessary research and to cover the administrative expenses in running the Primary Latin Project. From the start *Minimus* was more than just a book. It is a campaign and mission. Latin has given me such joy all my life and I wanted to make it possible for another generation of children at least to sample the language, literature and culture which are so rich and influential.

Sponsorship – from classical organisations, the business community and many generous individuals – was accompanied by encouraging letters. People did not think I was crackers after all! As soon as I had enough money to pay for a replacement, I was off – in the summer of 1997. But where to start? I had taught secondary children all my life. What arrogance, then, to attempt to write for children at Key Stage 2 (aged 7–10). I needed help and was fortunate to have made many useful contacts in the primary sector through my work for JACT. I had soon assembled five experts – Jean Cross, Wendy Hunt, Martin Forrest, Tim Wheeler and Helen Forte, all of whom had valuable experience. *Minimus*, plus the accompanying Teacher's Resource Book, owes a very great deal to this talented team. They soon helped me to realise that I was aiming far too high, that young children must have plenty of repetition and practice if they are to grasp abstract concepts.

In particular, the addition of Helen Forte to the panel radically changed the whole project. Her superb illustrations have made this Roman family come alive for thousands of children. Her attention to detail and charming sense of humour have shone through in every picture.

What is it about?

Primary teachers are phenomenally hard working, not to say overworked. They have to be experts at ten National Curriculum subjects. I reckoned that if I were to say, 'Here is yet another new subject to master – Latin', their reply might be none too polite. So I started by looking at the National Curriculum programmes of study in English and history to see how *Minimus* might complement and extend what pupils were already studying.

Minimus is about teaching English grammar – parts of speech, word derivations, prefixes, suffixes etc. – through simple Latin. The Latin is illustrated in a cartoon format. The characters in the book are based on a real family which lived at Vindolanda, near Hadrian's Wall, at the beginning of the second century AD. We know a lot about this family from the famous Vindolanda writing tablets. Every story in the book is based either on an artefact in the Chesterholme museum on the site or on material contained in one of the writing tablets. The story of the discovery of these tablets and their subsequent translation is a fascinating one, which grips the children. Obviously, the family's cat and the mouse are invented, but we know the names of the father and mother and that they had three children. The slaves are based on real slave names from Vindolanda. One slave is of Greek origin, the other Celtic. Thus the children are made to think about different cultures. Furthermore, the family were not Roman but came from Batavia (the Netherlands) and studying them helps children to have a better understanding of the Roman empire – and perhaps of the European Union too.

Greek mythology

The idea of incorporating some Greek myths came from teachers. One myth is told, in English, in each chapter. For example, in the first chapter the mother of the family is invited to a birthday party. The content of this comes from perhaps the most famous writing tablet. I was never taught that the Romans enjoyed birthday parties! Lepidina decides to take as a present a beautiful gold and onyx ring, which can be seen in the museum. Her friend's son asks about the stone in the centre of the ring – it is the head of Medusa. Since he doesn't know what this is, Lepidina sits everyone down and begins, 'olim…' Unsurprisingly, since these are some of the best stories ever told, the myths are proving very popular with primary pupils. They lend themselves to many cross-curricular projects, involving drama, creative writing and art.

What support material is there for teachers of *Minimus*?

The Teacher's Resource Book contains thirty-five photocopiable worksheets. These range from a dot-to-dot picture (a peacock!), word search on Roman weapons, a chart of the Olympian gods and a card game matching animals with appropriate adjectives (teaching adjectival agreement). It also contains historical information about Vindolanda and the tablets plus many cross-curricular suggestions. The two main books were published by Cambridge University Press in September 1999 and by the spring of 2003 had sold over 42,000 copies (pupil's book) and comfortably more than 2,000 (Teacher's Resource Book).

Many of those teaching *Minimus* felt hesitant about how to pronounce the Latin. The recently produced audiocassette should help here. I wanted it to sound like a family: hence the animals and youngest child were read by young children from Clifton High School. We also used some older children from Gordano Comprehensive School and Bristol teachers, including Niall Rudd, Emeritus Professor of Latin at Bristol University.

In addition, teachers of *Minimus* are excellent at sharing ideas. Hence the Project office holds many sheets to support the teaching such as dialogues and plays, booklists, Roman recipes, Latin carols and songs. *Old Macdonald* sung in Latin never fails. Great for a school assembly!

What is the 'Granny Latin' scheme?

At a *Minimus* training day in London, I was outlining the problem that many schools are finding: when they offer a Latin club, far more children want to learn Latin than the school can handle. Stories of waiting lists, disappointed children crying in school, and even Latin lotteries where the lucky ticket holders are allowed to join the Latin club, are heart-warming – but what about those who don't win a lucky ticket? An inspired idea came from one of those attending: she helped listen to children read and do cookery; she would love to offer them half an hour's Latin per week. It seemed such an obviously good idea to make use of the generation that had done Latin and perhaps had a little time on their hands. Thanks to brilliant publicity, masterminded by Peter Jones, the idea took off in spectacular fashion. When *Minimus* featured on the front page of the *Daily Telegraph*, I received 1,200 letters, 600 e-mails and 500 phone calls in six weeks. Hence there are now battalions of eager grannies (plus grandpas, undergraduates, postgrads, young mums at home, even a 16-year-old in the middle of his GCSE exams) who have signed up to help this campaign. A database of these volunteers has been compiled and many have already made contact with local primary schools to offer their services. They are formidable in their enthusiasm for Latin; I am full of admiration for their inventiveness in the classroom. Those who were not formerly teachers have usually attended a training day – and then armed with the book, they have assailed head teachers. So one hears of Oliver, a retired businessman, teaching 20 per cent of the pupils at Peppard Primary School in Oxfordshire. He is assisted by the Chair of Governors and also by Kate, a 16-year-old who has just taken GCSE Latin. The children respond with enormous enthusiasm and love 'Oliverus', who has written a *Minimus* play for them. Oliver now finds himself on the Management Committee of the Primary Latin Project and regularly speaks at training days. As he says, 'When I read the piece in the *Telegraph*, I began my second career.'

Who is teaching *Minimus* and who is learning it?

Minimus was designed for children aged 7–10. It is currently being used by pupils aged 2–87! One of the most pleasing aspects of the whole Primary Project is the variety of situations in which the book is being used. It is being used to stretch our 'gifted and talented' children; equally, dyslexic children and those with other learning difficulties are enjoying it. A head of a maintained primary school in Kent, now seconded to work with her LEA's Primary Excellence team, writes,

> I use *Minimus* as an enrichment activity with children aged 7–11. I had originally intended it as a project to be used with Gifted and Talented Children, as these are now the focus of DfES policy. However, my motto is 'What's good for the best is good for the rest.' All children have loved using the book, and the very able have explored the material in greater depth. It can be used very effectively in the National Literacy Hour, where it offers splendid material for Word, Sentence and Text Levels, as well as for etymology, an important part of the work in Literacy.

Much to my surprise, it is being used in Years 7 and 8 in inner-city comprehensives, as a language awareness course – I had imagined it would be too juvenile. There are some exciting partnership schemes taking place, where teachers from both independent and state sectors are working together to deliver *Minimus*. One such is in Surrey, which is now into the third year of such a scheme, funded by the LEA. Harrow teachers run a *Minimus* club in the area on Saturday mornings. In many parts of the country sixth-formers are teaching *Minimus* in local primary schools as community service for the Duke of Edinburgh scheme or the International Baccalaureate. It is being taught in the USA and Canada as well as in many parts of Europe, and there has been much recent interest in Australia.

I receive wonderful post from teachers and children, who kindly keep me informed of the various *Minimus* schemes. I was particularly pleased to hear of the book being used in the Isle of Canna, in the Inner Hebrides. When the three pupils at the school (!) are waiting for the boat to take them to the mainland, they fill in the time by studying *Minimus*!

It was always my hope that non-Latinists would be able to teach *Minimus*, given sufficient support. This has proved to be the case. As one head teacher wrote to me, 'I have never done a word of Latin but I am looking forward to learning with the children.'

What does the 'Primary Latin Project' mean?

The mission to make Latin available for young children is gathering momentum: *Minimus* has its own website: www.minimus-etc.co.uk; five training days are held around the country each year; a grant fund has been established to help schools set up *Minimus* clubs; I write a newsletter three times a year, which is distributed by Cambridge University Press to over 3,000 people all over the world; a small business has been established – *Minimus et cetera* – to provide pencils, stickers, badges and the other small items which children love; there is a constant need for fundraising. The various activities have grown at such a pace that a Management Committee has been established, under the expert chairmanship of Brian Sparkes, Emeritus Professor of Classical Archaeology at Southampton University. Moreover he has spearheaded a major fundraising campaign to make it possible for me to write the sequel.

What of the future?

As I write this, I am on sabbatical working on *Minimus secundus*, which will be aimed at slightly older children (10–13). Due to be published in spring 2004, it deals with the same characters, now five years older, but takes them away from Vindolanda via Catterick to York. All the key ingredients of Book 1 will still be there, but the stories will be more complex with a steeper linguistic gradient and considerably more Latin vocabulary. The grammatical emphasis will fall on verbs.

Other repeated requests from pupils and teachers, for a video, a CD-ROM and IT software, will all have to be considered in due course.

It would be living in Cloudcuckooland to hope for Latin as a subject on the National Curriculum. All I ask is that any child who wishes to know about the ancient world and the Latin language should have the chance to do so. The next generation must not be deprived of the stimulus, challenge and sheer enjoyment of learning Latin.

8 | Classics in prep schools

Bob Bass

Rather more than 500 preparatory schools provide privately funded education for children between the ages of $7\frac{1}{2}$ and $13\frac{1}{2}$ in the UK and overseas (Europe, southern and eastern Africa, South America and Australia and New Zealand). It is a competitive, commercial business subject to 'market forces', and this certainly has its implications for the teaching of classics within the sector. It is a brave, enlightened but possibly foolhardy head teacher, for example, who is prepared to hire a classicist rather than buy a roomful of computers with which to woo the prospective parents on whose cash his school's future depends. In fact the prep school sector is unique in the disparate (and sometimes desperate) nature of its classics provision, and this makes generalisation hazardous at best.

As in other sectors, classics provision is subject to pressures on the curriculum. Prep schools with long-standing classical traditions and generous staffing may be able to give their pupils as much as five years' worth of Latin at five periods per week: whether the academic curricula of such schools offer breadth and balance is another matter. At the other extreme is the department consisting of just one person – the usual situation – who has to manage on perhaps only two lessons a week for two years and who is expected to deliver good results in the appropriate exams.

Exam pressure too has a significant part to play. Whilst some children will move on to their senior school at 11+, others will gain entry to the independent senior school of their choice at 13+ by passing Common Entrance (CE) in the usual academic subjects. The CE papers are set by the Independent Schools Examinations Board (ISEB), and though recommended marking schemes are published, adherence to them by the markers, the staff of the senior school for which the child is entered, is not mandatory. A review of all ISEB's syllabuses and papers has recently been completed, a major aim being to move the emphasis from the simple recall of knowledge to the acquisition of skills, and the syllabuses and exams in the classical languages have been revised accordingly. The grammatical content of the Latin syllabus has been pared, and the vocabulary prescription reduced from 500+ items to about 350. Competence in comprehension, translation, grammar, manipulation of the language and even simple English–Latin work are tested.

The Common Entrance Latin paper also includes a classical background question, with a choice from a broad range of topics. The attitudes of senior schools to this background section vary. Some ignore it altogether on the grounds that it is a child's linguistic competence rather than recall of, say, a Greek myth in which they are interested; others read the responses with interest but do not allow marks gained in this section of the paper to influence the overall grade; others adhere to the recommended marking scheme. Its inclusion at all provides prep school teachers with some leverage to justify to their head teachers pursuing the Common Entrance syllabus (the Key Stage 2 modules on the Greeks and Romans provide useful aperitifs to the CE syllabus, but generally don't impinge on the post-KS2 CE preparations).

In Greek also the grammatical and vocabulary prescriptions have been revised to more realistic levels and this, together with the introduction of transliteration exercises and a gradated paper, has now made the Greek CE paper more accessible than ever to those even with only an elementary knowledge of the rudiments.[1]

A child's results are published only six days after exam week. Some schools will issue percentage scores, others grades with grade boundaries, and some – incredibly – grades without grade boundaries. The quality of feedback to prep school classics teachers therefore leaves room for improvement: nationwide the system certainly lacks the transparency which characterises the National Curriculum Key Stage tests or GCSE.

The brighter prep school child will be coached towards senior school scholarship exams. Each school sets its own paper, though more and more are now adopting either ISEB's Common Academic Scholarship (CAS) exam or at least its syllabus. The demands vary from school to school, but the linguistic level is usually around that of GCSE. In the case of the most prestigious senior schools the level is even higher than this, which drives the typical prep school Latin teacher, faced with the practical impossibility of meeting such demands, to distraction. This also applies to Greek scholarship papers, though more and more senior schools, aware of the varying nature of and constraints upon prep school Greek provision, are now producing more humane, gradated papers which offer something for the near beginner as well as the more advanced.

Such is the examination structure which drives the curriculum of many prep schools and on which most prep school classics teachers,

---

[1] Specimen papers and syllabuses for Common Entrance and Common Academic Scholarship papers are available from ISEB, Jordan House, Christchurch Road, New Milton, Hants BH25 6QJ. Tel: 01425 621111. Fax: 01425 620044. www.iseb.co.uk

under pressure from head teachers and governors to produce outstanding academic results to include in the school's publicity materials, must focus.

As is clear from the changing nature of senior school Greek scholarship papers, an air of pragmatism is gradually overtaking teachers in the senior sector. They are coming to terms with the fact that, however glorious the past, not all 13-year-olds entering their schools will be able to read Thucydides or write Latin like Cicero. There has in recent years been a reaction to prep school pupils entering senior schools after being crammed for exams and not knowing the basic elements. The demand now being made of prep school classics teachers, reflected in revised CE and CAS syllabuses and papers, is that their pupils make the transition from prep to senior school with a thorough knowledge of a little rather than a superficial acquaintance with a lot.

One of the first questions a prep school classics teacher will ask a colleague from another prep school is, 'What course book do you use?' It is more than a polite enquiry of casual interest: the wide diversity of prep school classics provision and the demands which vary from school to school make the production of the ideal universal prep school Latin course a pipe dream. Perhaps this is why prep school teachers have, generally speaking, been poorly served as far as textbooks are concerned.

Between them, the well-known mainstream Latin courses – the Cambridge Latin Course, Oxford Latin Course and *Ecce Romani* – account for about 40 per cent of those used in prep schools. But these and other courses are targeted at the secondary market, and what may work well with a 15-year-old will not necessarily do so with an 11-year-old. The disparity between the content and grammatical sequencing of these courses and the linguistic requirements of Common Entrance means that those using these courses with youngsters will need to produce much supplementary material of their own. In any event, the use of these courses in prep schools is often frowned upon by senior school classics staff: if the senior school uses one of the same courses it is inconvenient if incoming prep school pupils have overlapped with some of the senior school's anticipated coverage. A series of course books aimed specifically at the prep school market, written by the late Dick Marshall under the umbrella title *Disce Latinum*,[2] came on-stream in the mid-1980s and captured a sizeable share of the prep school market, about 30 per cent by the late 1990s. By this time something like 20 per cent – a remarkably

---

2 *Disce Latinum* is available from Mrs Maria Price, 39 Kennedy Road, Shrewsbury SY3 7AA. Tel: 01743 341817. Fax: 01743 354541.

high figure – of prep school Latinists were producing their own teaching materials. The disparate nature of provision and the changing expectations of CE and scholarship papers over the past fifteen years or so have led teachers to be eclectic in their use of textbooks, cherry-picking what they like from each, if they do not develop their own. Necessity has mothered some fine inventions, but what satisfies the needs of one school may not be successful elsewhere.

Greek is taught in only about one prep school in five where Latin is offered, and the course book situation is even more stark. (For full details of the course books referred to in this paragraph, see pp. 104–5.) Wilding's *Greek for Beginners* and Balme and Lawall's *Athenaze* between them account for about 80 per cent of the prep school market, but each course has its disadvantages from the prep school perspective, quite apart from the overlap problem in common with Latin course books. The predominant position of *Greek for Beginners* is largely *faute de mieux*. Having first appeared in the late 1950s it has several disadvantages from the modern beginner's viewpoint: the grammatical sequencing is odd (the perfect and even the pluperfect are introduced too early, participles too late) and there is no guidance as to the learning of vocabulary; strong aorists are not mentioned; syllabic and temporal augments are not explained properly; the vocabulary is at times uncommon (e.g. πιέζω) and of dubious atticity (κόρυς, Βόρεας, Ἀθήνη); it is necessary to rely on the antiquarian format of Abbot and Mansfield's grammar (when it's in print) – the list could be extended. *Athenaze* also is inappropriate for the prep school beginner. Too much grammar is covered too early (e.g. contracted verbs, which occur at the end of the CE syllabus, are introduced in chapter one), the vocabulary is idiosyncratic (e.g. βοῦς, ἄροτρον and λίθος), the grammar is unnecessarily obscure (e.g. μάχαιρα [knife] as the model 1st declension feminine noun, p. 34), there is too much grammatical jargon (e.g. φησί, chapter 3, is described as a 'postpositive enclitic'), and the paralinguistic material can appear off-puttingly dense for prep school boys and girls. For intelligent 16-year-olds with a sound Latin base behind them *Athenaze* may well be the answer, but for the prep school market it is not.

The new Common Entrance syllabus, and most senior school scholarship exams, have moved away from the world of tongues, yokes and stewards, rendering both Wilding and *Athenaze* irrelevant to this particular sector. They were not intended to be CE textbooks in any case, of course. Prep school teachers desperately await a course to do for prep school Greek in the first decade of the new century what *Disce*

Latinum did for Latin in the mid-1980s. Will the publication of Kris Waite's materials provide the answer (see p. 101)?[3]

One-person departments, constraints of time, exam pressure, lack of dedicated course books: these factors, some of which are of course not alien to senior schools, would seem to conspire against a successful prep school classics sector. Such a pessimistic view, however, is belied by the reality. Limitations breed ingenuity. A wealth of quality unpublished material exists in prep schools; and there are many exciting approaches which appeal to children of this age group – who are fascinated by words, who appreciate logic and relish simple challenges like reciting *hic haec hoc* within ten seconds or completing a communal oral exercise before the end-of-lesson bell goes in five minutes' time. Teenage cynicism is still just over the horizon here. At meetings, conferences and in the termly prep school classics newsletter,[4] an *esprit de corps* and a unity of purpose are discernible which transcend quibbles over methodology and syllabus. Yes, stereotypical humourless pedants using outdated course books (because they have used them for the past twenty years), oblivious to the arrival of ICT and boring their pupils rigid, still exist out in the backwoods, but generally speaking professional fervour and an evangelical belief in what prep school classics teachers are about are all-pervasive.

There are still prep schools where Latin is taught to children in only the brighter sets. Those not 'good enough' to do Latin will usually do extra English, maths, French or a classical civilisation course. An emerging trend, however, is that Latin should be for all and not confined to those who are perceived as the academic élite. In recent years slow learners or pupils with special learning difficulties have been allowed to drop Latin, in the fallacious belief that the extra time made available to them will result in a miraculous improvement in their progress in 'the basics'. The spin-offs of learning even a little of the language, however, are wide-ranging and enormously beneficial, and are gradually becoming more widely acknowledged by head teachers and enlightened parents. Young children struggling with written and oral French find comfort and security in a language whose basics are structured, consistent and predictable. Indeed it could be argued that it makes much more educational sense for those with learning difficulties to drop the modern rather than the ancient tongue.

Paucity of resources in this department, as generally, is a problem, but the advent of *Minimus* (now in use in more than 1,000

---

[3] Kristian Waite, *Greek, a New Guide for Beginners* (ISEB, 2002). For further details contact Kristian Waite, Hazelwood School, Limpsfield, Oxted, Surrey RH8 0QU. Tel: 01883 712194; fax: 01883 716135; e-mail: hellenikon@hazelwood.surrey.sch.uk. For ISEB see note 1 above.
[4] SATIPS (Society of Assistants Teaching in Preparatory Schools) www.satips.org.uk

primary-level schools) with its cross-curricular approach has given fresh impetus to the Latin-for-all rallying cry not only in maintained primary schools but in this sector too. It certainly provides younger prep school pupils with an appetising *hors d'oeuvre* to the more traditional linguistic courses.

Prep schools, of course, are not immune from the ICT revolution. Certainly the advent of CD-ROMs and online resources has made life easier for teachers who want to compile their own materials on the ancient world. Prep school pupils, however, have been less well served in terms of linguistic software. Professional linguistic programmers are understandably reluctant to expend the necessary time and effort to produce software that will be of appeal to a niche market from which the commercial returns will never be great. Rote-learning, self-testing programs based on CE vocabulary and the related grammar have always existed in various guises, and recent innovations have included the labour-intensive production of electronic texts at the appropriate linguistic level, every word of which can be dissected semantically and grammatically: ideal for the pupil working independently as well as for the teacher anxious not just to teach classics but to comply with his school's pan-curricular ICT policy.[5] Transmission of teaching materials to pupils via e-mail and making such materials available via the internet or a school's intranet are already areas of expansion. Paradoxically the harnessing of modern technology to the promotion of the most traditional subject of the curriculum will be vital to the subject's status in the years ahead.

The decline in prep school classics, as in other sectors, has been noted for several decades now. Problems still remain. There still exist out there unenlightened head teachers who need to be convinced of the value and diverse spin-offs of exposing youngsters to the basics of the classical languages, even if the senior schools to which those youngsters are progressing cannot carry on the torch. Even at age 13 the surrender value of classics is high. Teacher recruitment is also problematical. Extinction, however, is kept at a distance thanks to established, dedicated enthusiasts, those keen young graduates who do enter the profession and the biddable youngsters who do actually love to learn classics and can see the satisfying personal benefits that accrue as a result.

---

[5] The best summary of the available software is the catalogue produced by Julian Morgan, 81 High Street, Pitsford, Northants NN6 9AD. Tel: 01604 880119; e-mail: julian@j-progs.com; www.j-progs.com

9 | The theoretical underpinning of the main Latin courses

Brenda Gay

The early 1970s saw a significant change in the approaches to Latin teaching, with the publication of the Cambridge Latin Course (CLC) (1970) and *Ecce Romani* (1971) which were followed fifteen years later by the Oxford Latin Course (OLC).[1] No course or textbook is produced in an intellectual, political or social vacuum. The authors of these three courses talk about the principles underlying the courses in terms of linguistic theories. However, it is also important to examine the broader educational context of the late 1960s, the time when work began on CLC and *Ecce Romani*, and the theories of learning, and of language learning in particular, that underpin both these courses and which are reflected to some extent in OLC (1986). This should give users of the courses a greater understanding of the rationale behind the approaches to Latin teaching which the courses adopted and raise awareness of the complex process of language acquisition and learning.

The political, social and educational context of the 1960s

Looking at the wider political, social and educational context of the 1960s and 1970s, we can see a number of trends that impacted on the need for a fresh look at ways of teaching Latin. Forrest describes the two crises that threatened classics in the 1960s – the abolition of GCE O Level Latin as a compulsory entrance requirement to Oxbridge and the reorganisation of secondary education.[2] These crises acted as a catalyst for a major reappraisal of the role of classics in the curriculum and for ways of making the subject more attractive, and led to the setting up of the Cambridge Classics Project. However, it was not simply a pragmatic response to crisis that led to a radical rethinking of Latin teaching.

Education does not operate in an ivory tower isolated from the world around it. Therefore we need first to reflect on the *Zeitgeist* of the late 1960s and its effect on education, in terms of organisation,

---

[1] The Cambridge Latin Course (Cambridge University Press, first published 1970 and revised in a colour edition 1999); *Ecce Romani*, (Oliver and Boyd, 1971); M. Balme and J. Morwood, The Oxford Latin Course (Oxford University Press, 1986).
[2] M. Forrest, *Modernising the Classics* (University of Exeter Press, 1996), 13, 16.

pedagogy and the curriculum. The 1960s and early 1970s saw exciting and innovative developments and considerable questioning of the status quo in many spheres of life. Part of this was a questioning of traditional roles of authority, including that of the teacher. The period was also marked by a mood of anti-élitism and egalitarianism, which in education manifested itself at an organisational level in the accelerating move towards comprehensive schools. Fundamental questions were asked too about the nature of knowledge and what should count as valid knowledge to be transmitted via the school curriculum. Certain kinds of knowledge were perceived to be linked to social class. There was also a move to embrace more exotic modern foreign languages, such as Russian and Chinese, partly as a response to the Cold War. Anti-colonialism and immigration from former British colonies meant that, in a society which was becoming increasingly multicultural, old assumptions about cultural and political hegemony were questioned. Rapid change in science and technology meant that working patterns and practices were changing and that new skills were going to be required. *The Crowther Report on Early Leaving* (1959) pointed to the fact that an individual was likely to change jobs every seven years and this did not mean simply change within the same workplace or even the same area of employment.[3] It was against this background that a considerable amount of curriculum development and innovation took place in all school subjects.

Learning theories

Pedagogy and curriculum content are influenced by and reflect theories of learning. Learning is a complex, multi-faceted process, which involves cognitive, social, affective and neurological factors. Those who wish to pursue the different theories that have impacted on our understanding of teaching and learning in greater depth should use the bibliography at the end of the chapter. All I can do here is to provide a brief summary of some influential theories of learning and their impact on teaching and learning in classics.

In the climate of the 1960s certain educational philosophies and ideas of learning gained ground. One of the key thinkers, whose work was to influence developments in pedagogy in all areas of the curriculum in the 1960s, was the Swiss psychologist, Jean Piaget. Working in the early part of the twentieth century Piaget had conducted extensive observations of his own and his friends' children. From these studies Piaget advanced a theory of cognitive development as an inherent, unalterable, evolutionary process. He

---

[3] Department of Education and Science (DES), *A Report of The Central Advisory Council for Education in England* (Crowther Report) (HMSO, 1959).

suggested that, like physical maturation, thinking develops in a fixed sequence of stages through which individuals pass at their own rate. By assimilating and accommodating to the information coming from the environment the individual builds up cognitive schemata. Thus the brain is not a passive receptacle but an active, organising, directing system. Piaget argued that until about the age of 11 children are not capable of abstract thought, and need to work on concrete materials rather than deal with the abstract.[4] Attempts to show or explain things to children before they are mentally ready cannot foster development, although the child may learn empty procedures. Premature teaching and questioning may demoralise or frustrate a child who cannot begin to understand what he or she is being taught.

Piaget's picture of children as active builders of their cognitive reality has some similarities with the ideas of another educationist whose views also gained popularity in the 1960s – John Dewey. Like Piaget, Dewey emphasised that the acquisition of knowledge was an active and exploratory process rather than one of passive contemplation. He saw the learner as an active being, an experimenter, and not a contemplative theorist. The process of teaching therefore becomes that of enquiry, in which the learner is a participant in a common quest which relies not on rote learning or mechanical drill, but on a perception of meaning.[5] It is not difficult to understand why such child-centred views of learning gained increasing credibility in the climate of the 1960s and had a significant impact, particularly in primary schools, following the publication of the *Plowden Report* in 1968.[6] Their impact may be seen too at both secondary and primary levels in the development of materials and approaches in all subjects that shifted the emphasis from rote learning to learning based on an understanding of meaning and from reception to discovery learning, and favoured group work and cooperative learning over individual and competitive learning.

This dynamic concept of the learner contrasted with the theories of the behaviourist school of psychologists whose ideas gained ground in America in the early part of the twentieth century. The behaviourists saw learning as a process whereby the individual responds to stimuli from the environment. Behaviour is shaped as acceptable or correct responses are rewarded and thus reinforced. Thus, as a result of his experiments with animals, Skinner developed the concept of stimulus and response learning with the notion of operant conditioning in which the behaviour of the operant sets in

---

[4] J. Piaget, *Le Langage et la pensée chez l'enfant* (Delacahux et Nestlé, 1923).
[5] J. Dewey, *Democracy and Education* (Free Press, 1946).
[6] Central Advisory Council for Education, *Plowden Report* (HMSO, 1968).

train the stimulus–reward sequence. Skinner placed rats in a maze with a tray of food in the centre, which they could reach only by operating a series of levers. By being rewarded for correct responses with food pellets, the rats quickly learned to find their way to the centre of the maze by the most direct route. In the same way, Skinner argued, cognitive behaviour can be shaped by structuring learning in such a way that right responses are rewarded and thus reinforced. Rewards in the school context include praise, favourable comments on marked work or good marks. Incorrect responses atrophy as a result of either negative reinforcement, such as poor marks or unfavourable comments, or children being ignored. Motivation is thus extrinsic rather than intrinsic and the teacher is responsible for structuring the learning into easily manageable, discrete chunks.

Theories of language learning and language acquisition

Like the earlier behaviourists, Skinner extended his thesis to language.[7] He saw language as a form of verbal behaviour, which consisted of acquiring the correct habits through reinforcement of the correct responses. Just as the rat learnt to press the correct levers to be rewarded by food, so the human learns to use vocal signals to satisfy his/her needs. Pattern practice, drills and habit formation were seen as crucial parts of the process. Errors were thus the result of 'bad habits', which could be eradicated by rote learning and drill using target language models.

A robust attack on Skinner's ideas and on behaviourist theories about language came from Noam Chomsky, who was to become a key figure in examining the process of language acquisition and learning. In his review of *Verbal Behaviour*, Chomsky argued that theories which attempted to explain language learning in terms of stimulus–response were totally inadequate for explaining such a complex process: 'I have been able to find no support whatsoever for the doctrine of Skinner and others that slow and careful shaping of human behaviour through differential reinforcement is an absolute necessity.'[8]

Chomsky argued that human language is too complex to be learnt from the performance data available to the child and therefore each individual must possess an innate disposition to process linguistic data, a language acquisition device (LAD) which leads him/her to expect languages to be organised in a particular way. This innate core of abstract knowledge about grammatical form is Universal

---

7 J.B. Skinner, *Verbal Behaviour* (Appleton–Century–Crofts, 1957).
8 N. Chomsky, 'Review of *Verbal Behaviour*', in *Language* (1959), 35: 26–58, cited by H.H. Stern, *Fundamental Principles of Language Learning* (Oxford University Press, 1983), 300.

Grammar. Chomsky argued that the LAD makes it possible for children to acquire knowledge of both the surface and deep structures of a language. As children internalise rules from hearing language spoken, they acquire a generative grammar, that is, they use their knowledge of the deep structures to generate an infinite number of new sentences and phrases. By being immersed in a linguistic environment children become active in organising their language without formal instruction, apart from correction, so that between the ages of 2 and 7 they acquire generative grammar of their own native language. Thus Chomsky emphasised the rule-governed and creative nature of human language. Chomsky used this model of intuitive learning for the acquisition of the child's first language but it was also seen to offer a way of understanding second language acquisition. The question of how far a second language can be acquired in the same way as the mother tongue has been contested, chiefly because of the difference between total immersion in one's first language and the conditions under which second language learning takes place. The ongoing debate is outside the scope of this chapter to review but the reader will find a good account of this in Stern, Ellis, and Mitchell and Myles.[9] Whilst it is difficult to reproduce the conditions of first language acquisition in the acquisition and learning of a modern foreign language, the problem is compounded when dealing with ancient languages. However, Chomsky's theories had a major impact on the approaches adopted by CLC and *Ecce Romani*, and to a lesser extent on OLC, as will be discussed later.

Latin courses: changing times and ideas

A useful way of showing how the socio-political climate and pedagogical theories impinged on the development of new Latin courses is to examine the contrast between Wilding's *Latin Course for Schools* as an exemplar of the traditional courses and CLC, as an exemplar of the new courses. First published in 1949, Wilding's course is very much in the tradition of a textbook produced for public and grammar school pupils, particularly boys.[10] One of the traditional arguments for learning Latin was for its instrumental value in training the mind – a form of mental gymnastics. Thus for Wilding one reason for learning Latin is 'that the Romans expressed themselves with the utmost clearness. One of the chief objects of education is to learn how to express ourselves clearly, and there is no better way of reaching this goal than by studying Latin'.[11]

[9] Stern, *Fundamental Principles*; R. Ellis, *The Study of Second Language Acquisition* (OUP, 1994); R. Mitchell and F. Myles, *Second Language Theories* (OUP, 1998).
[10] L.A. Wilding, *Latin Course for Schools* (Faber and Faber, 1949, 2nd edn 1955).
[11] Wilding, *Latin Course*, 2nd edn, p. 10.

Language learning

If we look first at the approaches to the way in which accidence and syntax are introduced in Wilding's course and CLC we see a contrast between deductive and inductive models of learning. In the preface to the first edition, Wilding highlights the importance of the principle that explanation should precede use. 'Care has been taken not to bewilder him (the pupil) by the premature use of any forms that have not already been explained; on this principle, for example, the adjective is not introduced until it can be fully declined, i.e. until the neuter noun has been reached.' Thus each piece of new grammar is preceded by an explanation; this is followed by practice in translation from Latin into English and English into Latin. However, Wilding does acknowledge the importance of beginning continuous translation early on within the confines of the first few grammatical forms.[12] Translation from English into Latin runs parallel to translation from Latin into English throughout the course.

By contrast, in his discussion of CLC, Sharwood Smith pointed out that a major part of the hypothesis was 'that a pupil could, from a skilfully designed course, develop within three years an intuitive grammar without the help of explicit grammar learning'.[13] Fundamental therefore to CLC is the concept that reading and understanding should precede grammatical explanation. In CLC the learner first meets a new piece of syntax, accidence or vocabulary in the context of a passage or as a caption to a drawing. From this the learner then infers rules and patterns. However, John Wilkins, who acted as the language consultant to the Cambridge Latin Project, argued that it is impossible to reproduce the same conditions for acquiring a second language as those for the first, because Latin is not a spoken language. He saw that the solution lay in a 'passenger' grammar in the materials. 'The grammar has to migrate inside the material. In other words the LT (language teaching) principles are built up not at random but according to a carefully designed grammatical plan. Significant patterns are rehearsed to the point that habits are formed in the learner.'[14] Whereas rote learning and grammatical drilling are essential features of the approach adopted in Wilding, in CLC they are replaced by immersion in a highly structured language experience. This notion that the learner is able to infer meaning and apply rules is characteristic of what Piaget describes as the stage of abstract thinking. This develops gradually, with learners being capable of more abstract patterns of thought earlier or later than the Piagetian 'watershed' of 11 or 12 years of age and

---

[12] Wilding, *Latin Course*, cited from 2nd edn, p. 7.

[13] J. Sharwood Smith, *On Teaching Classics* (Routledge and Kegan Paul, 1977), 39.

[14] J. Wilkins, 'Teaching the classical languages: towards a theory', *Didaskalos* 3:1 (1955), 192.

switching between abstract and concrete modes of thinking. As the capacity for abstract thought develops children are able to see patterns and apply rules more easily.

The focus in Wilding is on form and productive accuracy and in CLC on insightful learning. This is partly a reflection of the different aims of the courses. The Teacher's Handbook to CLC makes it clear that it is presenting 'the language not as a means in itself, nor as an instrument of general training but rather as a means of gaining access to a literature and the culture from which it springs'.[15] Although Wilding does state the importance of the culture and reading passages in Latin, he follows the long-established tradition of emphasising the need for pupils to acquire a facility in translation from English to Latin, partly as a result of his view of Latin as a rigorous mental training. By contrast CLC was designed as a reading course and concentrates on developing the skill of reading in Latin without translating from English into Latin. Thus the problem becomes that of developing correct recognition of Latin forms and structures, not recalling or generating them.

Whereas in Wilding's course the initial exercises consist of single words, then phrases, then sentences and finally short passages, CLC follows Chomsky and makes the sentence the smallest linguistic unit. This also reflects the ways in which each course aims to motivate pupils. Wilding follows a more behaviouristic model of learning whereby the learner is rewarded for making the correct response to the stimuli (the discrete words, phrases and sentences) and thus tends to rely on extrinsic motivation. By contrast, in CLC from the outset of the course pupils begin to read connected passages which are designed to be intrinsically interesting, as they are episodes or chapters in a continuing story. Thus pupils' interest is likely to be aroused and motivation becomes intrinsic. However, CLC does not ignore the role of extrinsic motivation, as the variety of techniques for practising the language attests.

Ecce Romani, first published in 1971, followed similar aims and principles as CLC. Like CLC it was intended to be a reading course which aimed to 'bring pupils quickly to the point where they can read Latin with confidence, and also give them some insight into the early Roman empire'. However, unlike CLC, *Ecce Romani* used the traditional nomenclature for noun and verb parts and set out the paradigms in the traditional manner.

The approaches to language teaching of CLC inevitably drew criticism. Commenting on the first edition of CLC Sharwood Smith claimed: 'The most damaging charge against it is that its pupils do

---

[15] CLC (1973), 2.

not develop an intuitive grammar of Latin sufficiently effective to enable them to read unseen texts of even modest difficulty.'[16] One problem seemed to be that when pupils did not gain understanding through intuitive grammar, they did not have the linguistic basis on which to analyse sentences in the traditional way. In response, the second edition of CLC included more explicit grammatical sections. Published in 1986, the Oxford Latin Course took cognisance of the problems raised by the intuitive approach to language learning. It claimed to 'combine the best features of both modern and traditional methods of Latin teaching'. The authors stated that, where the complexity of a construction demands it, explanation will precede reading, and even in the early stages added footnotes to the cartoons to aid understanding. Like CLC, OLC seeks to engage readers in a continuing narrative. In this case the focus is on the life of Horace but opportunities within this framework are found for moving into Greek and Roman mythology. Unlike CLC, OLC introduces authentic Latin from an early stage and gives some exercises that involve translation from English into Latin.

Language and culture

That language and culture are inextricably linked was highlighted by Sapir and Whorf.[17] A 'hard' Sapir-Whorfian approach would claim that language determines thought, whereas a 'soft' Sapir-Whorfian approach suggests that the syntax available determines the modes of thought. This interconnection between language and culture is recognised by Wilding, CLC, OLC and *Ecce Romani*.

One reason Wilding gives for learning Latin is to benefit from the 'study of a practical people who have given many good things to our own civilisation and have expressed themselves in a literature that is always stately and often beautiful'.[18] Wilding chooses to start with passages that deal with Roman Britain as 'there are few parts of the country from which Roman remains of some kind cannot be reached; most museums have an interesting Roman section'.[19] Later passages are set in Italy and Rome.

Likewise the authors of CLC state the second aim of the course is 'to develop from the outset an understanding of the content, style and values of Roman civilisation, with particular reference to the first century AD'.[20] In Wilding's course it is the passages for translation from both Latin and English that convey the history and culture. The

---

[16] Sharwood Smith, *On Teaching Classics*, p. 41.
[17] B. Whorf in J.B. Carroll, ed., *Language, Thought and Reality: Selected Writings of Benjamin Lee Whorf* (MIT Press, Cambridge MA, 1956).
[18] Wilding, *Latin Course*, 2nd edn, p. 9.
[19] Ibid.
[20] CLC Teacher's Handbook, p. 2.

transmission of Roman culture in CLC is through both the Latin passages and the inclusion in each chapter of cultural material in English on a related theme which is intended to be read 'alongside' the Latin.

However, when we look at the content of the passages in both Latin and English we see significant differences in the approaches to culture adopted by the two courses. In Wilding the content of the passages in both English and Latin is for the most part dominated first by the campaigns of Julius Caesar in Britain and later by the heroic exploits of Roman men and boys. For, like earlier, traditional textbooks, Wilding appears to have been written for boys who were expected to be more interested in matters military than girls. The passages, with some exceptions, focus on the events of political and military history and the expansion of the Roman empire rather than on the social and cultural life of Rome and her empire. The emphasis thus is on 'high' culture as opposed to culture as social practice.

Both the socio-political climate and the child-centred approaches to learning impacted on the choice of materials in CLC. Firstly, with the development of a comprehensive system of education there was a shift in the perception of Latin as an academically and socially élite subject to the perception that classics should be made available to a wider audience. In the anti-authoritarianism and anti-imperialist mood of the times, to focus exclusively on the élite and powerful and on the military might and hegemonic nature of the Roman empire would hardly have been thought appropriate. Set in the early empire, CLC does show aspects of imperial rule such as the client king Cogidubnus, the governance of Egypt, Masada, and political and social life at the court of Domitian. However, CLC focuses too on the everyday and domestic aspects of life in the Roman empire and on its cultural legacy. CLC was interested in developing character and plot in both 'high' and 'everyday' settings with the protagonists in the stories being drawn from all strata of life. There is a parallel here with innovations in the curriculum in English, with working-class literature being introduced into the curriculum alongside or in some cases instead of Shakespeare.

CLC, *Ecce* and OLC acknowledge the importance of making their materials attractive to girls as well as boys. Whereas in Wilding males tend to be the leading characters of the stories, women are given greater prominence in the new courses. Thus CLC in its early editions focused mainly on the domestic roles of women, but in the latest edition (2000) has given more prominence to women in other contexts, in response to criticism from women teachers and girls. In the first books of *Ecce Romani* we are introduced to Roman life through female characters.

The focus on the non-militaristic and the everyday was also a response to child-centred approaches to learning and awareness of the need to motivate pupils by arousing their interests and engaging them with material that could be seen to relate to their own lives. CLC, *Ecce Romani* and OLC start with the theme of a family. Hence in CLC Unit 1 we start by getting to know the members of the family of Caecilius in their domestic setting right to their deaths in the eruption of Vesuvius and, on the way, progressively move outwards from the domestic to the public arenas of life in Pompeii. Through looking at a family located in a very different time and place there are clear points of contact and a rich source of possibilities for making comparisons and contrasts. CLC then moves from Pompeii to the Roman empire, which adds a multi-cultural or global dimension. In a similar way *Ecce Romani* starts with Cornelia and her family and OLC with Horace, a storyline which enables the authors of OLC to introduce some Greek and Roman mythology and authentic Latin. Unlike OLC and CLC, *Ecce Romani* retains the focus on the domestic and everyday life in ancient Rome.

Semiotics: conveying meaning through words and pictures

A recent approach to looking at textbooks is that offered by semiotics, which shows how meaning is conveyed through layout, illustrations and format. Kress argues that 'many texts are becoming multimodal in a pronounced way, using visual and verbal elements in quite new ways. Textbooks are increasingly now visual rather than verbal objects.' Discussing the use of images in extracts from textbooks published in the 1940s and 1990s, Kress concludes that, 'Where before written language was the medium of information, in many texts there is now a new code at work which consists of both verbal and visual elements, which are used in specialised ways.'[21]

Learning involves the use of all our senses and it is well to remember the adage that one picture is worth a thousand words. We can see this close inter-relation between the verbal and the visual, and between form and content, in CLC and OLC, particularly in their new colour editions. In its original format CLC was produced in pamphlets. This was partly pragmatic – to get the trial materials in school and receive feedback – and partly to give the pupils a sense of achievement in having reached the end of a stage. This division into stages has continued throughout all the revisions including the latest colour edition.

[21] G. Kress, 'Internationalism and globalisation: rethinking a curriculum of communication', *Comparative Education* 32:2 (1996), 193.

The original and all the subsequent editions of CLC and OLC have used visual images to serve a variety of purposes. Firstly, following Piagetian principles which stress the importance to learners of experiencing the concrete before they can move on to the abstract, CLC and OLC link words to pictures of objects and thus use visual images as an aid to decoding meaning. The concrete image accompanies/reinforces the abstract learning and at the same time serves to engage interest.

Another important function of the images in CLC and OLC is to help locate the language in the culture with illustrations of landscapes, artefacts and buildings of the Roman empire. CLC and OLC were both originally produced in black and white. In 1996 OLC produced its second edition in colour and this was followed in 1999 by the colour edition of the first book of CLC. OLC uses its original cartoons in colour and CLC uses the original black and white line drawings for the cartoons, often in enlarged format, in the same way as before. Where both OLC and CLC have made a significant advance is in the use of high-quality coloured illustrations and photographs to reinforce the idea that this is a course about a culture with its artefacts and locations. It conveys the message that following the course is going to be a pleasurable experience. Indeed, the textbooks have the appearance in some places of holiday brochures.

The size of the books is comparable to that of textbooks in other subjects and is more akin to that of a magazine. In CLC the text is broken up so that language work and pictures are interspersed on the same page, with a clear signposting in the different background colours used for different aspects of the language work. Indeed the colour editions of CLC and OLC recognise the need identified by Kress who argued that 'young people are formed and form themselves in the totality of their semiotic environment. If that environment is one in which the modes of writing are less significant than other modes, then that is the environment which we, as curriculum planners, need to consider'.[22]

Summary

This chapter has tried to set the changes in Latin teaching that came in during the early 1970s into the context of learning theories and the socio-political background. We have seen that the changes in pedagogy in the 1960s impacted on all subjects in the curriculum, including classics. Because of the threats to Latin in the 1960s the impetus for developing more innovative and imaginative teaching materials and styles was perhaps felt more keenly by classics teachers than those in other subjects. The courses that were produced in the early 1970s and

---

[22] Ibid.

the 1980s and have continued to be revised, drew rather eclectically on a variety of theories about teaching and learning to produce materials that have continued to engage the learner. The continuation of Latin in both state and independent sectors is in no small measure due to the responsiveness to change on the part of both the authors of the courses and classics teachers who embraced the changes in content and pedagogy.

References and further reading

Balme, M. and Morwood, J. The Oxford Latin Course (1986). OUP

The Cambridge Latin Course (first published 1970 and revised in a colour edition 1999–2003). Cambridge University Press

Chomsky, N. (1959) 'Review of *Verbal Behaviour*' in *Language* 35: 26–58

Central Advisory Council for Education *Plowden Report*. HMSO

Department of Education and Science (DES) (1959) *A report of The Central Advisory Council for Education England (Crowther Report)*. HMSO

Dewey, J. (1946) *Democracy and Education*. Free Press

Ecce Romani (1971). Oliver and Boyd

Ellis, R. (1994) *The Study of Second Language Acquisition*. Oxford University Press

Forrest, M. (1996) *Modernising the Classics*. University of Exeter Press

Good, T. and Brophy, J. (1990) *Educational Psychology: A Realistic Approach*. Longman

Kress, G. (1996) 'Internationalism and globalisation: rethinking a curriculum of communication', *Comparative Education* 32: 2, 185–96

Mitchell, R. and Myles, F. (1998) *Second Language Theories*. OUP

Piaget, J. (1923) *Le Langage et la pensée chez l'enfant*. Delacahux et Nestlé

Sharwood Smith, J. (1977) *On Teaching Classics*. London, Routledge and Kegan Paul

Skinner, J. B. (1957) *Verbal Behaviour*. Appleton–Century–Crofts

Stern, H.H. (1983) *Fundamental Principles of Language Learning*. OUP

Whorf, B. in J.B. Carroll, ed. (1956) *Language, Thought and Reality: Selected Writings of Benjamin Lee Whorf*. MIT Press, Cambridge, MA

Wilding, L.A. (1949) *Latin Course for Schools* (2nd edn, 1955). Faber and Faber

Wilkins, J. (1969) 'Teaching the classical languages: towards a theory', *Didaskolos* 3:1

10 | The development of the Cambridge Latin Course

Pat Story

Since the Cambridge Latin Course was produced by the University of Cambridge School Classics Project and began publication in 1970, it has gone through four editions, two of them involving major changes of content and format. Additional publications, not originally envisaged – graded tests, independent learning materials, worksheet master exercises and a suite of computer programs – have also been produced over the last thirty years. It is the purpose of this chapter to examine the evolution of the course in the light of teachers' experience and the changing circumstances of Latin teaching. The development of new electronic resources is described in David Goodhew's chapter and elsewhere in the volume (pp. 113-14, 143 and 165) .

It is now difficult to understand the strong reactions that greeted the announcement of the two objectives of the Cambridge Latin Course at its inception.

> The first (objective) is to teach comprehension of the Latin language for reading purposes. The second is to develop from the outset an understanding of the content, style and values of Roman civilisation, with particular reference to the first century AD. The course presents the language not as an end in itself, nor as an instrument of general mental training, but rather as a means of gaining access to a literature and the culture from which it springs.[1]

Traditionalists had their worst fears confirmed when they scrutinised the textbook. Why was there no provision for English into Latin translation? Why was there so little explanation of grammar? What was this nonsense about Forms A and B? Where were complete tables of nouns and verbs and adequate supplies of exercises? If the unusual content of the stories and oddly named paralinguistic sections evoked less comment, it was because the subject matter of Latin courses had previously played a subsidiary role. The idea that language and culture were inextricably linked and that the intensive study of both was necessary for any adequate reading of literature was an idea whose time had not yet come, at least in schools.

---

[1] CLC Unit I Teacher's Handbook, 1st edn (1971), 1.

However, a large number of teachers, who had recognised the need to change and had been influenced by the advocacy of the Project's director, David Morton, embarked on the highly experimental course with enthusiasm. First impressions were very favourable. Teachers commented on the fluency students developed in reading, the way they identified with the characters and the interest they showed in life in Pompeii as it was exemplified in the stories, the illustrations and – an innovation at the time – the specially commissioned set of slides. Anecdotes told of girls weeping at the death of Caecilius, instant recognition of Pompeian sites on school visits, re-creations of Roman dinner-parties, masked plays and elections and cross-curricular work with chemistry departments resulting in working models of the eruption of Vesuvius.

However, when students reached the end of Unit II, unease and sometimes disillusionment set in. As the Latin of the stories became more demanding, students continued to translate fluently but their translations, although sometimes making sense, often bore little relation to the text. The problem was compounded by the steep linguistic gradient of Unit III and the later Units and the general lack of advice in the Teacher's Handbooks. These were good at making suggestions about how to introduce new linguistic features, but did not emphasise sufficiently the need for constant reinforcement of those that had been encountered previously. Beyond re-reading stories in various ways and working through the few manipulation exercises supplied, little practical help was given. The underlying assumption that by extensive reading students would formulate their own adequate personal grammar of the language did not take into account that this would require more time than was available and that students might actually welcome more explicit explanations and examples.

An exhaustive survey of a large sample of teachers confirmed what the Project had already learnt from its many contacts with schools and provided the foundation for the second edition of the course. The revision editor, Robin Griffin, addressed the problem of consolidation by increasing the number of exercises in the course and by making more detailed and helpful suggestions in the Teacher's Handbooks. He tackled the steep gradient of the course by providing more reading material which both skilfully incorporated linguistic features at a more measured pace and maintained the high standard of writing that was one of the strengths of the course. This new material also sought to provide a more structured and smoother transition to the O level prescribed texts by introducing extracts of verse and notes on typical features of verse into the later stages. This preparation was completed by a new Unit containing an anthology of Latin verse and adapted prose, with introductions to the literature, questions on critical appreciation and notes that completed the linguistic scheme of the course.

The controversial Forms A, B etc. disappeared and nominatives and accusatives were reinstated, much to the relief of many teachers.

The new edition was hailed as a success, but the full implementation of its reforms was not possible in many schools because of the decreasing amount of time allowed for Latin in the curriculum. One of the effects on the course was that the new last Unit, intended as an introduction to O level Latin literature, became itself a prescribed text. Even this was not enough to make the course manageable in many schools. Teachers were forced to omit reading passages, particularly in the later stages of the course, at the very point when more practice was needed with complex structures. Some abandoned the text-based consolidation recommended by the Handbooks and fell back on recitation of paradigms in the hope that students would be able to apply their knowledge to unseen passages.

Eventually the fourth edition would attempt to address the problems, but in the mid-eighties and early nineties the Project embarked on three new initiatives stimulated by developments in secondary education.

The first of these was the growth of criterion-referenced attainment tests, particularly in mathematics and modern languages. It was hoped that these tests would provide a sense of manageable, short-term goals on the long haul to O level and subsequently GCSE, which would motivate students to continue their efforts. Those who for reasons of incapacity or option choice 'gave up' a subject before GCSE would have something to show for their investment of time, literally so, if success in a test were rewarded by a certificate. The application of such schemes to Latin teaching was obvious. Moreover, the Cambridge Latin Course, with its clear aims, highly structured linguistic scheme, well-defined cultural content and organisation in separate Units, lent itself to assessment by graded objectives. For the administration of the tests the Project had the advantage of being able to examine a number of existing schemes in modern languages and was influenced by the general principles of the Hertfordshire scheme, which combined a degree of flexibility for the schools, while maintaining control over standards of attainment and the award of certificates.

The Cambridge Latin tests have proved very popular, despite the extra work involved for teachers and moderators. Students certainly have a sense of achievement – in some cases certificates have been framed and proudly displayed at home. The fact that the certificates are signed by the head teacher and presented on a public occasion also helps to give greater prominence to a subject that is often marginalised. Since the beginning of the scheme in 1985 nearly 180,000 have been awarded.

The second influential development in education was the promotion of independent or self-directed learning which was a major feature of the government's Technical and Vocational Education Initiative (TVEI). At the time the writer and a fellow classicist, Jean Hubbard, were teaching Cambridge Latin in after-school classes to students of different ages and at different stages of the course. Even without the stimulus of TVEI, there was an urgent need to evolve methods and produce materials which would enable students to work independently with only occasional help from the teacher. The result was the publication of the Independent Learning Manuals with accompanying Answer Books, which guided students through the course, providing explanation of new language items, comprehension questions, exercises on language and background, and end-of-stage tests.

It has been unexpected and gratifying to find that the Manuals are used not only by students who have to work on their own, but also by teachers of normal classes who value variety of methods and materials. The ready-made lessons have proved a godsend to teachers who have to set work for classes during an absence and likewise to students who have had to 'catch up' with their fellows after illness or transfer from another school. More recently the Manuals have played a key role in developing an e-mail distance-learning programme.

The materials have also been used by a handful of students educated at home and a few interested adults. Hitherto it has not been possible for the Project to launch a campaign to reach more students in these categories but with the advent of the Project's website the problem of publicity and access to materials should be largely solved.

A further national development was the provision of computers in schools. This prompted a few enthusiastic teachers and sixth formers to devise computer programs for some of the early stages of the course. Eventually a varied package of programs for Unit I was published. It was predictably popular with those students who enjoyed being questioned on screen about a theft in the baths or discovering their own fate (in Latin) in the eruption of Vesuvius; but its use was never widespread because of technical problems with computers or simply the difficulty of getting access to a computer room at the right time. It is somewhat depressing that a decade later the efforts of teachers in some schools may still be frustrated for the same reasons.

A further influence on the Project during this time was our sister organisation, the North American Cambridge Classics Project (NACCP), whose course materials included a series of workbooks and worksheet master exercises. Thinking that attractive photocopiable exercises would be useful to teachers in this country, the Project produced sets of exercises for Units I and II, which included work on derivatives and background topics as well as consolidation of language features. As in the Independent Learning Manuals, many exercises were based on pictures.

By the mid-nineties the resources described above were available for the early Units of the course and work had started on much-needed additional materials for the later Units. It was at this point that our publishers suggested a new edition. The initial proposal to introduce some colour illustrations, but with minimal changes to the text, was soon superseded by a more ambitious plan. There was certainly a strong case to update the presentation of the course, which had remained largely unchanged since the beginning of the eighties and was now looking drab beside its more colourful rivals, but here was also an opportunity to make the course more manageable for schools with their ever-decreasing time allowances. Reading passages have therefore been pruned and the vocabulary to be known reduced in line with the new GCSE word lists. Relatively few changes have been made to the language notes: new linguistic points continue to be discussed in the context of complete sentences, but in view of the more formal approach to English teaching in primary and secondary schools some traditional grammatical terms are introduced earlier. Exercises have been revised, but not appreciably increased. Instead, the Teacher's Guides, extensively revised by Jill Dalladay, contain a large number of new comprehension questions and exercises based on the reading passages. This generous provision helps to satisfy a long-felt need for additional support, particularly in the later stages of the course.

The most obvious change in the fourth edition, however, is the appearance of the students' books. Their size has been enlarged to provide a more spacious layout for the text and the numerous colour photographs selected by Roger Dalladay. Like the line drawings retained from the previous editions, the photographs are not merely decorative, but are meant to convey information about the Roman world, which is essential to its understanding. This is not a passive process: the pictures are there to raise questions and provoke discussion. For example, in studying a relief showing an accident in a chariot race, students are asked why they think the accident has happened (the crash has occurred at the turning-point) and what urgent action the charioteer should take now if he is to survive.

In revising the Cambridge Latin Course and developing supplementary materials one is confronted by two major problems, which need to be considered by teachers whatever course they use. The first concerns the balance to be struck between 'reading for sense' and explicit analysis of the language. Over-emphasis on the first to the virtual exclusion of the second may lead, as we have seen, to plausible but inaccurate translations, while concentration on linguistic forms removed from a coherent context may result in incomprehension, boredom and consequent lack of motivation. There may be no one right answer: the balance may be different for different students. Most, in the writer's experience, are more interested in what a passage has to say than in the mechanics of language and will tolerate language notes and grammatical tables on a 'need to know' basis. But there is a minority who wish to go further than this and are fascinated by the organisation of the language. The Project's response to the problem in recent years has been a largely pragmatic one; there remains a need for more discussion of the issue, informed by teachers' experience and recent research in applied linguistics.

The second problem is caused by the requirements of the GCSE examination and the time allocated to Latin in schools. The latter of course has always varied, even between schools in the same sector, but over the last forty years it has shown some startling reductions. Whereas it was difficult in the sixties to recruit an adequate sample of schools with three-year courses for the Project's pilot group, such courses are now commonplace and, indeed, two-year courses are not unusual.

In response to this situation GCSE boards have modified their syllabuses: the amount of required accidence, syntax and vocabulary has been reduced, as have the length of the prescribed texts and the number of cultural topics to be examined. These syllabuses are more or less manageable for schools that still have reasonable time allowances and able students. Even so, teachers tend to omit the parts of the course that are designed to ease the transition to original Latin and struggle to initiate their students in literature that is linguistically and conceptually demanding. Nevertheless they rightly argue that the reading of a selection of Catullus poems or part of a book of the *Aeneid* is a memorable experience and a fitting end to the course. And certainly this is often acknowledged by students, who feel that they have not been challenged or inspired by anything comparable at this stage in their education.

Students who can achieve this goal with pleasure should of course continue to do so. But what of the others who may not be as able and have only two or three years to study Latin? They and their teachers are being asked to do the impossible. Would they not be better served by an option in the GCSE examination (perhaps an alternative to the Foundation Tier) which did not require the study of one or both set texts, but substituted an extra topic or literature in translation?

This would mean that a minority of students would no longer read Latin in the original, one of the objectives of the course, but there would still be other worthwhile goals to achieve. Schools in which Higher and Foundation Tier students were taught together would have problems, but these might be resolved by the use of independent learning materials – in print or online – and a different organisation of lesson time.

It hardly needs saying that the flexibility and resourcefulness that have enabled the Cambridge Latin Course to meet the challenges of the last forty years will continue to be needed in the future. In particular the success of the trials of the new electronic resources offers the prospect not only of enhancing the teaching of existing courses but also of extending the subject to schools where there is no Latin teacher.

This chapter would not be complete without an acknowledgement of the support and encouragement the Project has received over the years. First, the Nuffield Foundation, which with the Schools Council provided the initial funding, generously gave its share of the royalty income to the Project to disseminate and develop its materials; more recently the Department for Education and Skills financed the creation and trials of the electronic resources. Second, none of these developments would have been possible without the enthusiasm, constructive criticism and hard work of so many teachers who answered questionnaires, attended courses, tried out new materials and served on working parties and examination panels. To them the Project owes an immense debt of gratitude.

11 | The Oxford Latin Course

Maurice Balme and James Morwood

When we started writing the Oxford Latin Course in the early 1980s, the Cambridge Latin Course had been out for more than ten years. We had used it in our school with mixed success. We shared its authors' convictions that reading Latin must be the overriding objective of any Latin language course, that we must aim at reading some of the great Latin authors, in particular Virgil, and that some understanding of the Roman world which produced this literature was a key to reading their works with appreciation. We admired the radical novelty of their approach and agreed that in a world in which Latin was almost always an optional subject, motivation of the students was of vital importance. The Cambridge course saved Latin from a premature demise, giving many thousands of students a chance to attempt to learn the language with pleasure.

But we found that the course had significant weaknesses. The assumption that an inductive approach would lead students to form a 'personal grammar' proved false: without supplementary assistance they could never tackle real Latin with any confidence. (Of course this defect has been increasingly rectified in successive editions of CLC. See pp. 86–7.) Placing the context of the stories in the first century AD, a brilliant success in Unit 1, provided no lead into the authors of the Golden Age. Of the target prose authors, undoctored Tacitus proved too hard and Pliny too bland. The virtual absence of any mention of myth or of the Greek background to Roman literature meant that much Latin poetry was scarcely intelligible.

We therefore decided to try again. The principles on which our course is constructed are explained in the Introduction to the *Teacher's Book*, Part 1 (Oxford, 1996). In brief, linguistically we make a compromise between the traditional analytic method and the inductive method of Cambridge, insisting that reading with understanding comes first but must be followed by an analytical grasp and thorough learning of new grammatical features. Translation from English into Latin is included but only as an adjunct, to practise grammatical forms and concepts; for this purpose, we believe it has an important role to play in the early stages. And like the authors of CLC we believe that the Latin language should be taught in a Roman context, so that understanding of the language and of the culture may proceed *pari passu*.

We were delighted to have the opportunity to tighten up the material in a second edition produced ten years after the first. There was expansion too. The role of women was enhanced, to the course's considerable advantage. We included a succession of *fabellae*, playlets for the children to enact. (Such dialogues had been one of the great strengths of CLC from the outset.) And we pioneered *Responde Latine* questions on the passages demanding crisp answers to Latin in Latin. Our constant aim was to produce a course that works, avoiding any doctrinaire application of principles and aiming to combine the best features of the modern and the traditional methods of teaching Latin.

The course follows the life of the poet Horace. We felt that this had a number of advantages. First of all, much of what happened to him is well documented and as the course progresses we are able to move ever closer to historical fact and quote from contemporary sources, including his own poetry. Secondly, his life covers the end of the republic and the Augustan revolution, the period of the Golden Age of Latin literature, which is the reading target at which we aim and the literary area covered in the *Oxford Latin Reader*. And since Horace was involved in these great events, students acquire some understanding of the historical background to this literature. His unsophisticated boyhood in rural Apulia allows us to start with simple vocabulary, and his service in Brutus' army, culminating in his ignoble flight at Philippi, enables us to include the traditional vocabulary of Roman warfare.

Thirdly, Horace was an exact contemporary of the younger Marcus Cicero (the orator's son), to whom, at the cost of some bare-faced fiction, we give a major role in the story. This enables us to introduce Marcus' famous father, the one man about whom we know at first hand even more than we know about Horace himself. Fourthly, his friendship with Virgil enables us to prepare the way for the extracts from the *Aeneid* that appear in Part III (and of course in the *Reader*). By the time students come to read extracts from Caesar, Cicero and Virgil, the writers will be old friends, or at least acquaintances, whose social and historical background is already familiar. The literature will not, we hope, seem remote or unreal but related to what they have already read and relevant to their own experience.

Lastly, Horace's stay at university in Athens enables us to sketch in some of the Greek background to Roman poetry. This, as we have said above, struck us as essential, since without some knowledge of this, Roman poetry simply does not make sense. As Horace himself says:

Graecia capta ferum victorem cepit et artes
intulit agresti Latio.   (*Epistles* 2.1.155–6)

And so we intend that everything in the course should contribute to the overriding aim of preparing students to read the literature of the Golden Age with sympathetic understanding and intelligent appreciation. At the same time, we hope that the events of Horace's life and his attractive personality are sufficiently interesting to motivate them to want to learn more. This hope has not, it appears, been disappointed.

The authors of the course have produced a significant amount of supplementary material. We published a workbook for Part I of the first edition, but came to the conclusion that pressures of time meant that there was little need for yet more exercises, however entertaining some of them might be. Morwood edited the *Pocket Oxford Latin Dictionary* in 1995 (also published as the *Oxford Latin Minidictionary*). This is now available in electronic format (http://www.cambridgescp.com /pol/pol_home.html). In 1999 he published a Latin grammar (*A Latin Grammar*, Oxford University Press). The tables of accidence in this are based on those in OLC, though since the book is designed to be used after the course has been completed, they are somewhat fuller and the grammatical explanations are more thorough, while still giving opportunities for practice. Readings from the course appeared on two cassettes in the same year, and these are now also available in CD format. Julian Morgan has independently created excellent CD-ROMs on Rome (http://www.j-progs.com/) and on the travels of Horace (*The Horace Trail*, OUP, 2002), in which he follows the poet on his travels. And Balme and Morwood have assembled a reader entitled *On the Margin* (OUP, 2003), which begins with passages on the Roman family and moves out to the area of 'the other': women, children, freedmen, slaves, convicts, gladiators and Christians. A thriving North American group produces a wealth of valuable home-made material, and the Oxford University Press is ever supportive. The OLC show is very much on the road.

12 | Learning Greek

John Taylor

Introduction

The study of Greek in English schools has a long and distinguished history. Greek was first taught at St Paul's School in the sixteenth century. It has always been a minority pursuit, and that minority is now very small indeed. But the Greek enterprise has a disproportionate vigour and influence, and a future about which its devotees are cautiously optimistic. Greek, like Latin, has seen a significant decline in pupil numbers over several decades. Not all the causes and effects of this are a matter for regret. Many pupils in the past had little to show, in attainment or enthusiasm, for their enforced exposure to the rudiments of classical languages. Classics departments are now leaner and fitter, and to Greek in particular both teachers and pupils typically bring an unusual degree of commitment.

The health of a subject is, however, inevitably measured by public examination statistics. In 1994 the number of candidates taking A level Greek dropped for the first time below 300, and in 1996 the number taking GCSE dipped below 1,000. In response to concern over this, the Greek committee of JACT set out in 1997 to survey the Greek teaching going on in schools, and to investigate ways in which teachers might be helped and pupil numbers increased. A preliminary request for information was sent out with the JACT Bulletin, a one-day conference on 'Greek in Schools' was held in London in 1998, and then a detailed questionnaire was sent to about 100 teachers who had responded to these overtures. The main finding was an almost unanimous desire for new textbooks and teaching materials. Greek has until now been alone among school subjects in having no textbook aimed specifically at GCSE. Of course there is no desire to emulate the dumbing-down seen in the books publishers offer (and examination boards endorse) for GCSE in some subjects. And it may be admitted that many classicists take a sneaking pride in using books which have acquired a cachet, a patina of period charm, from having been first published a century or more ago. But from the viewpoint of teenage pupils in the real world, faced with curriculum options and glossy publications galore, Greek has been handicapped and made unnecessarily forbidding.

As will be described below, much has already been done to address this problem (though there is room for more). The wider picture revealed by the surveys contained much that was impressive and encouraging. The retention rate of GCSE candidates choosing to continue Greek at A level is probably the best of any subject. Greek is certainly ahead in the percentage of candidates awarded the top grades. It is true that Greek is offered in the first place to an untypically able minority. But outstanding results reflect also the enthusiastic commitment of both teachers and taught to a shared enterprise of great intrinsic fascination. Greek is cherished and vigorously promoted in schools where it still exists. Those schools are of course themselves an untypical minority. Most are independent. State schools have found it harder to keep Greek, though some remarkable pockets survive, especially in Roman Catholic schools. And pupils who have no opportunity to study Greek on the official timetable can often be offered it unofficially (referred to as 'broom-cupboard' Greek, though it is usually the timing not the location that is improvised, during lunch breaks or after school). Remarkable results are obtained every year in this way, illustrating again the unusual dedication Greek inspires. There is some indication that the kind of independent-minded teenage intellectual who in the 1960s demanded to be taught Russian is now more likely to clamour for Greek.

Beginners' courses

Practically all course books ever published can be made to work, given an enthusiastic teacher and willing pupils. Every book has strengths and weaknesses, friends and critics. Of existing courses for pupils beginning Greek, two are far ahead of any rivals: L.A. Wilding's *Greek for Beginners* (originally Faber, 1957, now Duckworth) and Maurice Balme and Gilbert Lawall's *Athenaze* (OUP, 1990 onwards).

Wilding remains the favourite overall for school use. Almost continuously in print for forty-five years, this book has given countless pupils a solid grounding in Greek. Of course its age shows (from its recommended pronunciation onwards). It is old-fashioned and dry in approach, but thorough and generally logical in order of presentation. Most exercises are sentences for translation (both ways round). Easily parodied ('We are sacrificing on the island, O sailors'), these are satisfying and enjoyable for pupils bright enough to do them quickly and get them right, but dispiriting for others. By modern standards there are too few reading passages, especially in the early stages. The passages (many adapted from Herodotus) were generally liked by respondents to the JACT questionnaire: they are cleverly written, and better integrated into the chapters than appears at first sight. But they are fairly demanding, and no lexical help is given. Vocabulary in the book is not a close match with GCSE requirements (though a better one than *Athenaze*). Chapter-by-chapter vocabularies would improve the book. It has, of course, idiosyncrasies and weaknesses. It is closely tied to Abbott and Mansfield's *Primer of Greek Grammar* (see below): pupils have an inevitable sense of being left in the lurch when (from Chapter 8 onwards) they are referred for all new grammar to that not very user-friendly book. The early learning of several tenses is generally liked, but Wilding gives too much emphasis to the perfect, knowledge of which is no longer required by OCR (one of the two boards offering GCSE Greek), and more bizarrely to the almost non-existent pluperfect. Excessively heavy weather is made of the third declension, where all that is needed is presentation of a basic paradigm along with variants for study. Conversely some things needed for GCSE are not covered: no conditionals, and no -μι verbs (still required by AQA, the other GCSE board offering Greek). At a more philosophical level, it has been commented that Wilding makes Greek too much like Latin. Two nicely double-edged comments from respondents sum things up: 'It's like a pair of old slippers', and 'Students like it for its solid reassuring efficient dullness.'

Many courses have come and gone: *Deigma* (Walters and Conway, 1916), *Kepos* (Kinchin Smith and Melluish, 1951), *Lampas* (Rees and Jervis, 1970) – interesting what names people choose for Greek books – but of those still in print the next landmark is C.W.E. Peckett and A.R. Munday's *Thrasymachus* (1965, now published by Duckworth). Innovative in method, this book pioneered an inductive approach (presenting new grammatical features in a reading passage before they are explained). It thus paved the way for *Reading Greek* (see below) and *Athenaze*. Yet it is now used only by a handful of schools (though they spoke warmly of it). The problem is a familiar one with classical textbooks more than a few years old: childish tone and content allied to a grammatical learning curve of excessive steepness. Though it dates only from the sixties, one respondent spoke of 'the humour of an Edwardian prep school' (it is important to distinguish intentional and unintentional humour: the three-page *Agamemnon* passage – *Reduced Shakespeare Company* meets Housman's *Fragment of a Greek Tragedy* – is in fact hilarious, but presumably was not meant to be). Next after *Thrasymachus* came the Scottish *New Greek Course for Schools*: following on from the Latin course *Ecce Romani*, this was produced by a Glasgow-based team headed by W.A. Williams. It appeared in successive versions from the 1970s, but never in an officially published form: the 1984 revised edition in four booklets is still obtainable. This course makes effective use of background material, and in its later stages has good reading passages. But the grammar in the early stages is presented in an order unlikely to satisfy many, and the physical presentation inevitably looks homemade by the standards of modern desktop publishing.

The JACT course *Reading Greek*, in contrast, began with a big public appeal led by Archbishop Michael Ramsey, *Times* correspondence, and a steering committee of luminaries. A team led by Peter Jones worked full time in Cambridge for four years: they started by reading the whole of extant Greek literature of the classical period. The resulting *Reading Greek: Text* and *Reading Greek: Grammar, Vocabulary and Exercises* (CUP, 1978) took their place at once as the standard course for older beginners. *Reading Greek* is the backbone of Greek learning in universities, at summer schools and among adults. The text is a *tour de force*, pitching students into only lightly adapted passages of oratory, comedy and philosophy, and ending with extended unadapted extracts from *Odyssey* 6 and Herodotus 1. After a quarter of a century it hardly shows its age. The *Grammar etc.* volume has always been more open to criticism (as was confirmed by a recent CUP survey investigating the revision which is now underway): morphology tables go across the page when you want them to go down, βαίνω was an odd choice of paradigm verb, and the vocabulary designated for learning seems an arbitrary selection. But these are minor faults: consensus suggests the grammar book needs light revision whilst the text should remain unchanged.

Reading Greek is intentionally adult in approach. Only one school reported using it successfully with pupils aged thirteen or fourteen. But as a course for sixth-form students starting from scratch (and as speed-reading practice after GCSE) it has a significant role in school. Even more useful for sixth-form general reading are the two volumes of texts with running vocabulary which quickly followed: selections from Homer, Herodotus and Sophocles in *A World of Heroes* (1979), and from Euripides, Thucydides and Plato in *The Intellectual Revolution* (1980). 1980 also brought the very useful *Greek Vocabulary* booklet. The next volumes in the series were ancillary to the original text: *Teachers' Notes* (1986) and *Independent Study Guide* (1995). A new departure came with *The Triumph of Odysseus* (*Odyssey* 21 and 22, 1996): the facing vocabulary was now presented in sequential rather than alphabetical order, a practice continued in *New Testament Greek: A Reader* (2001) and *A Greek Anthology* (2002). The first of these is perhaps tangential to classics teaching, but it is hoped that the *Anthology* (twenty passages of varying length, covering authors from Homer to Plutarch) will be useful in a number of contexts: adult education, immediate post-GCSE reading (a gap identified by the JACT survey), and possibly as a set text (all words are glossed except a core of 350 common to the prescribed vocabularies of the two GCSE boards).

As a school textbook *Athenaze* has the huge advantage of modern and attractive appearance. In some respects it is a junior equivalent of *Reading Greek*. It presents a continuous narrative based on the fictional family of Dicaeopolis (borrowed from Aristophanes' *Acharnians*) in the 430s BC. Inset stories in the first of its two volumes take readers into the worlds of myth and of the Persian Wars; the second provides generous selections from a wide range of original texts. The first version of *Athenaze* was produced and privately printed by Maurice Balme at Harrow School in 1979. Though the 1990 OUP version looks back to its predecessor as 'skeletal', in some respects it was better as a school text than the American-influenced collaborative version finally published. The intended American market was presumably among undergraduates: features such as the use of technical terms, and the length and sophistication of background sections, do not obviously seem those of a book aimed at schoolchildren. Of course it might be claimed that in a small field a Greek textbook needs to target its stones at several birds. *Athenaze* gets a very good press from American universities (this emerged from the CUP survey, some respondents explaining why they preferred it to *Reading Greek*). Results of the JACT survey among English schools were more mixed. It is easy to underestimate how much of an obstacle the presentation of the cases in American order (accusative last) was in the UK in the 1990 version. OUP brought out a 'Special UK Edition' in 1995, but the anglicisation seemed grudging and piecemeal (the accusative back in its traditional place, but 'theater' retained). Respondents generally felt that *Athenaze* stays in the present tense too long (perhaps as an over-reaction from Wilding). Conversely, contracted verbs appear from the very start: presumably so that they hold no terrors – but most teachers felt it was better to learn the normal forms thoroughly first, then apply the rules of contraction. Similarly with other criticised features of grammar presentation (second aorist before first, middle participle before active): it is clear why these things were done, but on balance a more traditional 'building block' order (in the style of Wilding) is preferred.

The biggest problem with *Athenaze* for young beginners, however, is vocabulary: they are simply overwhelmed with too much. By the later chapters of Book I only about 10 per cent of the vocabulary prescribed for learning is relevant to the current GCSE. It is also unsatisfactory that vocabulary is presented in two separate places (at the head of the chapter, and below each passage), with no indication of where a particular item features. It is readily conceded that pupils should be encouraged to learn some words beyond the modest GCSE prescriptions, but for most the demands of *Athenaze* in this area are unrealistic. In Book II the level of difficulty increases sharply, though it is by no means necessary to cover its contents for GCSE: many respondents did not go beyond Book I, using their own material to plug the gaps (as people also do with Wilding). Despite all this, *Athenaze* has many merits. Maurice Balme in the 1979 version disarmingly conceded that the material in the early passages was 'jejune'. Stories about dogs and piles of stones are as easy to mock as Wilding sentences about naval piety (and at least tell us something about subsistence farming). No beginners' book is immune from this charge, and no great harm is done if pupils enjoy gently sending up what they are reading. At some level they realise and accept that this is a necessary preparation of the palate for more solid food, and *Athenaze* offers rich enough fare in its later stages. But it resists being done quickly. If a fairly generous time allocation is available the criticisms lose much of their force and *Athenaze* can provide a good route to GCSE. If something else is preferred as a beginners' text, it can come into its own later. For it is an axiom of pupil psychology that fresh books are needed at the start of the sixth form: Book II of *Athenaze* can then serve well as a post-GCSE course.

The problem of doing GCSE in limited time was a central concern of respondents to the JACT survey. As we saw, Greek is often an extra-curricular activity. Even where it is still studied as a separate timetabled subject, it is often started only two years before GCSE. In a crowded curriculum it is hard enough to protect one slot for a classical language, let alone two. Over the last few years a number of schools have begun to offer their brightest pupils both Greek and Latin within the periods normally allocated only to Latin. It was particularly to address these needs that a new course was planned: John Taylor's *Greek to GCSE* (Part 1 and Part 2, BCP/Duckworth, 2003). This concentrates on the essentials, the prescribed grammar and vocabulary of the two GCSE boards. It assumes most pupils will know some Latin, and does not eschew comparisons; but it aims to be usable without. It does not have any grand theory or linguistic dogma, but is simply based on experience of what pupils find difficult. It tries to remember that Greek is only one of nine or ten subjects being studied, yet at the same time give those who will carry on to A level a solid foundation. The approach is fairly traditional: there is a mildly inductive element in that constructions which translate naturally (indirect commands, some forms of indirect statement) are introduced before they are discussed, but no apology is made for the fact that new grammar begins each chapter. Every year examiners' reports comment that candidates muddle through unseen passages with too little attention to grammar: endings are ignored, and common constructions not recognised. The new book aims to address this. But it also aims to be user-friendly. It concentrates on the understanding of principles, in both accidence and syntax: minor irregularities are postponed and subordinated, so that the need for rote learning is reduced. In 1998 Peter Jones brought out *Learn Ancient Greek* (Duckworth), a very quick introduction for adults based on his popular *Daily Telegraph* series ('Read St John's Gospel by Christmas'). This is not in any sense a school textbook, but it contains valuable lessons about short cuts (however irregular nouns get, the article remains as a case marker). 'Purists will shudder,' Jones said; but people bought the book, and enjoyed learning Greek. The point applies more widely. Those same purists may think GCSE Greek is already watered down far enough. Yet bright pupils constantly say it is the hardest of their GCSE subjects. The new Taylor course aims to make things a little easier than existing books, so that pupils on a fast track to GCSE do not waste time on non-essentials and are not hampered by archaic conventions. The course does not have a continuous narrative, but after the preliminaries each section concentrates on stories with one source or subject: Aesop, the *Odyssey*, Alexander, Socrates and the Sophists, the world of myth, and (the target to which all this has led, occupying the last three chapters) extended passages of lightly adapted Herodotus. It aims to combine the merits of Wilding and *Athenaze*.

Another new development is a course aimed at younger children in preparatory schools: Kristian Waite's *Greek: A New Guide for Beginners* (Independent Schools Examination Board,[1] 2002). This was written and developed at Hazelwood School from 1997, again mindful of timetable constraints. The book already published by ISEB covers the basic level of the new Common Entrance examination. A second volume for the higher level of CE is expected from the same publisher: this has already been written, along with a final part of the course extending to scholarship level and in fact including all the GCSE grammar. Waite acknowledges a major debt to Wilding, but the material is presented here in a much more lively and attractive form.

Readers, grammars, dictionaries and prose composition books

There used to be a wide choice of Greek readers, many of them reprinted for decades: Sidgwick, Colson, and – the best of the bunch – Freeman and Lowe's *Greek Reader for Schools* (1917, American reprint available from Bolchazy–Carducci). Even more antiquated in feel yet still remarkably good (and inculcating a lot of useful Greek

---

[1] ISEB, Jordan House, Christchurch Road, New Milton, Hants BH25 6QJ. Tel: 01425 621111. Fax: 01425 620044. www.iseb.co.uk. *Greek: A New Guide for Beginners* is also obtainable from the Hellenic Bookservice, 91 Fortess Road, Kentish Town, London NW5 1AG. Tel: 0207 267 9499.

history) is Hillard and Botting's *Elementary Greek Translation Book* (still in print with Duckworth, along with the associated *Elementary Greek Exercises*). The style of a later age is reflected in Nairn and Nairn's *Greek through Reading* (1952, again still in the Duckworth list), which offers a complete course with particularly good grammar tables, though no schools reported using it (probably because of the excessively steep gradient, as with *Thrasymachus*). A staple of GCSE set texts has long been E.C. Kennedy's *Four Greek Authors* (1968, now Duckworth), with extended extracts from Homer, Antiphon, Euripides and Thucydides. Duckworth and their imprint Bristol Classical Press have kept available numerous older school editions of texts and selections which are also frequently set by the examination boards, for example Farnell and Goff's *Tales from Herodotus* and Doherty's *The Martyrdom of Socrates*. As noted above, the new Cambridge *Anthology* may have a role here. But there is still room for more accessible elementary reading material, and editions focused on modern examination requirements.

Among grammar books, the Victorian warhorse of Abbott and Mansfield (*Primer of Greek Grammar*) until very recently reigned supreme. Published originally (like so many nineteenth-century classics books) by the now-defunct firm of Rivingtons, it has been a steady earner for Duckworth since they took it over in 1977. Generations have known and loved it, but in practice most students only use a few pages. Many aspects are baffling to modern beginners: we simply do not talk nowadays about 'substantives' and 'conjunctives', and the declensions of words for 'mustard' and 'vulture' are not high priorities for learning by heart. H.J.K. Usher's *Outline of Greek Accidence* (Duckworth, 1981) aimed to present the essentials in friendlier form. Usher is certainly more accessible, but there are oddities here too. Many tables do not give the English for the word whose form is being shown, and it seems perverse that (for example) dual forms are retained whereas the list of principal parts is inadequate even for GCSE.

For students at school and university in almost every context, however, the obvious choice is now James Morwood's *Oxford Grammar of Classical Greek* (OUP, 2001). The presentation of accidence sets a new standard in clarity. There is a clear sense of proportion and priority: problematic irregularities are never ignored, but are kept in their place. The book is accessible to pupils at GCSE level (*Greek to GCSE* has its own Reference Grammar, but uses the same paradigms). Equally the *Oxford Grammar* contains everything needed at degree level. The syntax section, with clear explanations of individual constructions, will be widely used (unlike that of Abbott and Mansfield: Usher's title was significant). Inevitably this section of the book involved decisions on matters where other views are possible. It was a high-minded aim to have unadapted quotations from ancient authors as so many of the illustrative examples and practice sentences, showing students the rough edges of real Greek. The downside of this for beginners is that some of the sentences are made difficult by relatively obscure vocabulary or proper names, or by idiomatic usages not germane to the construction being illustrated. It is, however, easy for teachers to supply their own simpler examples for practice. The syntax section is extremely good on points of detail (particularly by the use of boxes drawing attention to idioms, helpful mnemonics, and potential pitfalls). It would perhaps have benefited from more discussion of general principles, for example by giving an overview of the uses of the subjunctive and optative, and by treating in one place the issue of tense and aspect in the aorist. But these are minor criticisms of a book that will serve the subject well for many years.

Dictionaries for school use have traditionally been the two smaller versions of the standard Liddell and Scott *Greek Lexicon*: the *Intermediate Lexicon* and the *Abridged* one. Smaller even than the latter is the Langenscheidt *Pocket Greek Dictionary* (edited by Karl Feyerabend, and translated from German). A completely new dictionary on approximately the scale of the *Intermediate* Liddell and Scott is currently in preparation under the editorship of Dr Anne Thompson, to be published by CUP. Available already is *The Pocket Oxford Dictionary of Classical Greek* (OUP, 2002), edited by James Morwood and John Taylor. This presents a Greek–English section of about 20,000 words (based on Langenscheidt, but thoroughly revised) along with an English–Greek section of about 5,000 words common in Attic prose. It is remarkable that there has not been a Greek–English dictionary both ways round since the mid-nineteenth century. Students undertaking very advanced composition in prose, and the tiny minority composing verse, will still need the large-scale *English–Greek Dictionary* of S.C. Woodhouse (Routledge, 1910), just as those tackling obscure passages of Greek lyric will still need the full-scale Liddell and Scott, but it is hoped that the new dictionary will serve the everyday needs of most students.

A little has been said in passing already about strategies for Greek teaching at immediate post-GCSE level. This area is likely to need more concentrated attention in the next few years. Students who have read only two short set-book prescriptions and learned a few hundred words are often not ready for a sixth-form diet as traditionally understood. The advent of AS level has been welcomed by many classicists (in contrast to their colleagues in other subjects) as a valuable halfway house between GCSE and A level, with a prescribed vocabulary, unseen translation in prose only, and the opportunity to study a greater variety of set texts. For unseen practice Moore and Evans' *Variorum* (now BCP/Duckworth, 1969) is useful, as is M. Hiner's *Greek Comprehensions for Schools* (BCP/Duckworth, 1989). But the standard of both is fairly bracing, and there is room for a collection of easier, graded passages with systematic guidance about how to tackle an unseen. English–Greek sentences are offered by almost no candidates at GCSE, and composition is not an option at AS level, yet it has remained popular at A level and seems likely to do so in its new A2 form. Of composition books, the grand old Sidgwick *Greek Prose Composition* is now beyond almost all sixth-formers, and with the demise of S level has lost what place in schools it still had. The once-popular books by Lewis and Styler and by Nash-Williams have been outlasted by the Victorian North and Hillard *Greek Prose Composition* (now Duckworth): this might benefit from revision (ironing out oddities, and reducing the military emphasis in choice of passages). But there is also perhaps room for a book at this level with full-scale treatment of constructions but which is not geared so specifically to translation into Greek: indeed, perhaps this and an unseen book could be combined.

It will be apparent that many challenges lie ahead. But they will be met, because there is also abundant goodwill and determination to safeguard the future of Greek in schools.

Bibliography

Abbott, E. and Mansfield, E.D., *A Primer of Greek Grammar*. First published Rivingtons, Duckworth from 1977

Balme, M. and Lawall, G., *Athenaze*. Book I: 1990, Book II: 1991; UK edition of both: 1995. OUP

Doherty, F.C., *The Martyrdom of Socrates*. First published OUP, 1923, now BCP/Duckworth

Farnell, G.S. and Goff, Marie, *Tales from Herodotus*. First published Macmillan, 1963, now BCP/Duckworth

Feyerabend, Karl, *Pocket Greek Dictionary* (*Greek–English*). Langenscheidt

Freeman, C.E. and Lowe, W.D., *A Greek Reader for Schools*. First published OUP, 1917, now Bolchazy–Carducci

Hillard, A.E. and Botting, C.G., *Elementary Greek Translation* and *Elementary Greek Exercises*. Both first published Rivingtons, now Duckworth

Hiner, Martin (1989) *Greek Comprehensions for Schools*. BCP/Duckworth

JACT Greek Course (CUP):

(1978) *Reading Greek: Text*

(1978) *Reading Greek: Grammar, Vocabulary and Exercises*

(1979) *A World of Heroes*

(1980) *The Intellectual Revolution*

(1980) *Greek Vocabulary*

(1986) *The Teachers' Notes to Reading Greek*

(1995) *An Independent Study Guide to Reading Greek*

(1996) *The Triumph of Odysseus*

(2001) *New Testament Greek: A Reader*

(2002) *A Greek Anthology*

Jones, Peter (1998) *Learn Ancient Greek*. Duckworth

Kennedy, E.C., *Four Greek Authors*. First published Macmillan, 1968, now BCP/Duckworth

Liddell, H.G., *Abridged Greek–English Lexicon*. OUP

Liddell, H.G. and Scott, R., *Intermediate Greek–English Lexicon*. OUP

Moore, J.M. and Evans, J.J., *Variorum: A Greek Translation Book*. First published OUP, 1969, now BCP/Duckworth

Morwood, James (2001) *Oxford Grammar of Classical Greek*. OUP

Morwood, James and Taylor, John (2002) *Pocket Oxford Dictionary of Classical Greek*. OUP

Nairn, J.A. and Nairn, G.A., *Greek through Reading*. First published Ginn, 1952, now BCP/Duckworth

North, M.A. and Hillard, A.E., *Greek Prose Composition*. First published Rivingtons, now Duckworth

Peckett, C.W.E. and Munday, A.R., *Thrasymachus: A New Greek Course*. First published Wilding, 1965, now BCP/Duckworth

Taylor, John (2003) *Greek to GCSE*, Part 1 and Part 2. BCP/Duckworth

Usher, H.J.K. (1981) *An Outline of Greek Accidence*. Duckworth

Waite, Kristian (2002) *Greek: A New Guide for Beginners*. ISEB

Wilding, L.A., *Greek for Beginners*. First published Faber, 1957, now Duckworth

Williams, W.A. and others (1984) *A New Greek Course for Schools*, Books 1 to 4, privately printed, revised edition

Woodhouse, S.C. (1910) *English–Greek Dictionary*. Routledge

13 | Working at the chalk face

Julie Wilkinson

In 1990 I was asked to reintroduce Latin GCSE to a state comprehensive in North London where the subject had previously been offered but had been 'killed' owing to increasingly low numbers. For the past twelve years, a period of great change in the education system, I have tried to keep abreast of educational initiatives. At the outset this was motivated by the need to create a justification for including not only Latin but also classical civilisation in my school, but subsequently it proved a means of strengthening their tenuous position. It is the role of this chapter to outline the current position faced by those of us 'working at the chalk face' in the secondary sector. I intend to outline some of the strategies such teachers might wish to employ or have already employed to 'sell' the subject to establish and maintain such a position of strength. The chapter will endeavour to address issues surrounding the constraints of the National Curriculum; the inclusion of literacy, numeracy and citizenship targets; the introduction of AS and A2 levels *et al.* Naturally I am drawing primarily on personal experience.

I feel that I must begin by providing statistics on the current position of classical subjects in schools, if for no other reason than to provide a justification for writing this chapter. The first set comes from the AQA research and statistical unit at Guildford.

LATIN – GCSE entries 1997–2001 by type of school

year	comp	grammar	post 16	ind	other	TOTAL
1990	3792	2627	188	7774	128	14509
1997	2202	2083	115	7409	51	11860
1998	1996	1772	137	6966	37	10908
1999	1787	1833	118	6669	44	10451
2000	1840	1915	133	6642	31	10561
2001	1936	1852	62	6500	15	10365

LATIN – A level entries 1997–2001 by type of school

year	comp	grammar	post 16	ind	other	TOTAL
1990	295	319	102	1176	29	1921
1997	131	231	61	1097	19	1539
1998	111	261	42	1115	11	1540
1999	110	220	33	940	18	1321
2000	90	200	32	972	15	1309
2001	97	191	22	928	26	1264

GREEK – A level entries 1999–2001 by type of school

year	comp	grammar	post 16	ind	other	TOTAL
1999	2	17	0	192	1	212
2000	5	11	3	216	1	236
2001	1	10	0	190	1	202

CLASSICAL CIVILISATION – GCSE entries 1999–2001 by type of school

year	comp	grammar	post 16	ind	other	TOTAL
1999	1262	335	34	1890	12	3533
2000	1392	405	10	2040	23	3870
2001	1409	353	9	2121	12	3904

CLASSICAL CIVILISATION – A level entries 1999–2001 by type of school

year	comp	grammar	post 16	ind	other	TOTAL
1999	540	475	878	1415	65	3373
2000	564	431	779	1381	59	3214
2001	553	573	746	1266	50	3188

ANCIENT HISTORY – A level entries 1999–2001 by type of school

year	comp	grammar	post 16	ind	other	TOTAL
1999	128	214	185	193	38	758
2000	133	185	141	160	21	640
2001	92	200	152	151	19	614

The second set comes from an interim report on the DfEE Key Stage 3 Educational Services Pilot 'The Result Cambridge Latin Course – changing the face of Latin?' As the report states:

> Since the introduction of the 1988 Education Reform Act, it has been increasingly difficult to sustain classical subjects in maintained schools, both selective and non-selective: classics departments have seen their timetable allocation squeezed, and their resources (including staffing) reduced, to enable schools to meet statutory requirements in other subject areas. The seriousness of the situation is clear from the tables below:

Table 1: GCSE Latin entries 1990 and 2000 compared

GCSE	1990	2000	% change
Maintained, non-selective	3792	1840	−51.5
Maintained, selective	2627	2083	−27.1
Independent	7774	6642	−14.6

Table 2: A level Latin entries 1990 and 2000 compared

LATIN A LEVEL	1990	2000	% change
Maintained, non-selective	295	90	−69.5
Maintained, selective	319	231	−37.3
Independent	1176	972	−17.3

These statistics reveal the bleakness of the situation. When we add to this the growing number of classics teachers retiring, coupled with the reduction of new entrants to the classics teaching profession, the situation appears even gloomier. However, there are pockets of resistance to this growing trend, and those classics departments that have survived, particularly in the maintained sector, have done so through merit as well as dogged determination and a passionate belief that classics deserves a secure place in the school curriculum.

The intention of my chapter is to enlarge on the role of classics in *building upon* and *enriching* what is now, at least, a more uniform curriculum for secondary-school pupils. This is certainly the message that Ofsted conveys after inspections of schools containing successful and flourishing classics departments. So, what is it that classics offers over and above the National Curriculum and which might appeal to pupils, parents and a school's management team and governing body?

Classical subjects are in an almost unique position in the curriculum as they combine a variety of subject disciplines:

- a highly structured language when studied in the original
- the study of literature either in the original or in translation
- ancient cultures.

   Courses in classical subjects aim:

- to engender an enthusiasm for the personalities, ideas and achievements of the classical world and its civilisations
- to enable pupils to appreciate the influence of classical ideas on modern civilisation
- to enable pupils to develop a deeper understanding of today's issues through the discussion of ideas prevalent in classical times
- to develop an understanding of the classical world through the study of classical literature
- to arouse and develop an interest in classical literature and the ability to respond critically to it
- to enable pupils to compare and contrast outlooks of the classical and modern worlds.

   When studied in the original language, courses in classical subjects in addition aim:

- to arouse and develop an interest in the classical language, both in its own right and as an influence on English and other languages
- to develop an awareness of the power of language to form and express ideas and feelings
- to enable pupils to be aware of the nature and evolution of language and to gain insight into the structure of English
- to enable pupils to compare and contrast the classical language with English and/or other languages with regard to inflection, word order, linguistic structure and notions of register.

Why study a classical subject?

Classical courses, therefore, provide pupils with an integrated educational experience of the humanities, literature and language as they explore aspects of a classical civilisation through the medium of texts read in the original language or in translation. Classics could almost be said to be the *original cross-curricular subject* and as such helps schools provide for their pupils a curriculum that offers even more than breadth and balance. Classical subjects enable pupils to examine ideas from a different perspective and become an integral part of their understanding of the language they speak.

A course in Latin, in particular, can also help develop an awareness of the links between languages such as French, Spanish, Portuguese, Italian and Romanian, all ultimately derived from Latin. Since much of this cultural and linguistic heritage is shared by otherwise diverse nations of the modern world, Latin offers a useful perspective from which to develop an international awareness and to approach some aspects of multi-cultural education. With a considerable number of English words also firmly rooted in the classical languages, much can be done, of course, to enhance pupils' understanding and use of the English language itself.

What stimulates interest in classical subjects?

- Pupils are motivated by the subject matter of the classical world. They will have studied the Greeks and often the Romans in the early key stages and are often keen to discover more.

- The proliferation of television programmes on classical civilisation, art and archaeology such as 'Time Team' has generated considerable interest in the classical world. Hollywood has recognised such an interest by returning to the genre of 'Sword and Sandal' films of previous years through epics such as *Gladiator* which in turn has generated further media coverage and, of course, valuable teaching resources.

- Family visits to Roman sites in Britain and abroad can lead to questions about the meaning of the Latin inscriptions which some pupils may wish to be answered through a more extensive investigation of the language.

- Many are curious to learn the meanings of everyday Latin tags, mottoes and abbreviations and this may stimulate an interest for learning the Latin language and subsequently even Greek. Even 'made up' Latin such as that in Terry Pratchett's 'Discworld' series and spells cast in the Harry Potter books by J.K. Rowling has done the same.

- The introduction of Latin may be as a result of pressure from parents, teachers or governors. They look back on their own education, realise that Latin has helped their academic development in a variety of ways, and want the next generation to be given the same opportunities as themselves.

- Many who were not given such a chance feel that they have somehow 'lost out', often citing their poor understanding of grammar and spelling as a result of this loss, and do not want others to be similarly disadvantaged. A greater emphasis on grammar, grammatical terminology and reference skills in the National Curriculum orders for English and modern foreign languages, in addition to the recently introduced National Literacy Strategy, have supported such a view.

- In some authorities the introduction of Latin in one school encourages its inclusion in others to provide the equality of availability demanded by parents. In a few cases the introduction of Latin in a maintained school has even been a way of encouraging those parents who might otherwise be sending their children through the private system to consider an LEA school as an option.

In a later chapter, Judith Affleck will outline strategies for the survival of classics outside the curriculum. She would, however, be the first to grant that it is a top priority to keep the subject healthy *inside* it wherever possible. A key question is thus: once sufficient interest has been stimulated to create a place for classics within the school curriculum, how can teachers ensure it remains there? What help is at hand to support both the teacher and subject?

Elsewhere in this book Richard Woff covers the benefits for classics teachers of museum visits. The prime purpose of visits by schools, of course, is to enrich and extend the curriculum offered by the department by providing alternative learning environments to that of the classroom. A school visit should aim to provide opportunities for pupils to develop their social and personal skills, as they are likely to be faced with challenging activities and unfamiliar surroundings and groupings. Despite the increasing bureaucracy surrounding such visits, which now generally includes risk assessment amongst other delights, they are an invaluable way to gain supporters from accompanying staff from different subject areas as well as to promote the subject amongst pupils and their parents. Visits to the schools themselves from theatre groups, e.g. the Actors of Dionysus (dionysus@btinternet.com), whose members perform classical drama in English, and 'living history' groups, e.g. LEGIO XIIII (www.legion-fourteen.com), whose members provide demonstrations of Roman domestic and military life which pupils can take part in, are perhaps less stressful to arrange, but certainly just as valuable – as are talks on classical themes by speakers from universities.

My school has, for example, utilised overseas trips to Provence as a way of combining the talents of both the classics and MFL departments. The classics department provides the expertise at sites while my colleagues teaching French arrange the treasure hunts, French diary entries etc. In Britain, trips to sites such as Bath or

Fishbourne can form the basis of a piece of GCSE coursework. A trip to London with my Year 8 classics classes and their form tutors in the summer term includes a visit to The British Museum to see primary sources from the Roman period (the 'wow!' factor when they see for themselves images from their worksheets and text books), and a wonderful tour round the National Gallery with the education staff on the Roman influence on art.

Out-of-school visits are not, however, just for the pupils' educational benefits. Teachers in the maintained sector now have an entitlement to further their own knowledge through focused INSET (in service training). Teachers can acquire this through standards funds provided to each school by the government or needs they have identified themselves and negotiated with school managers to meet their performance management targets. The CSCP (Cambridge School Classics Project) provides a wide variety of training courses. JACT, its local branches (or ACTs!), ARLT (the Association for Latin Teaching), examination boards and enterprising classics departments from various universities also provide courses on many topics. However, there is often nothing better than to see the experts at work, and a day at a school where there is an accommodating and successful classics department will provide a wealth of ideas, paper resources and of course that much-needed human contact.

I do not think I could possibly have set up my own department without having previously been a member of the Harrow Association of Classical Teachers when still teaching English, and visiting each classics department in the borough to remind myself of teaching styles and techniques. In addition, I was given permission to 'acquire' ideas and worksheets from generous classics teachers in progressive and forward-looking London schools. Visits to a school in Yorkshire gave me the confidence to set up a 'speed course' in classical civilisation GCSE for my enthusiastic Year 10 Latin GCSE candidates. I now ensure that I make an annual 'pilgrimage' to a classics department each summer term to enhance my department's work.

There is certainly no substitute for excellent teaching, and because a school is not required to deliver a classical subject, the (often lone) classics teacher is invariably under considerable pressure. However, the classics teacher does not have to step outside the classroom to deliver challenging and stimulating lessons. This is because of the wealth of support material available in the form of supplementary activities that accompany most language courses, the high quality of the language courses themselves, and superb audio-visual resources produced both commercially and 'in-house'. Pupils are generally very competent computer users outside the classroom, and increasingly expect them to be used as a tool for both teaching and learning. Again the classics teacher has a variety of resources to hand and elsewhere in this book there is David Goodhew's chapter on using ICT in classics. There are numerous internet sites related to classical subjects that can be accessed by the teacher to enhance worksheet content and presentation, and by the pupil to develop a greater understanding of cultural topics for homework and coursework tasks. E-mail is enabling classics teachers to share individually produced resources more effectively than ever before. In addition, custom-built CD-ROMs are available, for example, to support the acquisition of vocabulary, develop translation skills and provide pupils with a bank of written and visual material on particular topics related to the classical world.

In fact, recent developments from the CSCP, with considerable financial support from the DfES, are utilising cutting-edge technology to enable pupils both to access Latin even if their school does not have a specialist Latin teacher, and to enhance their use of it within a Latin classroom where it does. The following is taken from the CSCP website and outlines how the new organisation set up to spearhead these developments is operating:

> The aim of the CSCP is to help make the classical world accessible to as many students as possible, whatever their age, whatever their ability. CSCP's Cambridge Online Latin Project (COLP) seeks to broaden that aim of accessibility by the use of electronic media, including the internet and interactive materials...
>
> ...From September 2000 to July 2001 CSCP was commissioned by Granada Result to provide subject specialist knowledge and strategies for the then Department for Education and Employment's KS3 Educational Services Pilot. This resulted in the production of electronic resources for Latin and introducing Latin into 16 schools where there was no specialist Latin teacher. In a further 5 schools specialist Latin teachers trialled the same resources.
>
> The number of schools involved in COLP currently stands at 23. This includes beacon schools, schools involved in Excellence in Cities and schools from an Education Action Zone. They are all non-selective schools with an interest in extending their curriculum through imaginative use of modern technologies.
>
> Most students taking part in COLP are in Year 8 or Year 9. Supervised by a facilitator in school, they follow the Cambridge Latin Course (CLC) with guidance and monitoring from an e-tutor, and further support from the CLC Independent Learning Manual. They also have access to a wide range of electronic materials for CLC Book 1 created with funding from the Department for Education and Skills.

Seven of the students from one of the original pilot schools are now working towards Latin GCSE as part of their Key Stage 4 studies. After some face to face teaching at the beginning of term, lessons are now delivered via video conference link. Through their experience of online teaching for the last two years, the students have the self-discipline and motivation to perform very well in their GCSE examinations.

This exciting development could do much to help schools where interest in a classical subject, in this case Latin, is present but a qualified teacher is not. However, ICT is not the only way to ensure that classical subjects are both accessible and relevant. It has, perhaps, been the fault of classics teachers themselves in the past that the subject is still seen by some as one to be taken only by an academic élite. Whether a school sets, bands or puts pupils in mixed-ability groupings, mixed-ability *learning* has always been the reality wherever class sizes have been greater than one. It is also true that in the majority of schools where Latin is taught, no matter what the setting arrangements of the school may be, small numbers choosing the subject may necessitate the grouping together of pupils of a wide range of ability.

It is generally recognised that in a mixed-ability situation a regular experience of success is possible for most pupils only if the management of learning is *flexible*, and allows for *differentiation* by resource, task, support or response. To some extent it may be possible to help the pupil who is finding the work more difficult by providing additional or differentiated resources, targeting teacher support or giving differentiated feedback.

One major advantage of not being a National Curriculum subject is that the classics teacher can tailor classical courses, in the early years of secondary schools at least, that reflect the interests, abilities and backgrounds of the pupils in their own schools without the need to conform to a rigid and externally imposed framework. In the post-16 sector, the recent division of traditional A level courses into AS and A2 levels has caused much consternation amongst teachers of all subjects. One of the significant drawbacks for classics teachers who had previously often combined small Year 12 and 13 classes has been the removal of this possibility because of different syllabuses. In some cases, especially in the maintained sector, this has effectively destroyed Latin or ancient history A level provision. Although there are similar problems across the curriculum with the AS/A2 division, at least now pupils are encouraged to study more than a narrow range of subjects, certainly in their first year of A level, so a scientist or modern linguist may have Latin as a fourth option. It is, of course, up to individual classics teachers to motivate them to maintain this into Year 13 once they have been hooked in Year 12.

There is no one correct way to ensure accessibility and relevance, but I will outline here just a few suggestions that I have used and that appear to have worked.

- Start with the pupil and what s/he already knows then move to the classical version, e.g. What would you expect to find on a modern-day tombstone and why? When discussing Latin literature at GCSE level, I introduced 'Elysium' (Virgil's *Aeneid* VI. 638–65) from the *Cambridge Latin Anthology* (CUP), by asking pupils what they considered a worthwhile life to consist of today. Such a discussion did much to gain the pupils' interest, contributed towards citizenship targets, and facilitated a non-threatening 'way in' to their knowledge of the Romans' views and thus their expectations of the content of the passage to be discussed in Latin, i.e. who would be found in Elysium.

- Involve the pupil so that active learning helps to 'fix' the subject matter. A slave auction always goes down well although care should be taken over making it too much fun! The humiliation faced by the slaves must, of course, be brought out. Before launching upon a classical studies module on the development of Roman government, I ask Year 8 pupils to imagine they have been given the opportunity to create their own government in Britain today. How would they organise it? After twenty minutes of small-group work they report back their ideas to the rest of the class, having considered the following points:
  - How many people would be in charge: one, more than one – why?
  - What type of people would you want in charge: rich, poor, male, female, old, young – why?
  - What jobs would each person have: why?
  - Who would elect / choose the government: why?
  - For how long would each government be in power: why?

- For homework after this lesson they are asked to compare their thoughts with those of their parents and we discuss any differences in their responses. The following lesson also involves active learning as they are given cards with the following information: names of types of government, i.e. democracy, monarchy, republic, dictatorship, fascism; definitions for each type; two advantages for each type of government and two disadvantages. Again in small groups using dictionaries and previous discussions they have to group the cards. A PowerPoint presentation in the next lesson with the correct answers from the teacher helps to frame the discussion. When we then move on to how and why the Romans changed their forms of government from Romulus to Augustus such activities enable the pupils to understand more clearly cause and consequence. There is also a considerable amount of citizenship and literacy work being covered for good measure.

There is no doubt that classics teachers in the secondary sector have to be experts in many areas apart from their subject. Without strong publicity from the department itself and support from the school management (which includes careful placing within GCSE option blocks, about which there is now at least more negotiation possible), pupils may well wish to take more conventional subjects. A classics department cannot afford to be an ostrich, ignoring developments that superficially appear not to affect them, but needs to take a leading role in its school's response to educational initiatives. I have, for example, recently been part of a small working party, funded by JACT, that has put together a number of 'National Curriculum' Latin level descriptors for teachers to make use of as they wish. In schools where reporting pupils' progress is by means of NC levels, teachers of classical subjects can now respond in line with other subjects.

The fierce commitment of classics teacher trainees is a most welcome sign of professional resilience. Yet it remains true that those of us who have been in the classics teaching profession for some time continue to worry about decreasing time, opportunities and numbers, while a new entrant has a challenging if exciting career in front of them. Without our perseverance, however, future generations will not have access to this still great subject.

14 | Ancient history

Robin Osborne and John Claughton

Ancient history in the sixth form

On 22 August 1966 *The Times* carried a long article on its Leader page (p. 9) by M.I. Finley entitled, 'New look at ancient history for sixth formers'. In this piece Finley outlined the rationale for the JACT ancient history A level syllabus, first examined in June 1968. Finley emphasised two positive points. The first was that history included not just questions about war and politics but about such things as the nature and manipulation of the Roman crowd or the influence of Athenian comedy on popular attitudes. The second was that students would be expected to read the ancient sources (in translation): 'A common reading of Thucydides and Tacitus – yes, and of Aristophanes or Horace – provides the basis for a dialogue between teacher and pupil,' he wrote. He also emphasised two negative points: 'outlines must go', and 'coverage is not a highly rated objective'.

The syllabus first taught in twenty schools in September 1966 involved pupils taking one period paper (either Greece 478–402 BC or Rome 81 BC to AD 14) and one 'special subject' (culture of Athens, Herodotus and the Persian Wars, the age of Augustus, or Claudius and Nero). Individual papers came and went (Finley already noted that 'there must surely be a place for Roman Britain'), but the JACT ancient history syllabus remained more or less in its original shape for more than thirty years. But while ancient history stood still, sixth-form education changed markedly. Finley's talk of giving 'much play to individual interest, whether of the pupil or of the teacher' smacks of a different world. A syllabus which began with the openness of idealism became a syllabus which left the teacher and pupil without any guidance except that provided by past papers. If the ideal was that 'No claims are here made for the primacy of any particular question', the reality became that only certain sorts of questions could be predicted and therefore only certain sorts of questions were answered. As for the extensive reading of the ancient sources to 'introduce the non-classicist to the Greeks and Romans on their own terms,' if it went on, it had insufficient effect to prevent examiners regularly complaining that candidates showed no awareness of the ancient sources.

The JACT ancient history committee began thinking about modest revisions of its syllabus in 1994 and was close to submitting it for approval when Dearing's report brought a complete set of new rules, including a demand that history candidates be made to study a period of 'at least one hundred years', so outlawing both traditional periods (100 years of solitude would satisfy the rule, 95 years of extraordinarily eventful Roman history would not). Rules changed again when Labour came to power, this time with regard not to content but to form: every A level had to have six more or less equal parts. Converting a march in two beats to a dance in six took more than a little ingenuity, and the JACT committee is justifiably proud, I think, that it was nimble-footed enough not to trip up over this, as the examination timetablers would so spectacularly do. But although there were times when simply conforming to the rules imposed from outside seemed challenge enough, the chief aim of the revisions was to retain the original ideal of providing the opportunity for a wide-ranging study of Greece and Rome from the original sources, but to give the sort of guidance appropriate for current-day sixth-form teaching.

The specifications which have been taught since September 2000 require students to study two sets of papers from two of the three groups 'Greek History', 'Roman History' and 'Roman World' – the last comprising papers on Roman Britain and the later Roman empire. All papers are available in AS or A2 versions, so as to assist those teachers who have to teach Years 12 and 13 together. Each set of papers comprises three papers. A 'Document Study' involves close study of a dossier of ancient sources in translation, chosen where possible from texts collected in a single sourcebook (e.g. a LACTOR) or from a small number of different authors readily available in paperback. Examination is by questions on set passages: for the first time knowledge of the source material is directly assessed. A 'Thematic Study' asks the student to look at a single topic over an extensive period, not just fulfilling the 100-year rule but giving a real chance to assess the nature and causes of medium-term historical change. A 'Source-based Study' completes the set. This tends to be a relatively short period, studied intensively in a wide range of different aspects. Familiar friends from the old syllabus reappear in this slot (Herodotus and the Persian wars, the culture of Athens, the age of Augustus, etc.).

What is most obviously gained in the change from the old syllabus to the new specifications is specificity. There are specific sources that need to be known, there are specific themes that are studied, there is a lot of information about the sorts of issues that need to be covered. Indeed, in addition to the 126 pages of the

'Approved Specifications' there are several hundred more pages of Teachers' Notes, suggesting ways of approaching each paper in terms of weeks of teaching and providing teachers with ready access to material which it might otherwise be hard for them to come by.

But the new specifications are also more flexible. There are more different types of history to be sampled here and, with the advent of papers on late antiquity (as a direct result of the energetic advocacy of the late Professor Thomas Wiedemann), an enlarged chronological range. There is the chance to substitute coursework for one paper in A2. There is also the opportunity to do a certain amount of mixing and matching within the broader groups of papers, allowing, in a sensibly policed form, some of that individual choice that Finley envisaged – at least for the teacher.

The original JACT ancient history syllabus was launched in the belief that 'a study of the classical world … [has] something important to offer … educationally'. Behind the new specifications is the conviction that, in particular, study of Greek and Roman history has something to offer historically, indeed that, because of the quality and accessibility of ancient source material, and because of the possibility of studying on a small scale political, social, economic and cultural themes fundamental to more recent history, the study of ancient history is the ideal introduction to the study of history, period. The ability to read closely and to analyse situations both critically and imaginatively is fundamental to the successful and humane performance of any profession involving human interaction. No one will successfully study the new ancient history specifications without acquiring at least some competence in those areas.

If the current JACT ancient history specifications are better, for the purposes of twenty-first century sixth-form education, than the old ones, they are also bigger. '[T]he last thing the sponsors seek is a soft option for the idle,' Finley wrote. The new specifications have proved in some respects too big, and some modest reductions came into force from September 2002, but the idle must continue to look elsewhere.

R.O.

The learning and teaching of JACT ancient history (or at least the Greek bit)

I am not quite one of Finley's children, but for much of my life I have lived, as pupil and teacher, in the land created by the JACT ancient history course. As Robin Osborne's account above explains, that new course placed the primary sources at the centre of study. In so doing it marked out ancient history as being something different from, perhaps even better than, other history courses. That has remained a central part of the attraction of the course, and certainly a central part of the selling of it. However, my experience as a pupil in 1972 rather supports Robin Osborne's judgement that not everyone noticed that this was the point. The man who taught me Roman history certainly didn't. Untouched, if not unspoilt, by progress, he dictated his minutely written notes to us and, when he or we had had enough of them, he sent us to the library to read *The Cambridge Ancient History*.

However, a few classrooms away our Greek history man did as Professor Finley would have wanted. He gave us the primary sources, or at least Thucydides. Indeed, the sight of the Penguin *Thucydides* still stirs me: it might be the single most important reason why I wanted to do classics. But even this man doing the right things had to compromise. He couldn't just put the Pentecontaetia into our hands and presume that all would be well. He had to resort to notes. I still have them. Only when I came to teach the subject myself did I realise the compromise with reality that he, and all of us, have to make. Direct experience of the primary sources is a noble aim, and the scale of the sources makes the aim just about conceivable. But it isn't actually possible to read all of Thucydides or Herodotus, even in translation. And even if you could, you couldn't easily understand them or anyone else. Finley may have mentioned a shared reading of Thucydides, Tacitus, Aristophanes and Horace as a way to a wisdom discovered together by teacher and pupil, but it's not easy to think of four authors who are harder to pin down as historical sources, unless it's Herodotus. To name but one, Tacitus may have written *sine ira et studio*, but he certainly did not write without selection and judgement. Tacitus' *Annals* and *Histories* may be the central narratives of the Roman historical period, but it is no simple narrative. It is as if you need to know what happened before you read Tacitus, and that probably means you may have to own Scullard as well.[1] It's not easy to come to such opaque texts from the simple certainties of GCSE textbooks.

Those responsible for the JACT course were not unaware of my teacher's compromise and the difficulties of getting beyond textbooks to the primary text. Lactorification was the solution, a solution that took two forms. Many LACTORs have made remote texts accessible: where else could you get Pseudo-Sallust or the Old Oligarch or the Lyons inscription, preserving Claudius' speech to the senate? As time has passed LACTORs have made such texts not only accessible but also comprehensible, as they have delivered more detailed commentaries. However, some LACTORs were themselves a

---

[1] H.H. Scullard, *From the Gracchi to Nero: A History of Rome from 133 BC to AD 68* (London/New York, 1982).

compromise. They conceded that it wasn't actually possible to deal with the sources in a raw state. Thus some were made out of references to the major sources. Thucydides was filleted for the Funeral Oration and the Melian Dialogue, which at least saved wasting too much time on the role of Mantinea in the period after the Peace of Nicias. Others followed the ancient Oxford tradition of the gobbet. For example, *The Culture of Athens* is a collection of highlights from the great sources, like a compilation CD – *Now that's what I call Athenian Culture* – or *Goal of the Season*. This may be a necessity, but it is also a kind of failure. Such quotations lose their context and thus their meaning, or rather the struggle to find the meaning. A double page on the role of women with quotations from Aeschines, Plato, Aristophanes, Xenophon and Euripides, none of them speaking *in propria persona*, and a double page on religion which quotes Xenophon, Antiphon, Apollonius of Rhodes, Aeschylus, an inscription from a cave near Anagyrus, Cicero, Juvenal (with scholiast) and Demosthenes tend to lead in only two directions. You either treat each source as fact – the most likely route – and bolt them accordingly onto your essay. Or you spend a lot of time trying to explain the context when the sources have been largely deprived of context in the LACTOR. Perhaps the fault lay not in the LACTORs, but in the ambition of the aim, in hoping to understand Athenian society or the Roman economy with so little time. In the end the noblest goal is to teach the sources not as a succession of gobbets, but as continuous texts. But I doubt that many of us ever got as close as we would want to such nobility. Perhaps we might be able to do so if more LACTORs were like the best LACTORs, rich in guidance and thoughts. Perhaps the new series of Cambridge University Press annotated texts of tragedy (and soon comedy) also points us the way forward. Surely someone could do the same for Plato's *Protagoras* or Tacitus' *Agricola*?

However, it is this nobility, albeit flawed, that makes it worthwhile. Even though the world has caught up with ancient history, in that primary sources are now central to so many history courses, the JACT ancient history course has managed to reach parts which other courses have not reached, or not all of them. From my experience there are three such parts. I apologise that my examples come almost exclusively from the Greek half of the course: it's what I know best. The first is that the very nature of the sources teaches us to peer with great suspicion at them. It teaches us to question, if not doubt, everything. Whenever I watch a historical narrative on television, I find myself asking, 'How does he know that?' I am sure that JACT ancient history taught me that. It teaches pupils to see that every statement is made by a person, in a context, for a reason, and that reason isn't just to tell us the truth. Thus, if a pupil can learn to doubt, but also try to understand the speaker and the moment, that is a vital gift for judgement in life.

The second lies in the diversity and greatness of the sources which a pupil gets to experience. Anyone who is to write a good essay on the role of Greek women may need to use law-court speeches and comedies and tragedies and vase paintings and philosophical texts and sculptures. And when those tragedies are Sophocles and Euripides and those sculptures are from the Parthenon and the philosophy is Plato (and preferably not Xenophon) you might be judged to be thrice lucky. And at such a moment there is a chance of glimpsing a society, albeit fleetingly. I find it hard not to laugh at the simple humanity of the beginning of Plato's *Protagoras*, as it presents to us a world we can understand.

The third lies in the centrality of the issues of our own time which the course allows us to address. There are few more direct routes into the discussion of the nature of power and democracy and justice than through Thucydides and Plato's *Republic*, or the nature of autocracy than through Tacitus, or the nature of religion or sexuality. The study of Greek homosexuality can be a highly successful way to help boys and girls to see that sexuality can be and has been constructed differently. They may not quite see that Nomos is Lord of All, but some days you think that the beginning of *Charmides* is their best chance.

However, it is not always the case that these great parts combine easily in a forty-minute lesson: doubting and questioning aren't ideal when pupils want an answer, and there's a module to be covered in a fortnight; it may be a wonderful thing to study the *Republic* and Thucydides' Melian Dialogue side by side, but no one said it was easy, and it certainly takes time; the inadequacies of democracy and the variety of religious experience are not topics which can easily be resolved into simple answers. Thus there is always the tension between the need for simplicity and closure and the desire to open out alternatives. Perhaps the very range of the content leads to a high percentage of lessons that don't quite work. However, on a good day pupils may get the chance to think with some very different parts of their experience and their knowledge, to compare saints to heroes, Medea to modern child-murderers, Aristophanes to modern political satire, the Roman empire to the British empire, Athens to the United States of America.

In 2001–02 the world created by Finley met Curriculum 2000, the bringer of modules. The existence of modules has brought even greater diversity, so that tyranny can be taught alongside democracy.

The topic of tyranny seems to take JACT ancient history to the outer limits of what is possible at this level. There are almost no primary sources: even Herodotus might be judged to be secondary. A LACTOR on the subject, even with a full commentary, wouldn't run to much: there is only so much you can do with Anacreon. Our main hopes are Herodotus and Aristotle's *Politics*, but even these great names are, on this subject, telling a special kind of narrative. Much of what they have is nothing but the image of tyranny created by the world of the fifth century to set against their own world and their own values. The only sensible conclusion is that the writing of the history of the period is impossible. Truth, like time, is irredeemable. But that doesn't make valueless the struggle to question and see how our own times are similarly keen to make myths from history. In the study of tyranny, the method and the game transcend the content, and that sounds like a good form of education to me.

J.C.

15 | The teaching of classical civilisation

Catherine Hobey

At a time when fewer and fewer children were learning classical languages, the study of classical civilisation breathed new life into classics departments and gave gratifyingly large numbers of children the chance to learn something of ancient Greece and Rome. Classical civilisation, at GCSE and A level, has attracted students who are intrigued and enchanted by ageless stories dramatically told, stirring history and art of timeless beauty and influence.

Classics departments have little trouble recruiting eager students for this subject. However, while classical civilisation is a popular option for students and a pleasure for teachers, the GCSE and A level specifications are not easy either to prepare or to deliver. The diversity of available modules and the breadth of period, genre and geography which they cover present both teacher and student with a wealth of choice. However, problems arise in part from the need to balance the time available with the material to be covered. In addition, a teacher will want to play to her interests and experience, and will need to consider her school's resources when choosing which modules to study. Making the best choice both of examination group and of modules offered is crucial to a teacher's success. The challenge is worth taking up, the results potentially most gratifying for both teacher and student.

The classical civilisation GCSE and A level specifications are offered by two examination groups, AQA and OCR. Neither board expects prior knowledge at either level of Greek and Roman civilisation, culture or language. The courses are available to any student, and the subject's popularity is reflected in the numbers of candidates. In theory both examination groups encourage students to acquire a knowledge of classical civilisation which is broadly based, treating aspects of both Greek and Roman civilisations and texts by both Greek and Latin authors. The richness to be gained by such an approach is obvious: Homer may be compared with Virgil, Aristophanes with Plautus; Greek religion may be contrasted with Roman religion, Athenian democracy with the early Roman empire. However, it is frequently possible to concentrate wholly on the Greek or Roman world, excluding any consideration of the literature, history and physical remains of the other. The scope may be narrowed still further by choosing to teach, for example, a selection of Greek tragedies and Greek comedies, and to combine that reading with an examination of Greek religious festivals. One could add a module about Athenian social life. A student would certainly gain an admirably comprehensive idea of Attic drama, its text and performance, as well as the life of the audience that witnessed the plays, but would know little else about the ancient world. However, a scheme of work which covers a great deal of ground superficially is not inherently better than one which explores a smaller area more thoroughly. Such a limited scheme may better suit the teacher's strengths, the students' interests and the school's resources.

The International Baccalaureate does not offer a classical civilisation syllabus. However, schools which participate in the IB programme may devise their own classical civilisation syllabus and submit it to the IB board for approval. The process is not swift, and a successful outcome is not guaranteed, but an individual syllabus devised by a school would enjoy all the benefits of being custom made.

The appeal of myths, drama, ancient history and classical art is obvious and, for teachers of classics, wonderfully stimulating. However, the details of the worlds of Greece and Rome may seem oddly alien to a student, despite the fact that ancient Greece and Rome provide much of Europe's cultural heritage. Cultural and social assumptions often need to be dispelled and replaced by more accurate concepts. Even classical names may at first be difficult to pronounce and learn. A teacher needs to devise methods of delivery for each module which clearly describe the background, elucidate the material and make the whole memorable, and it may be useful to suggest such methods for the study of Greek and Roman epic and Greek art.

The epic poems of Homer and Virgil provide endless scope for study at GCSE and A level. Examinations at both levels require general awareness of an entire epic and detailed knowledge of specific books in the longer work. The first challenge is to impart a sense of the whole. The mythological background to the story recounted needs to be sketched in: the origins of the Trojan War as a prelude to the *Iliad*; the end of the Trojan War and the *nostoi* (return stories) for the *Odyssey*; the fate of Troy and the end of the Roman republic with the rise of Augustus for the *Aeneid*. Next, the time-consuming but unavoidable adventure: the entire epic must be read. There is no other way to acquire a true sense of the poem's story, structure and style. If students write plot summaries of each book, they learn the outline of the story and sort out basic misunderstandings: just exactly how was Patroclus killed; which suitor was rudest to Odysseus; what precisely happened during the hunt of Dido and Aeneas? In addition, of course, the structure of an epic becomes clear when it is read in its entirety. The *Odyssey* is, perhaps, the most obvious example of the importance of examining the rhythm of events in an epic. The reasons for Homer's use of flashback in books 9–12 when Odysseus tells the story of his adventures cast a revealing light on Homer's treatment of themes such as leadership and *xenia* (hospitality), as well as on Homeric style and the use of first-person narrative. A more detailed sense of rhythm may be noted in the observation that each book consists of two small adventures and one large one. Consideration of each of the blocks of four books of the *Odyssey* (the Telemachia, Odysseus' voyage to Scherie, his adventures, the return to Ithaca, Odysseus in his palace, the hero's revenge) also clarifies prominent themes. Each block, for example, has something different to say about the theme of *xenia*: Telemachus travels to experience the right and royal way to entertain a guest, while the suitors illustrate its antithesis; the Cyclops Polyphemus does not so much have guests to dinner as have them for dinner; Eumaeus has much to teach those more prosperous but not more noble than he. Finally, the sweep of an entire epic gives a matchless introduction to the styles of Homer and Virgil. A teacher can direct the reading of the entire poem in such a way that themes, characters and stylistic techniques central to the set books are brought out for preliminary consideration.

When a class turns to the examination of individual books, it will have at the outset an idea of what to look for: elements of style, themes, the structure of the narrative. Students will, for example, be familiar with epithets and extended similes. They can bring a general awareness of these devices to a more thorough consideration of examples within their set books: e.g. why does Homer describe Polyphemus and his blinding in terms a Greek craftsman would understand; why is Penelope described as a lion, a king, a shipwrecked sailor? If they have thought generally about the roles of the gods in the *Iliad* or the *Aeneid*, students will be ready to develop more subtle ideas about, say, the Olympian reflection of earthly life in the *Iliad* or the role of Fate in the *Aeneid*. The centrality of Telemachus as heir to his father and Odysseus' need for disguise are illuminated by the story of Agamemnon's murder at his homecoming, a theme articulated in the opening lines of the *Odyssey*.

There are many techniques by means of which a teacher can lead the examination of a set book. Reading passages aloud often brings out the pace of an episode, its colour and tone. Different students can present different aspects of the same scene. For example, the scene in which Penelope at last recognises and acknowledges Odysseus (the two may not be simultaneous) could be discussed from several points of view: the characterisation of impetuous Telemachus, subtle Penelope, patient Odysseus; the language used at each stage of the scene; the themes of identity/disguise and the testing of strangers. Debates ('Was Odysseus a good leader?' 'Was Aeneas a puppet manipulated by Fate?') can illuminate characters and their actions. The idea of heroism, the role of the gods, visions of the underworld, battles with monsters, similes and structure: if both Homer and Virgil are studied, the links to be made and the contrasts to be identified will enrich the study of both the oral and the literate poet.

Greek art provides perhaps the most obviously attractive module in the study of classical civilisation. However, because the material is diffuse and perhaps unfamiliar, it can be difficult to organise into an effective scheme of work. Each of the three areas of art which are studied – sculpture, vase painting and architecture – demands a different vocabulary and a different mode of examination. All require a similar approach: clarity of presentation, consistency of observation and description, aids to the establishment of visual memory. Whatever the object or building, it should be observed, described and discussed in class, preferably by means of a slide or CD presentation, so that teacher and students are examining the same details at once. Views which are different from those in the set textbook (Susan Woodford, *An Introduction to Greek Art* (Duckworth, 1986)) can add subtle elements to one's appreciation of the object. It is extremely useful to provide a photocopy of each object discussed in a lesson. Notes can then be taken on the photocopy: object and observations are then linked and provide an aide-mémoire. The fusion of object and observations also helps students to develop their own style of description. Too often, an authority's description is memorised – or half-memorised – and regurgitated without thought or understanding.

Sculpture is no doubt the easiest of the three areas to present to students. They can all name the elements of which a statue is composed: arms, legs and facial features do not need definitions. Moreover, the development of sculptural techniques and representations, at least from the archaic period to the fourth century BC, is relatively linear and straightforward. A few paradigms serve to illustrate each phase of sculptural history. The names of few artists are known, and so few have to be learned. Lines of development may be simplified: the nude male in terms of anatomy; draped females in terms of drapery; architectural sculpture as the effective use of a triangle, rectangle and band. In all those ways, sculpture is easy to approach and makes a pleasing introduction to Greek art, if the syllabus allows it, which is not, at present, the case: OCR, the only body which offers modules in Greek art and architecture, prescribes the study of vase painting and architecture for AS level and sculpture for A level.

The examination of all free-standing statues should be consistent. General observations come first: is the statue marble or bronze; is it an original or a copy; what is the subject depicted; where was its original site; and what was its purpose? Next, a teacher might describe the statue in detail: pose; anatomy and/or drapery; head, hair and features; any elements of torso, arms and legs not noted in discussion of the pose. Consistency in the order in which observations are made is important, both because it provides a complete description, leaving out nothing of significance, and because it offers an outline for comparing and contrasting two statues – a type of question beloved by the examiners. A few technical terms are important: e.g. types of drapery, chiefly the woollen peplos and the linen chiton; chiasmos or contrapposto, the balance of relaxed limb with tense limb, of bent with straight. In considering chiasmos, it is useful to point out that while a relaxed arm is straight, a tense arm bent, the opposite is true of legs.

One might, for example, compare and contrast the Apoxyomenos (a statue of a man scraping himself after exercise) of Lysippos (figure 1) and the Hermes with the baby Dionysos of Praxiteles (figure 2). Both are known from ancient authors. Both are made of marble, but the Apoxyomenos is a copy of a bronze original. The question of the status of the Hermes, whether original or a Hellenistic copy, can be usefully considered; both his lower legs and his left foot are modern restorations. Lysippos depicted an anonymous mortal engaged in a daily activity, while Praxiteles sculpted a pair of gods at one moment of a story: the former is single and universal, the latter a group and a narrative; the former emotionless, the latter emotional. The Apoxyomenos would have been an athletic dedication, the Hermes stood (oddly, given the story) in one of the alcoves along the walls of the temple to Hera at Olympia. Both statues are naked but for the exquisite sandals worn by Hermes. The Apoxyomenos stands upright, with each limb tense, although the right leg bears little weight. His left arm crosses his torso, his right arm extends forward: both block the viewer's access to a fully frontal view of his body. The Hermes stands in a languid double curve, his right arm raised (to hold grapes for the baby's delight), his left extended at a right angle to hold the baby: nothing impedes a view of his body. The original of the Apoxyomenos no doubt stood outdoors. Lysippos has tried to make the statue interesting from all angles by making no single view entirely revealing of the statue's anatomy. Its pose would have invited the viewer to examine it from

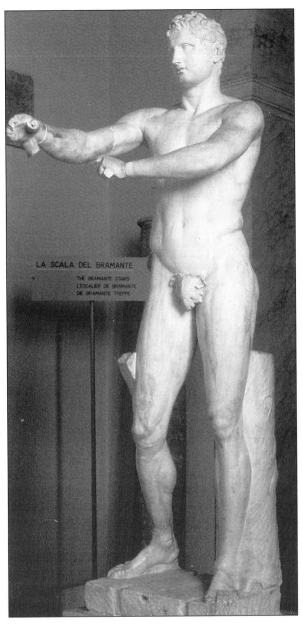

Figure 1. The Apoxyomenos of Lysippos

all sides. The Hermes is fully coherent only from the front, which is entirely satisfactory for a statue placed in an alcove. It may be supposed that the original Apoxyomenos had the well-defined

Figure 2. The Hermes of Praxiteles

anatomy which looked back to fifth-century statues of athletes, but the poor quality of the Roman copy forbids certainty. The surface of the Hermes displays the melting softness one associates with Praxiteles. The rumpled drapery and the rough trunk of the tree provide contrast. The round head and flat hair of the Apoxyomenos follow the example of fifth-century statues of athletes, while the small mouth and padded brow look more to the fourth century. The athlete looks straight ahead. The oval head of the Hermes, his deeply cut locks and deep-set eyes are what one would expect from a Praxitelean statue. The god's head turns to observe his young burden. Other details may be added to these basic descriptions. That sort of approach to the observation and description of sculpture helps to make a statue memorable and to link it to other statues.

Vases too should be observed, described and discussed in a consistent manner. General characteristics include technique of decoration, shape, painter, subject and date: e.g. a red-figure hydria by the Kleophrades Painter on which is depicted the sack of Troy (the Vivenzio hydria, figure 3), *circa* first quarter of the fifth century. (It is important to distinguish vase painters whose names are known, e.g. Exekias and Euphronios, from those whose names are unknown, e.g. the Brygos Painter and the Berlin Painter.) Examination of the scene illustrated on the vase might include: the story depicted, composition, details of individual figures. So, if one were to continue to explore the Vivenzio hydria, one would want to narrate the five episodes depicted: Aeneas bearing Anchises and leading Ascanius away from Troy; the lesser Ajax attacking Cassandra; Priam, holding the dead Astyanax on his lap, being murdered by Neoptolemus; an anonymous Trojan woman attacking a Greek; Aithra rescued by her two grandsons. Three scenes of violence, defiance and defeat are framed by two of salvation. In order to fit the diminishing space of the hydria's shoulder, the scenes are organised in compact pyramids which sometimes merge with each other to form larger triangles, e.g. the group from the lesser Ajax to the palm tree merges with that from Priam to Neoptolemus. Bodies, limbs, weapons and drapery link the scenes. The Kleophrades Painter's interest in the third dimension may be observed: the back view of Neoptolemus' right leg; the foreshortened legs of the Trojan lying dead at Neoptolemus' feet; the interior, shaded view of the shield carried by the Greek attacked by a Trojan woman. The chronological context of the vase may be significant: the Kleophrades Painter's majestic and sympathetic vision of the fall of Troy may be linked to his experience of the Persian sack of Athens.

Because the set textbook illustrates so many vases painted by almost as many vase painters, it is important to try to impart a sense of development in vase painting. The transformation from the black-figure to the red-figure technique and developments in the depiction of anatomy and drapery are the most obvious indications of progression. Although they will not be part of the syllabus, slides and photocopies

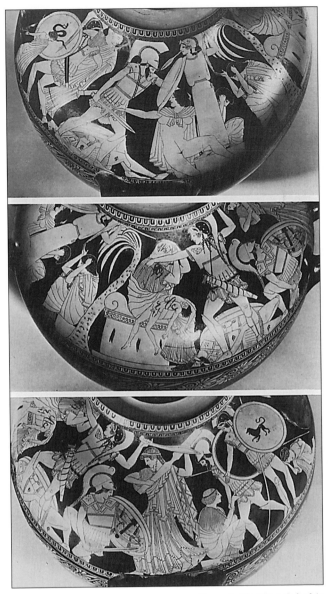

Figure 3. The Vivenzio hydria

of other vases painted by the most significant Attic vase painters give a fuller sense of an artist's style and *oeuvre*. John Boardman has written an admirable series of books about almost every phase of Attic vase painting. The books, published by Thames and Hudson, offer a compendium of the most characteristic vases by the best-known Attic vase painters.

The architecture of Greece is difficult to teach not only because the subject is abstract and the vocabulary unfamiliar but also because there are no truly excellent introductory textbooks for GCSE and A level students. Once again, consistency of approach and aides-mémoire are important.

The appearance of both individual buildings and sanctuaries is controlled by their site, their function and the material from which they were constructed. So, for example, squared stone blocks and rectilinear roof tiles give rise to buildings which emphasise straight lines and right angles and discourage curves, arches and apses. Individual buildings are best described as they would have been experienced. Even rather complex buildings benefit from such an approach. The Propylaia to the Acropolis of Athens (figure 4), for example, was built on land which rose steeply from west to east. The gateway to the Acropolis was designed to evoke awe by its size and lavish use of marble and decoration. It would have been entered at the lower, western end. From that position, the visitor would have been faced with the sternly intimidating Doric façade of six columns standing in front of the side walls (hexastyle prostyle) and the three steps of its entrance. From there, a central roadway lies below the level of the two passageways which flank it. While the roadway accommodated animals, chariots and processions, the passageways would have been used by pedestrians. The central roadway rises gradually from west to east. The level of the passageways achieves a similar adjustment in a different manner. Initially, the passageways extend eastward from the western hexastyle façade. The ceiling of this section is supported by three majestic Ionic columns along the inner side of each passageway, flanking the roadway. Ionic columns can sustain a greater height from a smaller lower diameter than can Doric columns, and so are elegantly appropriate in this position. Steps then lead through a cross-wall across each passageway. The cross-wall is pierced by a narrow opening and a wider opening at each side. The pillars which mark the inner openings are exactly as wide as the lowest diameter of the Ionic columns with which they are aligned. The passageways then continue to the eastern Doric hexastyle façade, where their level exactly equals that of the central roadway. The visitor would emerge from the huge shadowed Propylaia to a bright view of the Parthenon and the rest of the Acropolis.

The architect Mnesikles seems to have planned wings which would have flanked both the western and eastern ends of the Propylaia. Those at the east were never built, perhaps because of financial difficulties during the Peloponnesian War. Only that at the north west stood as an enclosed room: a dining room, its function defined by the off-centre

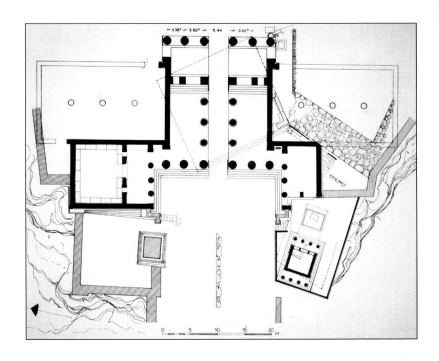

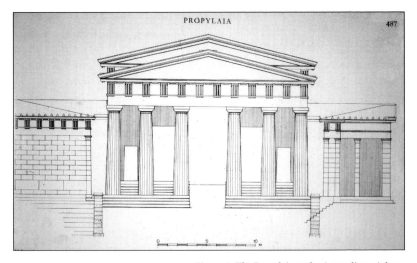

Figure 4. The Propylaia to the Acropolis at Athens

door, necessary for the accommodation of couches around the room's perimeter. The room was decorated with paintings. Three Doric columns, smaller than those of the western façade, stood prostyle along the façade of the wing. Religious scruples dictated by the proximity of the *temenos* (sacred precinct) of Artemis Brauron, a wall from the Mycenaean period and the area reserved for a planned temple to Athene Nike, none of which could be encroached upon, meant that, from the outset, Mnesikles had to design a truncated south-west wing which would nevertheless persuade the viewer that it was the partner of the wing opposite it. So, along the western side, a pillar stood as a false anta, as if it were the end of an actual side wall (*anta*, pl. *antae*), while another supported the entablature. A second false anta emerged from the eastern wall to balance that at the west and to frame the three Doric columns. (A similar false anta performed the same function for the north-west wing.) From the roadway and passages, the south-west wing would have given a similar impression to that of its northern partner. Mnesikles employed further visual sleight-of-hand in adjusting the proportions between the wings and the larger central core of the building.

A similar approach, from site and function to an orderly consideration of details, may be used in the discussion of sanctuaries. For example, the site of Olympia was an alluvial plain bordered by two rivers and a hill. The centrality of its religious function is reflected in the position of the temples and treasuries, the oldest buildings, at the heart of the site. Architecture to accommodate athletic events and spectators followed chronologically and lay nearest the religious buildings. Less essential structures came later: hotels for athletes and important guests, practice areas, administrative buildings. The architecture of the sanctuary developed as its needs and functions became more sophisticated. Development from the centre outward was facilitated by the flat geography of the site, which may be contrasted with the steeply rising site of the sanctuary of Apollo at Delphi.

Greek art and architecture present the student with groups of objects which initially seem difficult to understand and impossible to remember. Consistency of observation and description, together with annotated photocopies, develop a student's analytical powers and visual memory. What seemed to be a hopelessly disparate jumble becomes comprehensible and is not forgotten.

The study of classical civilisation is an encouragingly successful area of classical studies. It has grown and flourished in recent decades and seems set to continue to inform and inspire students. The popularity of the subject can be enhanced if teachers channel initial enthusiasm into deeper streams of informed appreciation and detailed understanding. The task is a challenge to be welcomed.

16 | Using ICT in classics

Or how I learned to stop worrying and love the computer
David Goodhew

Introduction

It is with some trepidation that I write this chapter, all too conscious that it may fall victim to 'Tomorrow's World' syndrome. Ten years ago only a minority of people had e-mail addresses or mobile telephones, home computers which ran at 66MHz were considered pretty fast, 32MB was a lot of memory, and the internet was burrowed, rather than surfed, by 'gophers'. How then to make this chapter future-proof? Certainly not by making confident predictions about the shape of things to come – *cave Betamax*. Rather I intend to examine ways in which currently available hardware and software may assist the study and teaching of classics; I assume a basic familiarity with computers on the part of the reader.

Equipment

In the late 1980s and early 1990s a key decision for a head of classics was whether to buy IBM-compatible (PC) or Apple Macintosh (Mac) computers – or indeed an Acorn: the software being produced was restricted to one kind of machine ('platform') or the other, and there was almost no intercompatibility with regard to hardware. Nowadays, this is less of an issue: for example, Perseus 2,[1] previously only available on Macs, was released in a PC-friendly version in 2000. Reasons for this change include the availability of internet resources via cross-platform browsers (e.g. Netscape or Internet Explorer), the use of platform-independent programming languages (such as Java), and the Mac's ability to emulate PCs. More relevant than the *kind* of machine one uses is the question of *distribution*: one or two stand-alone machines in a classroom are fine if one wants casual access to electronic resources (e.g. for researching a project), or a warm and fuzzy feeling if (when!) the school network goes down. However, for routine work with a large Year 8 class (e.g. language-drilling) a

---

[1] http://www.yale.edu/yup/Perseus2.html

computer suite of some description is a must; this may be used by the whole school or an individual department, depending on the size of the department and the generosity of the school bursar. The booking of the room and the disruption caused by taking a class out of their familiar territory, are drawbacks initially; however, if the suite is used regularly, then a session can be booked in the timetable, and it soon becomes part of the students' routine, and so things flow more easily. This still presents the problem of 'What do I do if the network's down?' Even if one has, with commendable foresight and efficiency, prepared a back-up lesson, time has been lost and expectations raised: one possible solution is to install software 'locally' (i.e. onto each machine individually) rather than running it via a network – this means pupils can still use specific programs even if the network is down; however, it makes installing, upgrading and maintaining the programs much more time-consuming and labour intensive, and the head of ICT support may quite reasonably disapprove of this.

Some schools have addressed the question of adequate access for staff and pupils to computers by investing in laptops: in theory this should be a good idea as it means everyone has a machine for use anywhere in the school. However, various practical problems present themselves: providing technical support to 1,000-plus machines, all of which have been 'customised' by inventive teen brains, will stretch all but the most lavishly staffed ICT support teams; wireless networks can still be temperamental; and teachers often find it disconcerting not to be able to see from the front of the class what a pupil is doing. Furthermore, if the school is flooded with machines before departments have had a chance to design specific tasks into schemes of work, then the chances are high that the machines will be used predominantly for e-mail, games, and watching DVDs. However, in a best-case scenario, pupils can be issued with relevant software/CDs at the start of term, very much as they might now be allocated textbooks (a good example is the CD-ROM which accompanies the OCR AS/A2 *Advancing Physics* course).[2] In a school where all departments are producing such resources, it is not unreasonable to anticipate that laptops will replace exercise books.

For any subject such as classics which makes use of slides and videos, a data projector is an increasingly desirable piece of equipment. The price has come down very significantly over the last few years, although it is worth scrutinising the number of hours for which the bulb is expected to last (replacement bulbs are still expensive) and the intensity of the light produced, which will greatly affect the quality of image produced in the ambient light of a typical classroom. Projectors

[2] http://post16.iop.org/advphys/

can convey images from a laptop or desktop computer, a VCR or DVD player: thus one can give presentations involving text, slides and video without having to chop and change between OHPs, slide projectors and VCRs. Some schools choose to have portable projectors, which can be taken from classroom to classroom: with practice, it takes only a few minutes to connect everything up, although it may not always be easy to find the best spot in the classroom from which to project. Other schools favour having the projector 'plumbed in', usually from the ceiling, which has the advantage of making the projector more difficult to steal and easier to use (no setting up required); however, this might mean that one needs to book the 'projector room' for specific lessons. The size of the image projected is attractive, and, as departments begin to digitise their slide and video collections, data projectors are likely to proliferate: on a recent visit to a museum, I was astonished to find sets of slides on sale for 50p per set – the assistant explained that the rise of PowerPoint has meant a decline in the sale of celluloid slides. Digitising images via a scanner, or converting video clips to digital format, has a number of advantages: the image is crisper, the lifetime of the slide is greatly increased, the images are easier to incorporate into other documents (e.g. presentations or handouts); it is also possible to create a 'thumbnail image' database, which makes it easier to search the department slide collection. The main disadvantage of a digital slide collection is the space it occupies on a school's server (even more so for video clips); this may become less of a problem as video-compression software improves, and in the meantime it is always possible to use CDs for local storage. Copyright regulations will, of course, continue to be an issue.

Resources

For most classicists, their first encounter with ICT is likely to be word-processing. Incredibly, it is not unknown for pupils to write out essays by hand before typing them into Word, printing them out, and handing them in; not a few colleagues still seem to regard word-processing packages as glorified typewriters. To do so is to miss the enormous potential for manipulating text that such software provides: not only can students' essays be improved by re-reading and re-drafting, but any text can be pulled apart and rebuilt in different ways – this is a powerful tool for encouraging reader-response critiques of classical texts. What would happen if Catullus 8 really did end at line 12 with the words *vale, puella*? What would happen to a Ciceronian speech if one put the *argumenta* before the *narratio*? A traditional objection to encouraging students to use word-processors is the fact that public examinations are still handwritten: this seems to be a perfect example of the tail wagging the dog. Whilst it is true that students will require practice in writing by hand under exam conditions, this does not mean that they should do nothing else throughout their school careers. A different problem has been posed by the typing of accentuated classical Greek: this requires a font (in which to display the characters) and a keyboard utility (to facilitate breathings and accents). A number of keyboard utilities are available (e.g. Greek without Tears)[3] – the problem concerns fonts. Although many are available, they are not compatible with one another: thus Greek text typed in WinGreek[4] will not display properly in GreekKeys.[5] A solution is provided by Unicode – a font standard whereby all characters would have the same code irrespective of whether they were in Times New Roman or WinGreek (a good review of the state of play is that by Rusten);[6] Unicode may also be able to make displaying Greek in web pages easier than it is at present.

The use of language-drilling software is one of the most obvious benefits of computer-assisted learning to the classicist. One advantage of computerised grammar or vocabulary drills (e.g. Latin Vocab Drill[7] or Lingua Latina[8]) is that students can work at their own pace, thus allowing the brighter ones to press on while the weaker ones consolidate. Another plus is the fact that the computer has unlimited patience, will not get cross, and will not cause a pupil to feel embarrassed for making errors; furthermore, the drilling can be done at any time, not just during lessons. Finally, the culture associated with computer games means that pupils will go far beyond a written test in order to achieve a highest score: a weak group might manage a twenty-item vocabulary test on paper, but I have seen such a group average 240–60 on a computer. Potential disadvantages include the need to make sure the list of meanings is accurate: pupils testing themselves on vocabulary from Stage 19 of the Cambridge Latin Course (4th edn) get remarkably tetchy if the computer expects them to know vocabulary from Stage 19 of the Cambridge Latin Course (2nd edn); furthermore, the failure of the computer to recognise typing errors or alternative (but valid) meanings can be frustrating. One solution to this is to ask students to pick a correct answer from a list of possible meanings (e.g. the CLC online vocabulary tester[9]): this has the advantage that it avoids the problems of typos and unanticipated answers, but the

3 http://www.doctor-flynn.demon.co.uk/gwthome.htm
4 http://www.classics.ox.ac.uk/software/wgreek19.zip
5 http://www.greekkeys.cornell.edu/
6 http://www.arts.cornell.edu/classics/Faculty/Rusten/unicode/review.htm
7 http://www.j-progs.com/
8 http://www.ucc.uconn.edu/~hasenfra/WLATIN.HTML
9 http://www.cambridgescp.com/vocab/voc.html

disadvantage that students have at least a one in three chance of being correct. In Greek it is possible to have one's cake and eat it, courtesy of the Eton Greek software project:[10] Stage One allows pupils to work Greek–English or English–Greek while testing vocabulary; Stage Two will drill grammar, and it is intended that Stage Three will cover syntax exercises. One can only applaud the decision of the Provost and Fellows of Eton College not only to fund a project that tries to remedy the comparative dearth of classical Greek software, but also to allow the software to be distributed free of charge via the internet, thus making a valuable resource available to students all over the world.

Computer programs can also be used to develop students' translation skills: in the case of Latin without Tears,[11] pupils work through past GCSE unseens, with as much or as little help as they require from the computer. The program tracks their statistics, so that both the pupils and their teacher can know exactly how much help was provided by the computer, and what sort (e.g. parsing, vocabulary, translation). The advantage of such a program is that it frees the teacher from answering the routine questions which arise from translation, and thus allows time to be devoted to more complex or subtle issues. Although translation software can provide right answers or correct errors, it is still not good at analysing why a pupil has made a given mistake: teachers may find it reassuring that artificial intelligence has not yet made a significant impact on classics software. Electronic dictionaries, such as the Electronic Pocket Oxford Latin Dictionary,[12] can help students read texts at considerable pace, are a real boon for those who struggle with inflected forms, and are much easier to navigate than their paper equivalents. Some teachers may object that pupils will succumb to the temptation to be lazy, and fail to develop both the skill of reasoning from inflected forms back to principal parts and the knowledge of irregular verb forms: this may be so in some cases, but one might draw a comparison with the use of calculators in mathematics – the fact that a calculator can add numbers faster than me does not prevent my knowing how to perform addition, but does allow me to do more complicated sums at greater speed.

The compilation of a complete corpus of electronic texts, whether Latin (e.g. Packard Humanities Institute CD 5.3[13]) or Greek (e.g. Thesaurus Linguae Graecae[14]), allows the classicist to analyse texts in

---

10 http://www.etoncollege.com
11 http://www.doctor-flynn.demon.co.uk/lwt1.htm
12 http://www.cambridgescp.com/pol/pol_home.html
13 http://www.packhum.org/
14 http://www.tlg.uci.edu/

ways hitherto impossible. Using a suitable search program (e.g. Musaios[15]), one can track down every instance of the noun 'praeceptum' (including inflections) in Virgil and compare the use of this word in Virgil with other (or all) Latin authors – in under half an hour! The ramifications of this, not just for stylometric analysis and textual criticism but also for literary criticism, are enormous. One small caveat: the value of search results will depend on how highly one regards the particular editions of texts which were scanned into the collections.

Classics is about much more than literary texts, and thus is particularly suited to multimedia work. A student of Greek drama may want to read the text of a play (in Greek or English), cross-reference depictions of the relevant myth on South Italian vases, or view different phases of the site of the Theatre of Dionysos: Perseus,[16] whether on CD or the internet, makes this not only possible, but quick and straightforward. CD-ROMs such as Olympia[17] or Pompeii Interactive[18] provide a wealth of absorbing material, through which students can navigate easily and profitably. The speed with which one can jump from one subject to another via hyperlinks is a great advantage of CD-ROMs: the *Oxford Classical Dictionary* (3rd edn) is much quicker to use in this format, despite one or two deficiencies in the software. Civilisation topics such as Roman technology[19] can be explained and tested very effectively using multimedia programs. Computer graphics can bring to life individual buildings (e.g. the Hadrianic Baths at Leptis Magna[20]) or whole cities – I vividly recall teaching *Iliad* 16 to a class of boys on a gloomy Saturday morning: courtesy of Metis[21] we were able to visit Troy and walk around the site in QuickTime VirtualReality. With practice, it becomes fairly simple to write multimedia presentations, whether using PowerPoint, HyperStudio, or Flash: the advantage for the teacher is the capacity to make text, image and animation/video work effectively together in one package. Lest this should seem to be too didactic in focus, one should observe that such presentations may be written by students as well. If such presentations are stored on a departmental intranet site, then they become doubly useful as a revision tool and a means for absentees to catch up missed work.

The internet, although limitless in its potential, poses a number of issues for classical teachers. Firstly, there is the problem of finding relevant and useful information: typing the search term 'homer' into

---

15 http://www.musaios.com/
16 http://perseus.csad.ox.ac.uk
17 http://www.j-progs.com/olympia.html
18 http://www.pompeii.co.uk
19 http://www.j-progs.com/RT3.HTML
20 http://archpropplan.auckland.ac.nz/virtualtour/hadrians_bath/
21 http://www.stoa.org/metis/

Yahoo! yields a staggering 10,101,000 web pages, comparatively few of which deal with the Greek poet ('doh!'). Secondly, even when one has found a useful website, it may be blocked by the school's filtering software (e.g. because it contains the Latin number six, or because it refers to the island home of Sappho). Thirdly, how is one to teach pupils to distinguish between academically sound websites and dross? Finally, how can one prevent unscrupulous pupils pasting large chunks of work from the internet into their coursework, or even downloading essays from subject-specific websites? To take these issues in order: searching can be made much easier either by using limited-area search engines (e.g. Argos[22]), which screen out non-classical material, or by using a page containing a general collection of useful links (e.g. the Oxford Classics site[23] or the Internet Resources for Classics page[24]). Problems caused by filtering software may be addressed by reporting to the network manager innocent sites which are blocked, when it happens: the problem with such an 'evolutionary' model is that it takes a long time, and the damage to pupil/colleague confidence is already done. Temporary exemption from filtering while pupils are in a supervised session is a better solution, but may conflict with whole-school policies on internet use. The issue of how pupils are to learn to evaluate material they encounter on the internet critically is in some ways no different from inculcating the skill of reading books critically. One urge which it is important to suppress is for pupils automatically to hit 'print' as soon as they come upon a page which looks vaguely relevant: not only does this waste paper, but the information has still to be read. Reading text on a screen does not come naturally – it takes time to leave the codex behind in favour of the e-scroll. One way of getting pupils to think critically about sites is to ask the group to review a list of ten sites on a given topic, and compare and discuss their findings. Alternatively, a list of trustworthy and useful sites can be put on the department web page, cutting down time wasted by pupils in searching, and allowing the teacher to have a fair idea of which sites have been used. Plagiarism is a live issue, partly because of the absence of handwriting clues, and partly because at least with books there was a fairly limited pool from which students might have drawn, and thus the chances that a teacher would recognise a given passage were high. Clearly some students will give themselves away on stylometric grounds: however, the existence of websites offering model answers is potentially alarming, not to mention the possibility of informal 'essay-sharing' networks which, thanks to e-mail, can extend nationwide. It

---

[22] http://argos.evansville.edu
[23] http://www.classics.ox.ac.uk
[24] http://www.sas.ac.uk/icls/default.htm

is difficult to see what can be done to prevent such abuses. On a more positive note, the internet does provide access to online museums (e.g. the Vatican[25]) and journals (e.g. *Bryn Mawr Classical Review*[26]): as with most tools, whether it is used for good or ill depends on the user.

A nice example of the potential for the use of ICT in teaching Latin is the Cambridge Online Latin Project:[27] this collaboration between the Cambridge School Classics Project, Granada Result and the Department for Education and Skills produced a variety of electronic resources which were used to introduce Latin into schools where there was no specialist teacher available. The test materials[28] include drills, exercises, 'media-rich' explanations and presentations, and combine many of the best features of the techniques outlined in the preceding paragraphs. Education need not be confined to teachers and classrooms: pupils of all ages and backgrounds might be keen to learn Latin, but the provision of the subject in schools is severely limited – the COLP seems a good attempt to solve an important problem. The use of e-tutors to track performance and provide assistance not only exploits the 'C' in ICT to broaden access to Latin, but also exemplifies the way in which the role of the 'teacher' changes positively when learners can use computers to work independently. The benefits of this project apply as much to schools with large, secure classics departments as those where no Latin is currently taught; the importance of the project for the survival of the subject should not be underestimated.

Conclusion

A study conducted in the 1980s[29] suggested that the use of computer-assisted learning was more effective in improving a school's results than either smaller class sizes or more time allocated to the teaching of subjects. Clearly current hardware and software have much to offer both students and teachers of classics: the challenge is making *high-quality* resources *easily* and *reliably* accessible to the learner. Ease and reliability of use are vital in order to avoid demoralising colleagues and pupils alike; quality of content is crucial if resources are to meet the exacting standards demanded by classicists, and stand the test of time (groovy graphics have a limited shelf life). A good example is the way in which e-mail has come to dominate communication in the UK over the last four years: e-mail is easy to

[25] http://www.christusrex.org/www1/vaticano/0-Musei.html
[26] http://ccat.sas.upenn.edu/bmcr/
[27] http://www.cambridgescp.com/cscpp/colp_main.html
[28] http://www.becta.org.uk/ks3online/
[29] H. Levin, G.V. Glass and G.R. Meister, *A Cost-Effectiveness Analysis of Four Educational Interventions*, Project Report No. 84–A11 (Institute for Research on Educational Finance and Governance, Stanford University, CA, 1984).

use, serves a useful purpose, and is swifter and (usually) more reliable than its earthbound counterpart: thus it has prospered. Nobody has had to go around the country proselytising on behalf of e-mail: it is a 'killer app<lication>'. Our challenge is not to convert pupils and colleagues to the cause of ICT – rather to introduce them to 'killer apps' (such as Perseus), which are straightforward to use, but more importantly *worth using*; there is little point in using computers for their own sake, merely to impress parents and inspectors. Encouragingly, in many schools and universities, classicists seem to be in the vanguard of employing new technology in academically profitable ways: *nobis computandumst, non computrescendumst.*

17 | Classics in the universities

James Morwood

There is a very real sense in which classics in UK universities has never been more thriving. Some 8,000 students are studying the subject with great relish and commitment in a wide variety of courses at three Scottish universities, two in Wales, one in Northern Ireland and fourteen in England.[1] Details of these can, of course, be found on the individual universities' websites, the valuable classics booklet in the CRAC Series of Degree Course Guides[2] gives the basic facts of what each and every university does,[3] and the Council of University Classics Departments (CUCD) is preparing a website with this information.[4] The situation looks enormously healthy. And the universities have certainly shown an imaginative response to the dramatically shifting nature of the subject in schools. In particular, as the teaching of Latin and Greek at the secondary level has become more and more restricted to independent schools where only between 7 and 10 per cent of the age group is taught,[5] the universities have found ways of welcoming students from across the whole social range by offering courses in classical civilisation and ancient history.

The kaleidoscopic vitality of the current classical scene in our universities[6] is thus a reflection of the profound change in the classical background of students who study at them. Twenty years ago a degree in classics meant that serious proficiency in Latin and/or Greek had been achieved. Nowadays, it is likely to mean much more – some would say much less – than that. All students then arrived at university with a knowledge of at least one of the languages and this enabled them to get on with the serious reading of texts in the original. Now they are very likely to have *both* to develop the knowledge of the classical world that has led them to university in the

---

[1] The most up-to-date information can be found in the Council of University Classical Departments' *Bulletin 31* (2002) in Graham Shipley's 'Classics at British Universities 2001–2: Statistics' – www.sun.rhbnc.cc.uk/Classics/CUCD/bulletin. The Northern Ireland classics department (Queen's University Belfast) is sadly no longer taking students. However, ancient history can still be studied there.
[2] Produced by the Careers Research and Advisory Centre and the Higher Education Statistics Agency – www.springboard.co.uk
[3] Save for the Open University. For this, see pp. 149–58.
[4] http://www.cucd.com/
[5] For a summary of relevant information see James Morwood, 'Classics in the UK in 2000' in Freddy Decreus (ed.), *New Classics for a New Century?* (Gent, 2002), 43.
[6] There have been so many lively initiatives in this sector in recent years that it would be invidious to single out any of them.

first place *and* to embark simultaneously on *ab initio* courses in one or both languages. And they will have no more time to do this than their predecessors. It is a serious mistake to assume that there has been a decline in the intellectual calibre of classical students. For one thing, we are liable to look back through rose-tinted spectacles at the actual level of attainment of their equivalents of two decades back. Many of them were not as linguistically strong as they should have been in view of the vast areas of time devoted to the study of the languages at some schools. For another thing, today's students can end up knowing just as much of the languages as the supposed giants of old ever did – and a lot more about everything else.

A valuable growth area is the availability of classics modules in the courses of other subjects. This interdisciplinary aspect is not only valuable in itself. It may also lead students who have dipped a toe in the classical pond to commit themselves to a deeper study of the subject. The importance of classics as a 'service subject' for other disciplines can scarcely be overestimated.

But the very wealth and range of classics has not proved free of problems and these can reach beyond the walls of the universities. In 1990 CUCD commissioned a history graduate to interview a number of employers in various fields of employment in order to discover what their attitude was to job applications from classicists. The responses were certainly reassuring, and *Classics in the Marketplace*, the booklet which resulted, played a significant role in persuading students at school that they would not be disadvantaged in the employment market by choosing a university subject that might at first sight seem decidedly remote from the modern world.[7] Indeed, a fairly recent investigation showed that classics graduates get jobs quicker than anyone else.[8]

The results of the CUCD exercise were to some extent based on the fact that the employers who were interviewed had a concept of what a degree in classics meant. Even in 1990 this may have been anachronistic, but in so far as there is any truth in the belief that a mind trained in the rigours of mastering difficult inflected languages can easily master other difficult areas as well, it was, as we have seen, a truth that was reflected in university classics courses far more then than it is now. And it was surely the belief that it was true that led to employer after employer saying, as they did, that they tended to give a warm welcome to classics graduates.

While there is certainly much cause for celebration in the way that university classics has broadened from its former linguistic

---

[7] T.P. Wiseman (ed.), *Classics in the Marketplace* (CUCD, 1990).
[8] Harriet Swain, 'What employers love the most' (*THES*, 29 August 1997).

centre, the fact remains that now we find ourselves faced with the problem of our brand description. Most universities where classics is studied offer language teaching. Some force their students to learn Latin or Greek or both of them. Others make it optional. Some teach a minimum, others aim to cover everything.[9] The products of all these varying systems are each and every one of them called classicists. By simply going on like this without a serious attempt to define what our students do or do not know, are we helping them, or the outside world, or ourselves?

One particular problem has been identified by Brenda Gay in an article entitled 'Classics teachers for the 21st century'.[10] She is writing of classics graduates who at their universities opted 'to take the minimum number of linguistic courses or literature courses in the original language' and who thus 'may acquire only a superficial understanding of the underlying structure of the language'. If these students wish to teach classics, it may be impossible even to admit them to PGCE classics courses since they may be unable to meet the demands of teaching Latin and Greek even at Key Stages 3 and 4. Since two thirds of the training takes place in school, to expose PGCE students to teaching Latin or Greek 'when they are not linguistically confident or competent is to do them and their pupils a disservice'.

The harsh fact is that teachers still need at least one of the languages. There is unlikely to be a sufficient amount of classical civilisation or ancient history teaching available in a single school to justify employment of someone who cannot teach Latin or Greek. And Gay suggests various avenues which could lead those who want to pursue a career in classics teaching to achieve the necessary linguistic mastery. Attendance at the intensive eight-week course now on offer at the University of Cork would be one obvious path to this.[11] The JACT Greek summer school is another. But we are still left with the problems caused in the outside world by confusion about what any particular classics degree actually means. It is dishonest to suggest, however unconsciously, that today's classics graduate necessarily has the same kind of well-trained mind that it was thought that she had twenty years ago.

And there is a serious problem for prospective students of classics. Faced with this enormous range of possibilities, how are they to choose their university? They should certainly feel no shame

---

[9] One university famed for its language instruction teaches *Reading Greek* to its *ab initio* students only up to the end of section 9 (i.e. before any exposure to the verbs in -μι). For some idea of the range of language teaching in British universities, see D.G. Fitzpatrick and L.P. Hardwick (eds.), *Practical Strategies in the Changing Environment of Classical Language Teaching at University* (The Open University, 2001).
[10] B.M. Gay, in *King's English*, vol. 2: Issue 1 (1999), 20–1. See also pages 40–1 of this book.
[11] The contact e-mail address for this course is n.humble@ucc.ie

if they are confused. It's a confusing situation![12] With any luck, they will have a teacher or former students from their school to help to guide them but such information soon gets out of date, and anyhow this will not always be the case, particularly for those from schools where there is no classics who have been fired with enthusiasm for the subject by an interest in mythology – or TV programmes, say, on Alexander the Great. For all students, and for the latter especially, constant visits to the websites mentioned in my first paragraph will be essential, and these should be followed up by literal visits to the universities which seem to offer the most attractive wares. Attendance at three or four open days is surely a worthwhile investment of time for anyone intending to commit herself to a place of study for three or four years.

If all my talk of problems seems off-putting, that will be extremely regrettable. The adventure of university classics is probably more exciting now than it ever was. Its reach and range are broader than they used to be. Students today are likely to view fifth-century Athens and the so-called 'Golden Age' of Latin literature not simply as areas to be studied but also as part of a vast cultural and historical continuum extending from the iron age to the fall of Constantinople. Any barriers between literature, history, art, archaeology and philosophy have tumbled down. And the problems can have their up-side too. University teachers need not only to recruit students but also to hang on to them in order to keep their jobs. In addition, they have to aim at the highest scholarship as well as publishing more than ever before. This means that the teaching at universities is overall far better than it was a generation ago. Classics at this level is a scene that students can be proud to be part of.[13]

---

[12] One factor not yet mentioned is that ancient history may well be part of a history, not a classics faculty.

[13] The recent collection of essays, *Classics in Progress*, edited by Peter Wiseman (Oxford University Press, 2002) to celebrate the centenary of the British Academy is just one indication of the quality, range and diversity of modern classical scholarship and the continuing value and vitality of the subject.

18 | For 'Anyone who wishes'

Classical studies in the Open University, 1971–2002

Lorna Hardwick

In 1971, anyone might have been thought to be suffering from delusions if they had prophesied that thirty years into the future over 4,000 students annually would be studying classical subjects in a university devoted to adult part-timers studying in their own homes. Furthermore, even the most far-sighted could hardly have anticipated that the Open University would become the largest single provider among UK universities of *ab initio* courses in classical languages and, in the case of classical Greek, would teach more students than all the other universities put together.

The factors which shaped the growth of classical studies at the Open University are complex. This was not a smooth progression and its successive phases map the contours of curriculum debate within the arts and humanities as well as highlighting the changes in the student body and the growing role of student choice in higher education. The issues and debates were often paradoxical and the eventual establishment of a focused classical studies strand within the Open University BA degree in some respects represents a microcosm of the restructuring of the discipline in general.

The beginnings

The Open University admitted its first students in 1971. Under the leadership of the founding Vice-Chancellor Walter Perry (previously a medical professor at the University of Edinburgh), small teams of academics had, in a period of only two years, created Foundation courses for each of the Faculties. Each course was structured round printed course units which were supplied to students and set books which they had to buy. BBC television and radio programmes were integral to each course (later largely replaced by videos, audiocassettes, CD-ROMs and DVDs). Assessment was by in-course written assignments (gobbets and essays in the case of Arts) and end-of-year examination. Course credits were to be built up over a period of years for the award of a degree. Face-to-face tuition was offered in local study centres and summer schools were held on the campuses of the conventional universities during their long vacation. The reality of the amount of work required from students (14–15 hours per week over an academic year of at least 32 weeks) provided a harsh contrast with the myth that somehow in the University of the Air (as it was called in Harold Wilson's original terminology) a degree might be obtained by lolling in front of the television. Following the defeat of the Labour government in 1970 the Open University only narrowly escaped being killed off by the incoming Conservatives.

The founding Dean of the Arts Faculty, Professor John Ferguson, insisted that classical studies had a section in the Arts Foundation course. The main focus of this section was a study 'Which was Socrates?' for which students had to analyse a large collection of primary source material relating to Socrates.[1] The teaching offered by the university was and is extremely public and the TV programme which dramatised scenes from Aristophanes' *Clouds* caused a particular furore. Projected into people's living rooms at 6.30 p.m. the combination of Socrates hanging in a basket and scatological language offended traditional conceptions of the gravitas of classics and confirmed the worst suspicions about an upstart university which admitted students on demand rather than requiring formal qualifications. Letters of protest appeared in the broadsheet newspapers.[2]

From 1972, students were able to progress from the Foundation courses to higher levels in order to complete their degrees. These included two classical studies courses, *The Early Roman Empire and the Rise of Christianity* and then *Greece 478–336 BC*. Both included material on the historical and intellectual context and the close study of a small number of canonical texts (such as Tacitus, Juvenal, the *Oresteia*, or selected books from Thucydides).[3] At this stage in the development of the Arts Faculty the emphasis was on the production of interdisciplinary period-based courses which were thought to offer a rounded education to adult students and the rationale for classical studies was that it fitted into that profile. All texts were read in translation and there was little effort to develop students' awareness of the Greek or Latin languages. It was commonly held that students would be anxious if told that translation was a problematic concept; better to let them admire uncritically the expertise of those who worked from the original languages.

---

[1] J. Ferguson (ed.), *Socrates: A Source Book* (Macmillan, 1970).
[2] This makes an interesting contrast with the position thirty years later when almost any production of Greek drama, however aesthetically flawed, is welcomed by classicists and traditionalists alike as a sign that the genre is still thriving.
[3] As a youthful part-time tutor on the course I contacted my supervisor to complain about what I considered to be an over-simplification of Stoic ideas. My comments were sent (unexpurgated) to the course author. I was invited to Milton Keynes to explain my ideas for improvement of the course.

The second phase – controversy and radical rethinking

The presence of classical studies in the course profile was perceived to be the result of a decanal fiat and when John Ferguson left the university in 1978 the position of classical studies was severely threatened. A new course, *Rome: the Augustan Age*, was then on the drawing board and barely survived attempts to suppress it (it became one of the Faculty's most successful courses ever and in its last year, 1992, recruited over 2,000 students). There were several reasons for the unpopularity of classical studies with the university decision-makers at that time. One reason was logistical. The Arts Faculty had grown quite rapidly and there was competition for the much-prized 'slots' for the presentation of new courses. The larger disciplines, such as History and Literature, wished to extend their empires further – and more courses meant the likelihood of more staff (and thus more votes at the Faculty Board). There was also a perception – openly articulated outside the Arts Faculty and sometimes within it – that the study of classical subjects was part of an outmoded and socially exclusive approach to higher education and should form no part of an Open University curriculum. Conversely, it was also argued that since the classical contribution to the Arts BA degree was quite small and did not include study of the languages it did not really deserve the description 'classical' and might bring the Faculty into disrepute.

At several points it seemed that these unholy alliances would win. Classical academics had to grow armour-plated skins and tenacity. However, the classicists did get crucial support from some colleagues in other disciplines and from classicists in other areas of the university. *Rome: the Augustan Age* duly appeared on schedule, followed by its Hellenic twin *Fifth Century Athens: City State and Democracy*. These courses provided important options in the BA degree during the 1980s and proved very popular with students. Both courses, however, had to overcome a further problem. The Arts Faculty refused to include a classical studies component in successive Foundation courses. This meant that at post-Foundation level no previous knowledge of classical subjects could be assumed and names, geography, methods and texts had to be taught from scratch (the only reasonable assumption could be that students progressing from Foundation level had university-level study skills of a generic kind). However, this apparent difficulty proved to have considerable benefits. The classical studies staff developed careful strategies for teaching the critical use of sources to inexperienced students and had to think more imaginatively about raising awareness of the subject and in particular how to make classical study more accessible to a new generation of students, many of whom had previously been unaware of its existence. A new course, *Homer: Poetry and Society* (presented from 1993), was designed to provide an effective follow-on from Foundation level. Its sections on archaeology and on Homeric refigurations in twentieth-century literature opened up the subject for new constituencies of students and helped them to make links between different subject areas in their degree study. At this point, too, Open University classical studies was receiving considerable encouragement from the classics community nationally.

The language gamble

Until the late 1980s Open University students had no opportunity to begin or return to the study of Greek or Latin. There was, however, evidence of considerable interest from students, mainly because they were so excited by the works they were reading in translation that they wished to read them in the original. The Arts Faculty resisted investment in language courses and in the staff needed to produce them, claiming (not unreasonably) that such courses would attract only small numbers of students and thus not be economically viable. It was therefore decided to develop some schemes of collaboration in which Open University students could enrol for languages courses at other universities and count any course credits obtained towards their OU degrees. Again there was opposition within the university and again the arguments were paradoxical. One set of opponents claimed that it was not academically respectable to allow students to *begin* the study of a language at university. These people were reminded that most academics researching in Hebrew, Sanskrit and other ancient languages had not studied them at school and that many other universities had instituted *ab initio* courses in Greek (and some in Latin also). A contrasting body of opinion held that classical languages were too difficult to be successfully tackled by adult students learning at a distance. To these it was pointed out that such beliefs undermined the principles of the Open University. In the usual spirit of academic compromise (and with the active support of the then Dean of the Faculty Joan Bellamy), a pilot scheme was authorised. A small number of students began to benefit from language teaching at the University of Warwick (which also developed an Open Learning route so that students could enrol wherever they lived) and at campus-based courses at Keele and University College London. The support of the classical departments at these universities, and especially the work of Stanley Ireland, Richard Wallace and Bob Sharples, established precedents on which the Open University could build.

The progress of the language students was carefully monitored and it became clear that mature students were just as likely to show aptitude for the languages as were conventional-age undergraduates. They also had the motivation to progress, some to outstanding performances at honours level. It also turned out that Greek was even more popular than Latin. Nevertheless, the numbers of students that could be accepted on collaborative schemes was small and most students really wanted the Open University system of course materials they could study at home in their own time with local tutorial support.

By 1993 classical studies in the Open University was sufficiently recognised to be made an independent department. This gave the subject a secure strand in the BA degree profile and was accompanied by a small increase in staffing. The next step was to introduce *ab initio* courses in classical languages into the Faculty curriculum. With the active support of the Dean, Professor Tim Benton (to whose energy and far-sightedness the department owed a great deal), classical studies took advantage of university provision for 'fast track' production of unusual courses and in 1997 *Reading Classical Greek* began, followed in 2000 by *Reading Classical Latin*. The production of these courses was preceded by detailed consultation with other universities and with members of the Joint Association of Classical Teachers. In each case it was decided to use existing teaching texts (*Reading Greek* and *Reading Latin* respectively), augmented by study guides and audiocassettes produced by the Open University. Here the principle was not merely economy (although it would have taken massive investment to produce a new course from scratch and the time scale would not have met the terms of the university's 'fast track' scheme) but also suitability. Both *Reading Greek* and *Reading Latin* had demonstrated their capacity to help students to progress fairly quickly towards reading original texts (which was the major aim of most Open University students). They also had currency in that they were used successfully by many university departments. This would help Open University students who wished to progress to more advanced language work at other universities by giving a benchmark against which their achievement could be measured.

Everyone, including the classical studies department, was staggered by the enrolment for these courses. In its first five years the Greek course regularly enrolled in the region of 500 students each year; the Latin course population varied between 700 and 900 each year. As expected, the student body initially included some students who had studied classical languages years before at school (usually Latin) but recruitment broadened to include many with no previous experience of studying an inflected language. The course teams responded to the needs of these students by producing 'Getting Started' leaflets to give help with basic grammar and encourage students to recognise and develop vocabulary links with English. An experimental series of interactive exercises to help students learn the Greek alphabet and form simple words was made available on the department's web page in summer 2002, freely available to all visitors to the site.

Expansion and consolidation

From the late 1990s classical studies also received a further boost from its participation in a new Arts first-level course, *Introducing the Humanities*. The course aimed to introduce new students to all the subjects taught in the Arts Faculty. Classical studies contributed sections on both Greek and Roman studies. These included a source-based investigation of the Colosseum and a study of Greek drama (*Medea*). Both these areas lend themselves to integrating study of the ancient world with modern debates on social and ethical issues so that students understand both the strangeness and the familiarity of classical culture. As a result, an increasing number of students went on to register for the higher-level classical studies courses and in addition to the 5,000-plus students taking the Arts introductory course about 4,000 students each year enrolled for the classical studies programme, making the subject one (together with literature) of the two most popular in the Arts Faculty. The classical studies profile was given additional breadth and depth with the enlargement of the courses on fifth-century Athens and the production of additional courses in Roman Studies (*The Roman Family*, an advanced project course, and *Culture, Identity and Power in the Roman Empire*). The enlargement of the classical studies profile enabled students to major in classical studies as part of a named degree and the move towards inclusion of more advanced work culminated in the introduction of the taught MA in Classical Studies in 2001. The MA consisted of a module teaching research skills, a special subject module on the Greek theatre and a dissertation. It provided a recommended bridge for students wishing to move on to a research degree.

Teaching and research

The department has a special commitment to part-time research students who work on a wide range of doctoral subjects and often benefit from having academics in other classical departments as co-supervisors. In addition to the individual research of its full-time academics the department also developed two larger group projects.

These were on the Arts and Society in the Later Roman Empire (including a major excavation in Carthage) and the Reception of Greek Texts and Images in Modern Drama and Poetry. The research of its part-time associate lecturers was also supported, especially through research associateships.

Like all other classical departments, the Open University underwent Subject Review by the QAA (Quality Assurance Agency) and in 2001 was awarded the maximum score under all heads (24). The reviewers' report commented on the commitment of the students and excellence of much of the work and on the qualities of the large body of associate lecturers (132 at that time) who undertake the seminar teaching all round the country and are responsible for supervising students' written work. The university's commitment to promoting excellence in teaching was also marked by its appointment in 2000 to host the national work in classics and ancient history for the Learning and Teaching Support Network. The LTSN is funded by the four Higher Education Funding Councils in England, Scotland, Wales and Northern Ireland. Its twenty-four subject centres are based in higher education institutions throughout the UK and it aims to enhance the status and excellence of university teaching and learning through promoting the dissemination of good practices and enhancing the quality of debate and development.

The work of the LTSN in classics and ancient history has been supported by close consultation with the subject associations, especially the Council of University Classical Departments and the Hellenic and Roman Societies and by extensive liaison with individual academics and departments and with its formal Advisory Panel which consists of classicists and ancient historians and includes members from all career stages. In addition to organising regional and national conferences on key issues in teaching and learning, LTSN classics and ancient history has also aimed to provide a forum for debate on strategic issues and to reach out to part-time lecturers and graduate teaching assistants. It provides small grants for teaching development and through its website publishes case studies and briefing papers contributed by academics. In this way it aims to establish a coherent practitioner-led body of literature on teaching and learning in classical subjects and its refereed publications of conference proceedings develop awareness of ways in which scholarship and practice bind research and teaching. Its underlying principle is to work towards the time when debate and exchange of ideas and approaches to teaching and learning will attain the same extent and depth that are taken for granted in subject-based research.[4]

---

[4] See further L. Hardwick, 'Classics and ancient history in the learning and teaching support network', *JACT Review,* 2nd series, no. 30 (2001), 5–7.

Challenges for the future

The major developments in the first ten years of the Open University from 1971 were the initial integration of classical studies into a broad-based interdisciplinary curriculum and the embedding of source analysis into study of the cultural history of the ancient world. The second ten years saw the overcoming of resistance to classical studies' role as a major Arts subject, a shift in the previous educational backgrounds of students and in their expectations of classical study and the beginnings of the development of language opportunities. The third ten-year period included a substantial expansion in student numbers, the development of language programmes and the move towards a named degree. The structure and content of the degree course became very similar to those of other universities. Yet by its nature the Open University also has to remain different from others. This is so not only in the need for course materials and study mechanisms suited to supported open learning and in its need to ensure a continuing supply of dedicated associate lecturers all over the country but also in its particular commitment to reach out to and provide opportunities for people for whom the Open University offers the only realistic possibility of discovering and studying classical subjects in higher education. There is also a need in the OU context to maintain the role of classical material in interdisciplinary courses. Nevertheless, because of the increasing alignment I have described, many of the challenges in the future development of curriculum and teaching are common to the Open University and other institutions. Three examples are discussed in the following sections:

Convergence between language and non-language courses

It is clear that language students in classical studies and ancient history can be motivated by linking their language work to other courses they study. There is a demand for learning strategies which, even at advanced beginners and intermediate levels, enable students to address key passages in original texts.[5] In courses which are read in translation, developments in the emerging discipline of translation studies enable students to compare different translations and thus encourage basic language awareness, especially in relation to key concepts and ideas. Research has shown that both classical and literature students benefit from reading glossed texts in which key words are kept in the original.[6] Furthermore, language and non-

---

[5] S. Phillippo, 'But that's not what it says! Using translations in beginners and intermediate Greek language teaching', in D. Fitzpatrick, L. Hardwick and S. Ireland (eds.), *Old Wine, New Bottles: Texts for Classics in a Changed Learning Environment at University* (Milton Keynes, 2002), 5–18; also electronically at www.hca.ltsn.ac.uk

[6] J. Parker, *Dialogic Education and the Problematics of Translation in Homer and Greek Tragedy* (Edwin Mellen Press, 2001).

language students alike need to be trained in the use of dictionaries and commentaries.[7] There is a demand for new kinds of commentaries that combine elementary linguistic help with university-level discussion of interpretation and evaluative criticism.[8]

Exploitation of ICT

As a learning medium, ICT can enable students to work independently and at their own pace in language learning and textual study. The Computer Assisted Text Reading project being developed in the University of Cambridge will, it is hoped, be licensed for use in other universities. This area will also be important for graduate students who need to achieve rapid competence in areas crucial for their research. ICT could combine with intensive summer schools as a fast-track medium.[9]

For Open University students and others electronic discussion groups and virtual seminars can add to opportunities for interacting with other students. For all students critical use of ICT can contribute to independent learning and reflective study.[10] The increasing importance of digitised research material needs to be followed by opening up student learning routes to such research collections. For Open University classical studies, the challenge is to build on these possibilities without excluding the older or poorer student who does not have ready access to reliable and fast computers (the latter may be a general problem for all universities). It is also necessary to think radically about how ICT can best be integrated with other learning tools and situations – classical studies is, after all, a humanistic discipline.

Outreach – raising aspirations

The Open University has a significant national role in providing opportunities for classical study for all who wish, wherever they live and whatever their previous educational background. It is clear from the OU experience in its foundation and introductory courses that 'learning through classics' has an important part to play in the intellectual development of all arts students, whether or not they go on to specialise in the subject.[11] Projects such as the Excellence in Cities scheme and other initiatives to encourage widening participation in higher education suggest that this is also the case

---

[7] J. Robson, 'Commentaries and post-beginners' language learning', in Fitzpatrick, Hardwick and Ireland, *Old Wine, New Bottles*, 51–9.
[8] C. Emlyn-Jones, 'Commentaries on philosophical texts', in Fitzpatrick, Hardwick and Ireland, *Old Wine, New Bottles*, 71–8.
[9] See further N. Humble in CUCD *Bulletin* 31 (autumn 2002).
[10] See L. Mitchell, 'Active and reflective learning', LTSN Briefing Paper (2002) (www.hca.ltsn.ac.uk).
[11] For discussion of the potential role of classical subjects in the new universities see Hardwick, 'Classics and ancient history' (see note 4 above).

with school-age students. Apart from its importance for cultural history, classical studies has a largely untapped potential to contribute to understanding of cultural exchange, comparative studies and popular culture and its interdisciplinary base can be developed to include these aspects.[12] The convergence between Open University courses and those in other universities must not be allowed to divert the attention of the OU department from its national role in outreach. It needs to consider radical approaches in curriculum development (including methods of language learning) in accordance with its founding aims. In the thirty years from 2003, classical studies in the Open University will need to increase its provision of advanced and post-graduate opportunities for part-time students but it will also need to continue to foster the grass roots of classical awareness through collaboration in national outreach programmes and through its advisory and induction programmes for new students.

---

[12] For discussion of the importance of interdisciplinarity in the developing classical curriculum, see S. Bassnett, 'Is there hope for the humanities in the 21st century?', *Arts and Humanities in Higher Education*, vol. 1 no. 1 (June 2002), 101–10.

19 | Twilight classics

Judith Affleck

Twilight /ˈtwaɪlaɪt/ n.
1. The soft glowing light from the sky when the sun is below the horizon, esp. in the evening. 2. The period of this. 3. A faint light.
4. A state of imperfect knowledge or understanding. 5. A period of decline or destruction.

Visiting the National Curriculum website for Britain in 2002 is a depressing experience for a classicist: thirteen brightly coloured buttons represent the subjects to be studied in schools and it will come as no surprise that none of these is for classics. A 'word search' on Latin results in two footnotes (Primary Literacy and Secondary Geography), three references to the Primary History Roman Case Study ('Why have people invaded and settled in Britain in the past?') and twelve to Latin America; Egyptians and Greeks get a look-in in primary schools, but at secondary level the only suggestion of classical learning is a history unit entitled 'From Aristotle to the Atom'; the Language button, entitled 'modern foreign languages', invites you to select Irish, Gujurati, Persian or Finnish (four of the twenty-five languages on offer), but no Latin or classical Greek. Ancient languages have no place in the critical years in which they were once absorbed so painfully or so easily, with such frustration or such delight.

Nevertheless, the study of classics remains important in many British schools, primarily, but not exclusively, in the private sector, where demand from parents, choice by pupils and freedom from government restraints have ensured its continuity. Two exam boards continue to offer GCSE, AS/A2 and AEA qualifications in classical subjects.[1] Scottish Highers and the increasingly popular International Baccalaureate also make good provision for classics at pre-university level. Entries from state schools are small,[2] but there are some that manage to fulfil the demands of the National Curriculum and still allow space for maintaining or developing a classical tradition within

---

[1] OCR and AQA; numbers, however, have plummeted: in 1965 33,396 students passed Latin O level and 6,012 A level (statistics quoted in *Didaskalos* vol. 2 no. 3 (1968), 163); in 2001 these numbers had dropped to 10,365 and 1,264 (number of candidates according to QCA; there were 774,364 A level candidates overall in 2000).
[2] There were only 310 state school candidates for A level Latin in 2001.

the curriculum. Many of these are Beacon Schools or Centres of Excellence.[3] In some cases Latin is offered explicitly as part of the school's provision for 'gifted and talented pupils'.[4] JACT is currently working on winning QCA[5] acceptance of 'grade descriptors' for Latin comparable with other National Curriculum criteria (see p. 116), and this, combined with recent initiatives allowing schools more autonomy, may help bring classics back into the curriculum.

Even when classics has a place within a school's curriculum, the tradition of teaching off the timetable is well established: at Harrow School (where I teach) Latin, Greek, classical civilisation and ancient history each have their place within the curriculum and yet 'twilight' teaching goes on all the time, for the boy who realises late that he wants to learn Greek, or for the musician who simply can't fit his chosen curriculum into the timetable. This 'Browning Version'[6] of teaching is rewarding, but it is time consuming and, even with a staff of five or six, wannabe classicists are sometimes disappointed. If this is the case in a school where classics is given such strong support,[7] it is inevitably true of smaller departments: between 1956 and 2001 E.F. Read at Southend High School for Boys taught Latin and ancient history, on his own in the latter stages of his career, in a school of about 850 pupils. Every single lesson slot was already taken, and so he taught Greek off the timetable. There is nothing unique about this example. This is the 'twilight classics' (or 'lunchtime classics') experienced by many classicists today just as it was by an army of those who have now put their lexicons away; stolen hours of half light and half-understanding in small numbers and odd corners. The shared commitment has often led the pupil to take the subject further. Many current classicists[8] educated since the subject came under severe attack (i.e. in post-war Britain) seem to have been fortified and, in some cases, kindled with missionary-like zeal by this sort of experience.

In this chapter I wish to consider the opportunities available for learning Latin and Greek to students who are not enabled to do so by their own school, on or off the timetable. I shall first consider the implications at tertiary level for someone who has not been exposed to classical languages at school.

---

[3] For example, St Anthony's Girls' School (Sunderland), Nower Hill High School, Harrow, Devonport High School for Girls and Kendrick School, Reading.
[4] For example, Beechen Cliff School.
[5] The Qualifications and Curriculum Authority.
[6] In Terence Rattigan's *The Browning Version*, Taplow is expected to turn up for extra help in Greek.
[7] Harrow School, for example, like most other Rugby Group schools, which were surveyed in 2002, permits tiny and 'uneconomical' divisions of A level Greek; the same survey revealed that many classics teachers voluntarily take on larger numbers of teaching periods than the average to keep the full range of classical subjects alive and healthy.
[8] The example of E.F. Read was affectionately recalled by J.D. Cooper, now Head of Classics at Summer Fields Preparatory School in Oxford.

No one wishing to study Egyptology at university would be expected to have learned hieroglyphics at his mummy's knee; you can start courses in Arabic or Persian at university with no prior experience and expect to leave three years later competent in both languages. Is classics any different? Traditionally it has been, but significant changes have taken place in recent years to widen the accessibility of classics at university: it is often possible, for example, to take a classics paper within a non-classics degree or as part of a joint honours course; all universities with classics departments now offer courses with *ab initio* language teaching in both Latin and Greek; even Oxford University, the biggest classics faculty in the UK, has recently introduced a new course which does not include any compulsory language-learning component.[9] There is plenty of opportunity in theory, therefore, for those who have not had the benefit of classics teaching at school to study some form of the subject at university. But it comes as no great surprise that the number of students opting for these courses is relatively small,[10] and that universities have a problem in making people aware not only of the existence of such courses, but also of their richness, diversity and value. The fact is that a vast number of people in Britain have no idea what 'classics' is. Of those who do, the number who have any confidence in its value or 'marketability' is even tinier. Universities in America and, in the UK, Scotland with arts foundation courses and established faculties have a great advantage in this respect because these courses give students the chance to make up their mind in an informed way. The gratifying statistics in Lorna Hardwick's chapter on the Open University might suggest that adults who have either got to know about the 'permanence' of classics through other subjects or for whom Latin was more of a household word recognise more readily the value of the opportunities on offer.[11]

An argument based on access and equality might suggest that tertiary level (possibly in conjunction with some exposure to Latin/classics at primary level) is the right place (if there is such a thing) for a classical education in the twenty-first century. Given the fact that far from every university has a classics faculty, there is still an element of inequity here: classics is likely simply to remain the prerogative of the rich or 'well informed' (i.e. middle classes).[12] Arguments based *only* on equality tend to have little to recommend

---

9 Classical Archaeology and Ancient History, introduced in 2000.
10 1,909 people enrolled on undergraduate classics courses in 1995/96. (Harriet Swain, 'What employers love the most', *THES* (29 August 1997).)
11 Although applications to read classical courses at university outnumber vacancies (in 1995–6 'by six to one': Swain, 'What employers love'), the numbers are nevertheless small.
12 A trend likely to be emphasised by 'top-up fees', if the threat of introducing these is realised in the next parliament.

them and this particular one is characteristic in being a knee-jerk response to an inequitable *status quo* rather than an educational argument. Here, then, are a few reasons for why classics *should* form part of the secondary curriculum. Not all are compelling individually, but collectively they seem to me to justify some sort of coordinated attempt to reverse the default 'policy' of the last fifty years.

1 **Developing literacy and linguistic skills**. Over half the words in our language derive from Latin;[13] understanding the original meaning of these words helps with spelling and precise usage; it also helps develop a vocabulary quickly when learning any other romance language; the fact that Latin is a highly regular inflected language means that learning Latin often provides a valuable analytical framework for approaching any other new language.

2 **Understanding man's place in the world**. Gaining a chronological and technological perspective on the history of mankind is important if we are to understand our own achievements and way of looking at the world. Recognising and learning to respect the similarities and differences between other people are vital elements of citizenship; the ancient world provides material that is stimulating, controversial and unlikely to cause any individual offence.

3 **Developing other analytical skills** (literary, historical, evidential). Classics involves a number of different disciplines, particularly linguistic, literary and historical: Latin and Greek are currently the only subjects at GCSE level which offer children a taste of literature in a language other than English. The fact that the creators of these ancient works were themselves highly self-conscious and allusive in their approaches makes their writing particularly well suited to developing critical skills. The quantity of material surviving, as well as the quality, creates evidential puzzles that appeal to a developing intellect.

4 **Challenging the bright**. Self-selection shows that the study of ancient Latin and Greek languages challenges the brightest: it is no accident that these subjects tend to be chosen at A level by high intellectual achievers.

5 **Firing the imagination**. Classics is now taught using a huge variety of approaches, which means it has something to offer everyone; the material and ideas encountered stimulate the

---

[13] An even higher percentage from classical roots, if Greek is also taken into account; much of this is technical scientific language. All the arguments that follow apply also to Greek.

imagination. The continued proliferation of popular films and books with debts to the classics, particularly those aimed at and loved by children, is evidence of the continued power of the classics to capture the imagination.[14] Once a child's interest has been caught, learning becomes more independent and effective.

6 **The classical continuum**. The western world has been nourished by the classics in almost every conceivable field, whether artistic, literary, philosophical or scientific. Like it or not, in order to understand the thought processes and appreciate the artistic and scientific achievements of the last five hundred years some acquaintance with the classics is essential. Learning about the past and living in the present are constantly enriched by familiarity with the classical world.

Classics is arguably unique in its holistic approach and in offering so compact an educational 'package'. Why should only a tiny percentage of the nation's children have access to it? Despite the reputation classics has acquired for élitism, at the beginning of the twenty-first century we can already look back on fifty years of rearguard action challenging the attack on classical learning within the curriculum. A good example can be seen in the efforts of Mr J.E. Hunt to block the tide of change in the early 1970s, found 'amazing' even by the energetic band of teachers at the ARLT's 49th annual summer school in 1972: he tried to thwart the fact that 'out of more than a hundred staff there was not one who supported Latin' by introducing a dynamic mixture of Greek and Greek civilisation at Westfield School in Sheffield (formerly Eckington Grammar; it became a comprehensive school in 1967), concluding that 'such a course will be the most effective weapon in the assault upon a barbarian world'.[15]

This chapter is in part a celebration of what has been achieved by people with the vision, passion and energy to fight the squeeze on classics. I shall focus on three areas in particular: the role of residential schools, recent developments for distance learning in ICT and community-based projects; it also, of necessity, offers a familiar but urgent warning about the darkness falling over the study of classics in schools. Not only is classics no longer taught in Westfield School. According to government statistics, only one person from a comprehensive school took A level Greek in 2001.

---

[14] A few examples: *Asterix, Gladiator; Harry Potter* and the *His Dark Materials* trilogy (both of which are steeped in the classics); prime-time TV documentaries on life as a Spartan or Roman legionary; interactive computer games; projected movies: Wolfgang Petersen's *Troy* (an adaptation of the *Iliad*) with Brad Pitt as Achilles and Baz Luhrmann's Alexander the Great epic starring Leonardo DiCaprio.
[15] *Latin Teaching* XXIV no. 3 (November 1972), 354–8 and 369.

Residential schools

It was to combat the alarming fall in numbers studying Greek at school that the first JACT Greek summer school (now located at Bryanston School in Dorset) was set up in 1968 by the newly formed JACT Greek committee. The principal aim was to teach Greek to beginners.[16] In practice, since the summer school's birth there has always been a healthy contingent of more advanced students who have benefited from the intensive experience and from meeting others studying this increasingly isolated subject. In 2002, 75 of the 253 students were complete beginners and over a quarter of students came from state schools. There has been a steady increase over the last ten years in numbers overall, in the numbers attending from state schools and in the numbers of beginners (in 1993, 38 of the 231 students came from state schools and 50 were beginners); the percentage of beginners has also been gradually increasing (22 per cent in 1993, 30 per cent in 2002). Other classical summer schools have also tried to target those who have not had the opportunity to study a classical language in school: in 1995 at the fifteenth JACT Latin summer school (now located at Wells Cathedral School in Somerset) there was an initiative to encourage state-school beginners, funded by Cambridge University (the Arthur Henry Thomas Fund) and Friends of the Classics. Although in its first year it attracted only one student, within five years it was necessary to create two groups. This is not the only classical summer school now to succeed in attracting more state than independent school students.[17]

The great problem, of course, with a summer school is that, while the experience may be intensive and stimulating – an opportunity to spend a week or fortnight studying what it might take a term or even a year to cover in school – the momentum is very difficult to sustain, and for beginners it is likely to be little more than a kick-start. One summer school that has addressed this problem head-on is the Rowley Regis College Latin summer school in the West Midlands, now approaching its thirtieth year. This offers follow-up lessons and aims to enable students to take GCSE Latin within two years. This ambitious programme is clearly challenging (and not only to the students!) and seems to offer a particularly valuable service by working through feeder schools; it is also advertised through the government's Excellence in Cities web page. Other residential schools, like the more exclusive Madingley Hall[18] courses for adults, reduce the problem of discontinuity by using weekend courses, a structure better suited to working adults, but gruelling nonetheless. The growth in the number of

---

[16] 32 of the original 52 students in 1968 were beginners.
[17] Another example is the JACT classical civilisation and ancient history summer school held at Repton.
[18] The home of the University of Cambridge's Institute of Continuing Education http://www.cont.ed.cam.ac.uk

summer schools over the last few decades, not only in classical languages but also in ancient history and classical civilisation, is testament to a demand for classical teaching; it is also witness to the dynamism of a number of highly committed teachers and to the vision of several vital grant-giving bodies. Whether by offering accommodation (as University College London has to the London Summer School), free entrance to sites (British Heritage) or generous grants to those who could not otherwise attend a residential course, the desire to keep classics alive and accessible is fierce, particularly among a great many of those who have had the privilege of studying it for themselves.

ICT and distance learning

It is only about fifteen years since computers started making a significant impact on schools, education and people's homes. During that time a wide range of initiatives in teaching and learning classics has been pioneered (see David Goodhew's chapter on ICT). There are now electronic texts, vocabulary testers and grammar drills available,[19] all of which, in theory, facilitate independent learning. In the USA you can learn Latin on the web through complete distance-learning programmes such as the one provided by KET,[20] and a British site maintained by Dr Neil Croally of Dulwich College now offers online assistance for those wanting to take GCSEs or A levels in classical subjects.[21]

A most important distance-learning initiative is currently being developed in Britain by the Cambridge Schools Classics Project, creators of the Cambridge Latin Course, in conjunction with Granada Media and Cambridge University Press. The Cambridge Online Latin Project (COLP), a DfEE/DfES initiative, is still in its developmental stage, but superb materials are being created and tested in partnership with a number of state schools in Britain, most of which do not currently offer Latin. The project makes use of a wide range of cutting-edge technology, for example video linking and message-boarding. It is hoped eventually to make the materials as widely available as possible, particularly within the state sector. Details of this initiative which aims 'to broaden … accessibility by the use of electronic media, including the internet and interactive materials' can be found on the project's website[22] and on pages 113–14 and 143 of this volume.

---

[19] For example The Perseus Project; the materials produced by Julian Morgan; Dr Flynn's *Latin without Tears* program; the Eton Greek Project, developed by Eton College in conjunction with OUP.
[20] Kentucky Educational Television (www.ket.org) provides distance-learning support in Latin, German and physics.
[21] www.latin-uk-online.com
[22] http://www.cambridgescp.com/cscpp/colp/colpaims.html

Community-based projects

It is a widely held belief that learning is best achieved (and assessed) through personal contact; that the computer will never replace the teacher (see Marion Gibbs' chapter, p. 38). Only time will expose this shibboleth, if it is one. In the meantime, the fact that people believe it helps to make it true. One of the reasons why community-based projects can be so effective, particularly when combined with good support materials, whether an attractive course book like *Minimus* or electronic resources like those of the COLP, is that there is personal contact. A full account of the heartening growth of Latin at primary level in Barbara Bell's chapter offers a number of models for this sort of teaching – models that need not apply only at primary level.

Initiatives stemming from a number of school departments have been proving successful, whether by sharing teaching resources between schools or by trying to reach out into the community. My area of north-west London provides a modest example: a group of Latin teachers has joined forces to offer Saturday morning *Minimus* classes to a small but committed group of nine to eleven year-olds with a view to helping them take the subject to GCSE and beyond if they wish. Harrow is an interesting case study: 'one of London's most attractive suburbs', it is a prosperous borough with a population of about 220,000; currently it has a system of first, middle and high schools; sixteen-plus students go on to one of three sixth-form colleges. Two high schools offer Latin to GCSE,[23] but since Harrow College closed down the option of Latin to the eight students who had expressed interest in 1999 (on the basis of insufficient numbers!) and made its classics specialist redundant, there has been no provision for A level Latin in the borough. In the last three years a partnership between Harrow School and St Dominic's Sixth Form College has made it possible for students to join Latin classes at Harrow School. Five students have so far emerged with AS or A2 qualifications in Latin and two have gone on to study straight or joint honours classics at university. This partnership, which has proved relatively straightforward because of the proximity of the two schools and the flexibility of the timetable in a large sixth-form college, has brought great mutual benefit. The long-term objective of the Harrow 'LEO Project'[24] was to make Latin available to anyone in the borough who wished to learn it. It currently falls far short of that aim for two reasons: one is the difficulty of raising public awareness of the courses; the other more pressing (and related) problem is teacher time. A similar project set up by a group of teachers in Leeds has gone some way towards solving one of these difficulties by using classics students

---

[23] Nower Hill High School, Rook's Heath.
[24] Founded in 1999; the acronym stands for 'Latin for Every-One'.

from the university; at Dartmouth Grammar School sixth-form pupils have also been encouraged to help at primary level. A number of current government initiatives are in sympathy with projects like these: here, it seems, is a genuine opportunity for 'public–private partnership'; for links between universities and the community; for ways of stretching the 'gifted and talented'; an opportunity for specialisation in schools that want to diversify and offer something to the community which is not otherwise available. The climate is potentially favourable for some sort of limited classical renaissance in schools, but what are the chances of this actually happening?

There are two critical factors that must be addressed if there is to be any chance of redressing the situation in schools. This, of course, must be *in addition* to the traditional types of trench warfare at which classicists have excelled: producing exciting and appropriate new courses,[25] teaching imaginatively, showing resourcefulness in combating economic arguments, adaptability, tenacity.

Teacher shortage

The more alarming of these two factors is teacher recruitment. 'There are very, very few Latin teachers around, and those who are seem to be getting on a bit, being polite,' as one punter delicately put it.[26] Currently the demand for classics teachers exceeds the number of teachers available: around 125 classics jobs were advertised in last year's *Times Educational Supplement*; a survey conducted by Bob Lister of Cambridge University suggested that at least 31 of these posts became available because of a retirement, about the same number as completed a PGCE in 2002. What this does not take into account is numbers leaving the profession owing to illness and other factors: this brings the figure of those stepping down from the profession in 2002 to approximately 46. Classics teacher training now takes place only at Cambridge University, King's College London, and Strathclyde University. St Mary's, Twickenham was the victim of the most recent cuts, and, before that, Nottingham University, which provided some opportunity for training outside the south and east of England.[27] Numbers are currently limited more by available training places than by candidates, despite the fact that teaching in the early twenty-first century is hardly perceived as a glamorous profession; prohibitive costs of accommodation intensify the difficulties of finding suitable training schools since students may have

---

[25] Courses like the Cambridge Latin Course, *Ecce Romani*, the Oxford Latin Course, *Athenaze*, *Reading Greek*; readers like *Aestimanda, The Millionaire's Dinner Party*, the *Cambridge Latin Anthology*, the *Oxford Latin Reader*, JACT's *Intellectual Revolution* and *World of Heroes*, etc.
[26] Student's view, quoted in the BBC website's news page under Education (Summer 2002).
[27] Of course, some classics teachers still enter the profession without a PGCE and either remain technically unqualified or train on the job. Henry Wickham's article in *JACT Review* (Spring 2003) gives an inspiring account of how this can be done.

to find accommodation not only near the training faculty, but also within reach of their training school if their teaching practice is distant from their place of study. The small number of schools with classics departments also creates difficulties. ('In 1984 there were still 3,400 full-time teachers teaching classics in maintained secondary schools and sixth form colleges. By 1992 this had fallen to 1,000.' [28]) In effect, a head teacher or governors may be unable to appoint a suitable person to an advertised post, however eager he, she or they may be to increase the amount of classics in a school. It is interesting to see that the USA is facing a similar crisis and that steps are being taken there to guard against a dangerous future: a National Latin Teacher Recruitment Week has been organised by the National Committee for Latin and Greek in conjunction with the American Classical League (ACL), the American Philological Association (APA) and various regional organisations to make up for deficiencies in numbers like those in the UK. Retraining is a prime strategy in the USA for recruiting Latin teachers.

Decreasing awareness of classics

The second growing problem is an increasing lack of awareness of the existence of the subject: the generation who had to take Latin in order to enter university is now beyond retirement age. Not all were necessarily fans of the subject (my father had to retake Schools Certificate Latin twice in order to study chemistry at university) or of the way they were taught it, but on the whole they had a grudging respect for what they learned from it and at least they had heard of it! Conversations with parents of children in the independent sector suggest that conservatism has been a major factor in keeping classics going amongst the upper-middle classes. The inclusion of some classics in Key Stages 2 and 3 may yet prove significant in raising national awareness that history extends back well beyond the First World War, King Henry VIII and even the Norman Conquest.

The fight over the body of classics is not over yet,[29] but strategies to combat its loss in schools need beefing up. I shall close by discussing two possible directions which could help to establish a brighter future for the subject.

Sponsorship?

There is much anecdotal evidence to suggest that top employers like

---

[28] Nick Tate, 'Ancient foundation courses', *THES* (19 May 1995).
[29] A view shared by Nick Tate, former chief executive of QCA: 'But is it too late to reverse the decline of classics? I think not. The position of Latin in some European countries, notably France, Italy and Spain, is much stronger than in England. This is true even where, as in England, Latin is an optional subject: in Germany, for example, 14 per cent of pupils take Latin. What happens there could happen here too, if there is a will.' Tate, 'Ancient foundation courses'.

graduates in classics, and that classics graduates are amongst the (if not the) most employable type of graduate.[30] The response attributed to an international petroleum company in answer to the question of why they were pleased to appoint classics graduates ('because they sell more oil') is a good example. Interestingly, a significant amount of money has been made available for classics at university level by the Leverhulme Trust in recent years;[31] could private sponsorship for classical 'Centres of Excellence' help some struggling departments to survive or even expand? Classics teachers might be able to serve a wider community if their skills were better coordinated.

As is abundantly clear from elsewhere in this volume, a great many exciting individual initiatives in classics are being pioneered in Britain today. But how far is there a coherent national strategy in place? Is the wheel being reinvented in a number of different corners? From where should such a strategy emerge – the DfES? JACT? the Classical Association? the universities? – and how might it look? Regional models, perhaps, based around the universities? Clusters of schools[32] or independently established centres?[33] Some sort of centralised advertising? One thing that seems certain is that initiatives too dependent upon individuals – like that of Mr J.E. Hunt – or small groups – perhaps like the LEO Project – are likely to founder and prove ephemeral.

---

[30] A recent study of graduates' first destinations showed people who had studied classics were less likely to be unemployed in the first six months after leaving university than those from any other subject. (Quoted in Swain, 'What employers love'.)
[31] Durham and Exeter universities have been able to make additional appointments.
[32] This model has been pioneered by the Jack Hunt School, Peterborough, with local Beacon Schools.
[33] A short-lived initiative along these lines was started in Clifton by the then chairman of governors of Clifton School, Andrew Thornhill QC.

20 | Classics and museums

Richard Woff

Museums have always been educational in some sense and thus they have been educational within the field of classics for as long as classical artefacts have been collected and displayed.[1] The collections of Greek and Roman material in the eighteenth and the nineteenth centuries were dominated by sculpture and vases. They provided essential resources for the education of artists and architects who in turn used their styles and motifs to communicate the cultural authority of the classical. In this period – and for most of the twentieth century too – access to a classical education was severely hierarchical and the opportunities afforded by museum collections for the demonstration and development of cultural knowledge certainly contributed to the broad processes of social and cultural distinction which operated through education.[2] However, the textual and linguistic nature of the classical curriculum meant that museums had little role to play in school classics.

This situation was not typical of the way in which the role of museums was being defined. As the nineteenth century progressed, museums and art galleries were increasingly seen as tools for social and cultural improvement. Many non-governmental educational institutions such as Mechanics' Institutes combined libraries, classrooms and museums.[3] The Museums Act of 1845 was motivated to a large extent by the belief that local museums could play an important role both in teaching the lower classes utilitarian skills and principles of self-improvement and in rendering them more civilised and enlightened. The first great age of museum education for schools began in the late nineteenth century when the transformational power of museums was harnessed to the new schools created by the Education Act of 1870. Museums were established with provision directed specifically at children, with pedagogies based on objects and material culture, with museum teachers and with boxes of specimens

---

[1] Adults have always been the main target audience of most museums. While there is much to say about how adults engage with classical collections in museums, the focus of this article is on school students. Nevertheless, my views about the use of a more varied and adventurous pedagogy in museums are as relevant to the formal education of adults as they are to that of young people.
[2] For a full and stimulating discussion of these processes see Christopher Stray, *Classics Transformed: Schools, Universities and Society in England 1830–1960* (Oxford University Press, 1998).
[3] See Eilean Hooper-Greenhill, *Museum and Gallery Education* (Leicester University Press, 1991) for a fuller account of the history of museum education.

and objects which could be loaned to schools. Such provision continued into the twentieth century in spite of a loss of momentum suffered after the end of the First World War due to an increased emphasis on research and academic interests. As yet, of the many educational programmes and projects that can be identified during this period, I have found none which deals with the classical world.

There were certainly changes taking place in the nature of classical education at the end of the nineteenth century. The reform of the Cambridge Tripos in 1879 led to the inclusion of the study of archaeology along with myth and religion, and in 1884 the Museum of Classical Archaeology was founded to house a collection of casts for use as illustrations in lectures. In 1880 the Keeper of Greek and Roman Antiquities at the British Museum was also appointed the first professor of classical archaeology at University College, London and in 1885 a professorship of classical archaeology was created at Oxford. A glimpse of attempts to cascade this reform into schools is revealed by the address given to the Headmasters' Conference in 1900 by the first professor of classical archaeology at Oxford, Percy Gardner, who argued forcefully for teaching archaeology in order to enliven and broaden classics.[4] Sadly such attempts failed and classics went on to redefine its purpose more in terms of mental discipline than cultural enlightenment. It is not as if the museum resources were not available to support this broader concept of classics: apart from the art-historical displays of classical art, in 1908 a Greek and Roman Life Room was opened at the British Museum to exhibit material from the classical world not as art objects, but as documents of social and cultural history.

By the late 1960s, the landscape of education as a whole was changing and the value of museums and other out-of-school experiences was also being re-asserted. This change did not exclude classics teachers. Both the linguistic and non-linguistic materials produced by the Cambridge School Classics Project emphasised the need to introduce children to the actual remains of the classical world through the use of museum collections. Such initiatives were reflected in teacher education courses, for example at Bristol and at the University of London Institute of Education, where John Sharwood Smith developed an innovative cross-curricular museums option in partnership with the education departments at the British Museum and other London museums. Three factors seem to have contributed to the development of this museums option. The first and most general was a broad, holistic conception of the curriculum in which the education of eye and hand was as important as the nurturing of the

---

[4] See Stray, *Classics Transformed*, 205–7.

cognitive and linguistic.[5] The second was a belief in the need to challenge the heavily text-based approach to the study of the past. In the case of classics, this meant providing young people with an understanding of the whole of the classical world, in which the literary texts took their place alongside art, artefacts and the built and natural environments. Finally, the reorganisation of secondary education meant that classics had to be made accessible to all young people, not just those in selective schools. The study of visual and material sources offered additional and alternative gateways into the ancient world for those students who found it difficult to access that world solely through the written word. These three dimensions remain as relevant to classics teachers now as they were thirty years ago.

The introduction of the National Curriculum after 1988 marked a sea change in the relationship between schools and museums in that its requirements endorsed and recommended the use of museums. However, the results of the Dearing review of 1995 rendered the change even more profound for classics by removing the Roman empire as a core unit at Key Stage 3. The effect of this was to transfer the principal onus for public education about the Greek and Roman worlds from secondary to primary schools. The continuing presence of Greece and Roman Britain in the Key Stage 2 programmes of study means that all children in state education, and probably the majority in private schools, engage in some study of both the classical cultures before the age of 11. For all but the tiniest minority of these children, that is the sum total of their experience of the classical world in formal education. That Greece and Rome featured in the National Curriculum orders certainly owed much to the persistence of the classical lobby. However, the success of establishing classics firmly in the primary curriculum was followed up with surprisingly little practical support in the world of classics education. The sole exceptions were the projects coordinated by Martin Forrest in Bristol and a series of six pamphlets published by JACT in 1989 and 1991 while the programmes of study were being developed.[6] The resources and training needed by the thousands of primary teachers who were now required to teach Greece and Rome, but who had no background in classics, were left entirely to history specialists in universities and local education authorities, to publishers and to museums.

The response from museums was prompted not by any crusading

---

[5] A seminal text for Sharwood Smith was Renée Marcousé, *Using Objects: Visual Awareness and Visual Learning in the Museum and Classroom* (Van Nostrand Reinhold, 1974). An education officer at the Victoria and Albert Museum, Marcousé was more concerned with material culture as aesthetic, experiential and expressive than as an ethnographic or historical document.
[6] The series was *Themes: The Use of the Classical World in the National Curriculum for Primary Schools*. It was edited by Wendy Hawkin, a practising primary school teacher, and Lesley Bedford-Forde, tutor in classics at St Mary's College, Strawberry Hill.

zeal on behalf of classics, but by the need to deal with a crisis. The impact of the National Curriculum's expectation that schools make use of museums was huge and immediate. In just two years, the number of primary visits received by the British Museum tripled and then continued to grow steadily until the museum is now at saturation point for visits to the Egyptian and Greek collections. Museums all over the country experienced the same expansion of demand which they catered to as best they could given their staffing and resource levels. Museums created direct teaching programmes for primary groups, developed teacher packs to support visits conducted by teachers, offered teachers training in how to use the collections and where possible produced resources for use in the classroom – these might be photographs of museum objects or actual objects as, for example, in the excellent loans provision still offered by Reading Museums Service. In spite of the flexibility permitted by Curriculum 2000, museums continue to register very high rates of visit for Ancient Greece, to the extent that even museums with only tiny collections of Greek material try to make it available for use by children in either displays or handling sessions. Romano-British museums and sites such as Chester, Colchester, Vindolanda and Verulamium also cater for very large numbers of visits from primary schools. Thus museums continue to provide the only non-commercial classics-specific training and resources for primary school teachers working within the mainstream of curricular provision.[7]

Up to now, museum educators have had to deal with the most pressing demands and those have stemmed from primary schools. Visits from secondary schools are at a much lower level. There are a number of reasons for this, including the greater formality and text-based nature of secondary education, the logistics of organising visits by whole year groups from large comprehensives and the extent to which head teachers and other staff are willing to tolerate the extraction of classes or groups from a more fragmented timetable. These are problems shared by all subjects in the secondary curriculum. Different museums have responded in different ways depending on the subjects for which they are most suited. However, classics is a subject which, more than most others, depends for its survival on the commitment and motivation of its students. In the past classics teachers were able to take advantage of a more flexible school context

---

[7] I refer here to resources and training targeted at the classical aspects of the programme of study rather than those for history in general which happen to use classical examples. The Cambridge School Classics Project's current *Iliad* Project coordinated by Grant Bage and Bob Lister may rectify this situation somewhat. The *Minimus* project, while having a relationship with the programme of study, focuses too much on Latin to be able to meet the needs of the majority of teachers and children working at Key Stage 2.

to use trips outside school to distinguish their subject from others and to motivate potential students. A hierarchy of curricular value from core to foundation to non-National Curriculum coupled with tighter requirements for accountability threatens what is in any case a high-risk strategy.

The risk in seeing a museum visit as primarily motivational is that it can tend to separate learning from pleasure, conceiving them implicitly as at opposite ends of a linear scale rather than as mutually independent variables.[8] Such a separation debilitates teachers by depriving them of their usual motivational tools, that is their teaching abilities, and forcing them back on vague beliefs that museums are valuable because they offer a change of environment and a chance to see the real thing. Unfortunately, what really motivates students about trips is seldom congruent with these underdeveloped aspirations. Classics teachers are not alone in this predicament. They share the same problem with secondary teachers in other subjects and with primary teachers. What is needed is for teachers in general to integrate motivation and learning in order to substantiate their claims for the value of museum visits. By and large teachers have all the skills they need in order to improve their visits, but are simply not exploiting them.

The main problem here is lack of confidence. Museums are daunting places for teachers and in the past this has not been helped by the attitude of museum staff and the lack of facilities suitable for use by schools.[9] Museums are full of objects about which teachers may feel they know little. The information the museums provide is often not what the teacher needs to know in order to make use of the objects for teaching. Where the teacher has taken the trouble to learn a lot about the objects, other factors get in the way of that knowledge being used effectively. In museums, teachers are outside their normal environment; they do not have their usual control over students' experiences and reactions; their students' and their own behaviour is under scrutiny from other visitors and from museum staff. A common response to these pressures is to base the visit on tightly structured worksheets or to take the students round on a tour or to combine a bit of both. Such a response, as well as attempts to react against it by setting students free to experience the exhibits in an unstructured way, tend to result in similar degrees of withdrawal and boredom. Here lies the irony: museum educators seldom see teachers employing any of the wealth of

---

[8] See Alan J. Friedman, 'Differentiating science-technology centers from other leisure-time enterprises', *Association of Science-Technology Centers Newsletter* (Jan/Feb 1986).
[9] Fortunately, the situation has changed considerably over recent years. Many museums now have lunch-rooms, cloakrooms and toilets for schools, and museum staff are becoming more aware of their importance in ensuring not only that the objects are safe, but that visitors have a positive experience in the museum.

pedagogical techniques they use in the classroom despite the fact that most of these would not disrupt the experience for other visitors and would greatly enhance the experience for the students.[10]

A key factor in releasing teachers' own potential is for them to re-conceptualise the museum itself. Rather than seeing museums as completely separate institutions from their schools with separate though vaguely worthwhile agendas, teachers might try to see them more as a different classroom, albeit one at some remove from the school instead of just along the corridor, and with a stock of resources that are not available in the usual room – not unlike the ICT Room![11] A change of classroom does not usually involve a rupture in the progress and direction of students' learning; teachers do not usually sacrifice teaching methods to control methods; they do not suddenly abandon the sorts of techniques and resources they usually use in class; they do not assume that the encounters in the new classroom cannot be carried forward into the next lesson in the usual room; they do not presume that the students will enjoy the lesson because of something other than the quality of their teaching. This is not to say that teachers do not need to make some modifications to the way they work in museums compared with classrooms, but that unless they serve some special purpose, the modifications need not be extreme. For example, if a teacher would find a whiteboard helpful to gather students' ideas in a classroom, there is no need to abandon that technique in a museum. There are alternatives such as large sheets of paper bulldog-clipped to a piece of hardboard or post-it notes and file cards on which students' views can be recorded, shared and taken back to school and sharing in the following lesson.

As with any lesson, teaching methods depend on the aims and intended outcomes of the lesson, which both affect the teacher's choice of resources and are affected by the range of resources available. It is here that the variety of audiences and the different expectations served by museums create a context radically different from that of the usual classroom in which resources are selected by teachers to meet specific purposes. Positive responses to this less controlled range of resources could be to see the visit as an opportunity for students to practise selecting objects relevant to an enquiry they have already embarked on at school, or to introduce them to the very idea of selecting and

---

[10] One word of caution is needed here. The amount of flexibility teachers have to run visits as they wish will depend on the museum or site. It is a good idea always to book a visit and to use that opportunity to check what the limitations might be on using certain teaching techniques or resources.

[11] Of course museums are separate and do have their own agendas. There is a wealth of literature on the issues related to museums' representation of the past and of different cultures. Good starting points are Carol Duncan, *Civilizing Rituals* (Routledge, 1995) for art galleries and Nick Merriman (ed.), *Beyond the Glass Case* (Leicester University Press, 1991) for history museums.

focusing in face of an initial excess of data, or to immerse them in the ancient world and allow them to gain an initial impression of its nature ready for this to be developed in further lessons. Each of these options would entail a different kind of preparation before the visit, a different structure to the visit itself, a different approach to following up the visit and a different stage in the course at which the visit would be scheduled.

I am not suggesting here that every aspect of the visit should be controlled to the exclusion of the accidental and the personal. Like all good lessons, the good museum visit allows for changes of direction prompted by unpredicted encounters. The vague open-ended benefits attributed to museum visits which were mentioned earlier are actually perfectly respectable, but teachers need to use targeted techniques to try and achieve them and must not rely on hoping for the best.[12] For example, that almost mystical experience of encountering The Real Thing can be and, especially in museums where students cannot touch ancient objects, needs to be, engineered. Somewhat paradoxically, one of the best ways of making it happen is to ensure that students are very familiar with the objects before their visit – they then come to the museum with strong preconceptions about the objects they are going to see. In challenging these preconceptions, the real thing makes its presence felt more powerfully. This does not need to be made into a specific phase of the lesson – if it is set up properly, it will happen and teachers see immediate evidence of its effect in the students' responses.

The preceding discussion is not intended to suggest that using museums well is easy any more than teaching good lessons at school is easy. Thinking of the museum as a classroom is simply a device which can unlock talents, skills and pedagogical know-how which all too often teachers put to one side when they plan their visits. The museum as classroom helps make absurd the notion that what happens on the visit does not depend on what happens before the visit and after it. Only the most adventurous use of a museum at the very beginning of a scheme of work challenges the concept of the museum visit as a tripartite entity of before, during and after. At the same time, the potential of the museum as not-a-classroom needs to be understood when teachers formulate their aims, methods and outcomes and when they think about the opportunities for new experiences that a visit offers. Similarly, the very nature of museums

---

[12] For a wide range of ideas for activities suitable for museums see Kate Thomson and Tim Copeland, *At Least 101 Things to do in a Museum* (Cheltenham & Gloucester College of Higher Education, 1996). For approaches to objects and how to prepare students to use objects see Gail Durbin et al., *Learning from Objects* (English Heritage, 1996). As with all such treasuries of ideas, it is vital to have an overview of the learning which the activities serve; otherwise perfectly good activities simply become time fillers.

as places that exhibit material culture needs to be respected – there is little point in bringing students to a museum to identify the causes of the Peloponnesian War or to find out who founded Rome.[13]

So far I have focused on how teachers might develop their use of museums for quite well-known purposes. Over the years museums have often been involved in the formulation of new ideas about classics. In 1816 the arrival of the Parthenon sculptures in the British Museum prompted a radical re-conceptualisation of Greek art and started Sir Charles Townley's renowned collection of Graeco-Roman sculptures on the slippery though very long slope down into the basement galleries. At the end of the nineteenth century, the establishment of the Museum of Classical Archaeology at Cambridge resulted from and was inextricably linked to a fiercely contested revision of the Classical Tripos.[14] In the 1970s, school classics changed almost beyond recognition and central to the new classics was a much greater role for archaeology, material culture and visual images. Museums have played and still play an important part in supporting the needs of primary schools in the radical redistribution of the opportunity to study classics that arose from the National Curriculum. During the last decade of the twentieth century, classics at university level underwent another re-conceptualisation as multiple -isms from structuralism to post-modernism were brought to bear on the discipline. Since the mid-1990s museums and the general concept of classical heritage, as opposed to classical art and archaeology as such, have come under scrutiny.[15] Beard and Henderson have used the analogy of the gap between the museum context of an object and the original context of the object as an analogy for the gap between our world and the world of the Greeks and Romans – a gap within which the subject of classics exists. They see classics as involved with both the discovery of the classical world and the exploration of our relationship to it.[16] In museum terms, the task is to uncover what we can learn from ancient objects about the world from which they come, but also to consider the histories prompted by their acquisition and presence in the museum, the museum's representation of the classical world and its construction of our understanding of that world and of our responses to it.

---

13 It would be possible to plan a stunningly clever course on the Peloponnesian War using a visit to the British Museum as its starting point, but the effort needed would probably not be worth it!
14 See Mary Beard, 'An archaeology of the Classical Tripos' in Christopher Stray (ed.), *Classics in Nineteenth and Twentieth Century Cambridge* (Cambridge Philological Society, Supplementary Volume 24, 1999).
15 So far Mary Beard, sometimes writing with John Henderson, has published most in this area. See their initial foray, 'That's showbiz/classics in the museum', *Bulletin of the Council of University Classics Departments* (1991) and *Classics: A Very Short Introduction* (Oxford University Press, 1995) and most recently, Mary Beard, *The Parthenon* (Profile Books, 2002).
16 See Beard and Henderson, *Classics: A Very Short Introduction*, 4–6.

Classics teachers have always claimed as one of the strengths of the subject that it challenges and encourages students to reflect on the significance of Greece and Rome for them personally and for culture in general. Apart from television, museums are the most important medium for the transmission and negotiation of classical heritage in our society. The principal challenges for classics teachers are to develop strategies for making the best use of museums for the purposes with which they are familiar and also to take advantage of the opportunities offered by new approaches to understanding museums and their role in the interpretation and representation of the classical world.

Epilogue

David Hargreaves

In 1932 the distinguished mathematician and philosopher Alfred North Whitehead published his influential *The Aims of Education and Other Essays*. The future of classics in this country, he argued, would depend on its adaptability to changing circumstances. The pleasure and the discipline of character to be derived from an education based mainly on classical literature and philosophy had been demonstrated by centuries of experience, but its supremacy in school and university depended on the lack of rivals. When classics was the road to advancement, it was the popular choice of study. In his own age, said Whitehead, classics could be defended only on the grounds that, now sharing the curriculum with many subjects,

> it can produce a necessary enrichment of intellectual character more quickly than any alternative discipline directed to the same object.

The essays in this volume display the many ways in which classical languages, literature and civilisation can indeed enrich education, and not just in the secondary phase. The fight to achieve the status of a foundation subject in the National Curriculum at the very time when classics appeared to be under the greatest threat after twenty years of decline was, in my view, misguided and destined to failure. Happily, however, the community of classicists has discovered a far more constructive response to the threat, namely innovation; and it is succeeding.

I believe that over the next few years there will be unprecedented opportunities for classics to build on these foundations. The tight constraints of the National Curriculum are being relaxed. Key Stage 2 is about to open up to the world of modern languages: this is the moment for the wonderful *Minimus* to expand, at the very time when (at long last) there is a recognition of the need for a better understanding of grammar at this stage. Indeed, clusters of primary schools committed to classical languages may well form mutually beneficial alliances with the rapidly expanding specialist language colleges. The Cambridge Online Latin Project is unusually well placed to take full advantage of the wider revolution arising from Curriculum Online, and especially the BBC's digital curriculum, through which the vast resources of the BBC could be brought to support the flourishing courses in classical civilisation. (I think of the few books with black-and-white photographs of classical art and sculpture in my own schooldays, compared with what is now available to today's student through the internet.) Key Stage 4 is about to be made much more flexible, reduced to a core of four subjects and with freedom for the rest of the curriculum devolved to the discretion of head teachers. The broadening of the A level structure opens the way to AS courses in classics. Even more importantly, an English baccalaureate, now under discussion, could – and in my view should – provide a Language and Literature option that includes classics. These opportunities, combined with the availability of *ab initio* courses in the universities, are surely grounds for a new optimism.

Some useful addresses

The following organisations give grants or other assistance to support classical activities over a wide number of areas:

Joint Association of Classical Teachers (JACT)
Contact: Clare Roberts, executive secretary, JACT Office, Senate House, Malet Street, London WC1 7HU. Tel: 020 7862 8706; fax: 020 7862 8729; e-mail: jact@sas.ac.uk

JACT aims to promote the teaching of classical subjects at every level in the public and private sectors of education. It offers summer schools in Greek, Latin and classical civilisation.

JACT Greek project
Contact: Dr Peter Jones, 28 Akenside Terrace, Newcastle upon Tyne NE2 1TN. Tel: 0191 281 1451; fax: 0870 052 3407; e-mail: pvjones@friends-classics.demon.co.uk

Royalties from the Cambridge University Press' *Reading Greek* series are ploughed back into grants furthering the spread of ancient Greek language, history and culture in schools, summer schools and continuing education. These are given to institutions, not individuals. Applications for grants should be as specific as possible.

Friends of Classics
Contact: Jeannie Cohen, executive secretary, Friends of Classics, 51 Achilles Road, London NW6 1DZ. Tel and fax: 020 7431 5088; e-mail: classics@friends-classics.demon.co.uk

Friends of Classics is a charitable organisation established primarily to raise funds to support classics in schools. In general it supports institutions, not individuals, and is keen to support new initiatives.

The Classical Association
Contact: Clare Roberts, executive secretary, CA Office, Senate House, Malet Street, London WC1 7HU. Tel: 020 7862 8706; fax: 020 7862 8729; e-mail: croberts@sas.ac.uk

The Classical Association (CA) will consider applications for: subventions to summer schools teaching Greek, Latin and classical civilisation; a bursary scheme for undergraduates attending the CA conference; bursaries for teachers attending courses abroad; support of academic conferences in the UK, to enable participation by graduate students and scholars from East Europe; support of reading competitions arranged by CA branches; support of regional Greek or Roman days or of schools conferences.

The Association for Latin Teaching (ARLT)
Contact: Robert West (Treasurer), 45 Thorpe Road, Thornton, Bradford BD13 3AT. www.arlt.co.uk

The ARLT runs a refresher day and a residential summer school for classics teachers. It also has a loan service of archaeological material for teachers to use for handling, and of tape and video material for use in the classroom.

Society for the Promotion of Hellenic Studies
Contact: The Secretary, Senate House, Malet Street, London WC1 7HU. Tel: 020 7862 8730; fax: 020 7862 8731; e-mail: hellenic@sas.ac.uk

Grants by the Society's Schools Sub-Committee are for books and other teaching materials, classics days or conferences, Greek plays and summer schools. Applications from schools planning to start courses in Greek are especially welcome. Applications should be sent by 15 February or 15 September each year.

The Jowett Copyright Trust
Contact: Professor Jasper Griffin, Secretary, Jowett Copyright Trust, Balliol College, Oxford OX1 3BJ. e-mail: jasper.griffin@balliol.ox.ac.uk

The trustees make grants to assist scholarly publication of editions of Greek authors or to promote the study of Greek literature. They have on occasion made grants for other purposes, such as the JACT summer school in ancient Greek, the Jowett–Sendelar essay competition, *Minimus*, and library purposes.

Gilbert Murray Trust
Contact: The Secretary, Gilbert Murray Trust Classical Committee, Institute of Classical Studies, Senate House, Malet Street, London WC1E 7HU.

The classical committee of this trust gives small grants towards travel in Greece, Greek reading and essay competitions in schools, and projects relating to Greek drama. The secretary to the committee is happy to advise potential applicants. Grants for attendance at courses run by the British School at Athens, to which the trust contributes, are administered directly by the School.

Society for the Promotion of Roman Studies

Contact: The Secretary, Senate House, Malet Street, London WC1 7HU. Tel: 020 7862 8727; fax: 020 7862 8728; e-mail: romansoc@sas.ac.uk

The Society's Schools Committee makes grants to schools to help promote Latin and Roman studies. Applications for grants should be as specific as possible. Priority is given to supporting the purchase of new books. The annual budget is approximately £6,000, and the usual level of award is £50 to £500. Applications should be sent to the Secretary to arrive by 1 February, 1 July or 1 November in any year.

The Hobson Foundation for Classical Studies

Contact: Mr Richard Short, Harvard University Classics Dept, 204 Boylston Hall, Cambridge, MA 02138, USA. e-mail: short@fas. harvard.edu

The objects of the trust are to advance education in and learning of the language, history and culture of ancient Greece and Rome and the classical world generally, primarily by enabling teachers to take Greek and Latin study groups to places of cultural interest in the ancient world. The trust also has a wider mandate to enhance the teaching of classics and make its study more widely available.

2004. 12. 11   35.00